OWLS

OF THE WORLD

OWLS

• OF THE WORLD •

WRITTEN BY
ROB HUME

ILLUSTRATED BY
TREVOR BOYER

PB

Parkgate Books

Artist's Acknowledgements

Trevor Boyer would like to express his sincere thanks to the following individuals and organisations who have helped him in the field and on his travels in search of owls, or have provided access to museum collections or live specimens of many of the species illustrated.

Tony Turk, Bernard Sayers, Alice & Tony Douglas, Ruth & Hayo Hoekstra, Erwin Wagner, Yossi Leshem, Eli Hoter, Ron Amiel, John Metclaf, Dr. Colin Bradshaw, Keith Boyer, Richard Swales, Mike Parr, Ken & Shaun Smith, Mark Armitage.

Staff of the British Museum, Tring, The American Museum of Natural History, New York and the University of Tel Aviv.

For translation of reference materials from overseas journals, thanks are also due to the following:

Janet Little, Liane Waters

LM ED WR

First published in 1991
This edition published in 1997 by

Parkgate Books Ltd
London House
Great Eastern Wharf
Parkgate Road
London SW11 4NQ
Great Britain

1 3 5 7 9 8 6 4 2

A catalogue record for this book is available from the British Library.

ISBN 1 85585 352 3

Printed and bound in Italy

CONTENTS

FOREWORD

Eric Hosking, O.B.E.,
HON. F.R.P.S., F.I.I.P., F.Z.S.

OWLS HAVE ALWAYS occupied a special place in our culture. The familiar figure of the owl is probably the most readily identifiable bird to the average non-ornithologist, and is frequently represented in many forms: in the Bible, in art, as a bird of ill-omen in Shakespeare, as Merlin's familiar, as the symbol of Athene, Goddess of Wisdom, and of course as the well loved character of 'Wol' in *Winnie-the-Pooh*. Across a wide range of cultures, from Aboriginal to Eskimo, owls are seen traditionally as wise, mysterious creatures set apart from other birds.

My own fascination for owls was established long ago, back in the days of my earliest observations of the Tawny Owls which nested in trees in playing fields near my boyhood home. Owls are, I confess, my favourite birds and without doubt those which have brought me the greatest pleasure. The highlights of a lifetime in photography have usually been associated with them: my first thrilling experiments with flash photography in the thirties and forties, which led to my well known photograph of a Barn Owl in heraldic attitude, one of hundreds taken in flight; the sheer elation of observing the African Marsh Owl at close quarters in Zimbabwe; photographing a splendid baby Eagle Owl in the Telki Hills of Hungary; and perhaps most exciting of all, my work photographing the Snowy Owls in the Shetlands in 1967, when a pair bred for the first recorded time in the British Isles.

Photographing owls has taken me around the world, through Europe and beyond to Africa, Australia and New Zealand, and the Seychelles. It also cost me an eye. While climbing into a hide in the dark where I had been photographing Tawnies, I experienced a sudden heavy blow to my face and a searing pain in my left eye — an accurate strike by a silent, unseen Tawny. This led to the eventual loss of the eye — but not to any loss of respect for the owl, which was, after all, only protecting its nest. I returned the following year to photograph the bird.

Any photographer or observer of birds faces a dilemma: pursuing his interest, while recognizing that he runs the risk of disturbing the bird or of attracting the wrong kind of interest from predators or other people. I hope that my own desire to share my enthusiasm and knowledge of owls has also helped to promote their conservation and protection. This book will, I hope, encourage the same response. One of my most satisfying recollections is of the part played by my work in protecting the Little Owl. Gamekeepers would insist that game chicks were its main prey, while ornithologists maintained it was primarily an insect eater. Detailed study of my series of photographs of Little Owls, taken in central Wales, revealed their diet to consist almost exclusively of invertebrates; not a single game chick was recorded. Such photographic information has helped alter the attitudes of those who manage our countryside.

The owl is under threat worldwide from man's destruction of its natural habitat and nesting sites, from the elimination of its natural prey by the increased use of pesticides and from poisoning and hunting. The Barn Owl, for example, has suffered greatly in recent years from the destruction of hollow trees and tumbledown barns where it nests, as the process of 'modernizing' the countryside continues. Vole-rich, rough grasslands have disappeared under the plough, forcing the birds to hunt along roadside verges where they are often drawn fatally into the slipstream of passing vehicles. The Barn Owl has also been particularly prone to the poisonous effects of chemical pesticides. Yet owls are generally beneficial to man — none is harmful and in many places they help to control pests such as rats and mice.

Conservationists are working to redress the balance. In Japan, Blakiston's Fish Owl was reduced to just 50 birds by 1984 and only two pairs bred. The old forests in which they nest were being rapidly felled. A crash programme to erect nest boxes has successfully halted the decline in numbers. Sadly, however, the overall trend for owls worldwide is still downwards — they need our help.

Some owls have proved particularly adaptable to a changing habitat; Tawnies, for example, have taken to city parks as the countryside recedes. The Vancouver Airfield authorities in Canada reported a massive increase in the number of Short-eared Owls, when they allowed grass between the runways to grow tall, in an attempt to discourage the gulls which were a hazard to aircraft. Inadvertently they created an ideal habitat for small rodents, and the owls were quick to take advantage.

Part of the attraction of owls for me lies in their surprising variety — over 150 species catalogued in the modern world, ranging in size from the tiny Elf Owl, to the huge and magnificent Fishing, Snowy and Eagle Owls. Equally interesting is the range of habitats and nesting sites they occupy — from the treeless, Arctic tundra, home of the Snowy Owl, to the underground nests of the Burrowing Owl beneath the hot American prairie.

But perhaps the most thrilling aspect of owls is their awe-inspiring ability to fly and hunt at night — on silent wings, pinpointing their prey with their phenomenal sight and hearing. There is no doubt that owls have a special magic, one which I am sure that readers of this book will discover for themselves. This really is a fascinating book.

INTRODUCTION

OWLS PRESENT a challenge to the scientist and ordinary birdwatcher alike. A few are easy to see and study and some are among the best-known, most intensively-studied birds in the world. Others are so little known, and have been so rarely encountered alive and free, that even the basic details of their biology are unknown or sketchy at best. Even some of the commoner species live in such remote places, or are simply so strictly nocturnal, that they are difficult to study, keeping themselves very much to themselves.

Some owls are adaptable and successful, surviving well in a changing world. There are surprising examples, like the enormous Great Horned Owl of North America which, despite past persecution and continuing habitat change, still manages to thrive. Few of the world's great owls have faced the almost universal influence of mankind with such success; smaller, less obvious birds seem to do better. Other owls are so specialized and so restricted in their habitat requirements or their range, that the least disturbance threatens disaster. Many species are in decline and a few are seriously endangered, mainly through loss of habitat, often linked to a naturally restricted range. The destruction of tropical rain-forests, as well as the loss of old, natural, temperate forests, causes the greatest concern.

Yet there are owls that cling on better than we once dared hope. The Seychelles Scops Owl was pronounced extinct in 1958 but we now believe that 80 pairs still survive and most are in a protected national park. Hume's Tawny Owl, once among the least known birds in the world, has been intensively studied and now appears to be more widely spread and more numerous than used to be imagined. Others are still being discovered — ornithologists in Peru have found over 20 birds new to science since 1963, including new owls.

CLASSIFYING THE OWLS

While some owl species have apparently remained almost unchanged for millions of years, others are in a dynamic state, rapidly evolving in changing circumstances. The variety of owls, combined with the isolation of many groups, especially on tropical islands, poses many questions for the taxonomist, the scientist interested in classifying them into a meaningful system of species and subspecies.

Deciding what makes an owl is little problem, despite their variety. They share some characteristics with diurnal birds of prey but are not simply nocturnal equivalents of the day-flying raptors. They have hooked

Tawny Owl looking over its back

bills and sharp, arched claws, but they differ, among other things, in not having a crop. They are actually most closely related to the nightjars, rather than to the daytime hawks and falcons. Owls are generally soft-feathered, short-tailed, large-headed birds with large eyes that face forwards and have little or no movement in their sockets. To look from side to side, the owl has to turn its head; indeed, some have a remarkable facility to turn the head through up to 270 degrees. The face is usually more or less flattened into a broad disc, which serves to focus sound into the ear openings. The bill points downwards, in the centre of this disc, creating a vertical break in the smooth facial feathering. The feet are characterized by a reversible outer toe, which usually points more or less sideways and gives a more secure grip on prey. Few species are not instantly identifiable as 'owls', even on a superficial examination.

Precisely what may best be treated as a species, or merely a subspecies (or race) is far less easy to decide. Lists of 'the owls of the world' vary in the total they include. There are a number of more or less well-defined groups of owls — particularly the barn owls *Tyto* which are rather different from the rest, and including such clear divisions as the eagle owls *Bubo*, the scops owls *Otus* and the fish owls *Ketupa*. They can be defined by

Barn Owl

their physical appearance, calls, habitats and behaviour and put into families and genera. These factors also help separate them into narrower categories – primarily, the individual species.

Any species of animal, such as a horse, a lion or a tiger, is theoretically clear-cut. Each is a recognizable entity, an animal that keeps separate from all others, breeding only with others of its own kind and producing young that are unquestionably the same. Hybrids are crosses between species and are usually artificially induced, like the mule, and are characterized by their inability to produce fertile offspring. Hybrids have to be specially bred every time – there can be no second generation.

This is the basic criterion for separating bird species – their ability, or inability, to produce fertile young. Where two very similar kinds of owls live in the same place but do not interbreed, they can safely be classified as different species. But where two closely similar forms are geographically separate, with one replacing the other in a certain direction, at a certain altitude or in a different habitat, deciding whether to 'split' them as two species or 'lump' them as races of a single species is a problem and sometimes a matter of opinion. The gradual adaptation of one group to higher altitude, or denser forest, or different food, may in any case eventually, over hundreds of thousands of years, lead to the evolution of a new species. The question is where or when to draw the line.

Many bird species are clearly very closely related – in the case of wildfowl, especially, even hybrids in the wild may not be uncommon. In a few cases, hybrids may even be able to breed, and the conventional species concept begins to break down. Owls are not prone to hybridization, but they are often not easy to 'test' for specific distinctions because they do not naturally meet in the wild.

There are many examples of very close relatives, however. The Scops Owl *Otus scops* and African Scops Owl *Otus senegalensis* are obviously very much closer than, for example, the dog and cat, and it is not obvious that they are really just as distinct. In terms of outward appearance they are very similar and it is an amalgam of factors that helps us to decide that they are separate species. These factors include different geographical distribution, habitat, migratory behaviour, colour and differing voices.

Owls present problems largely because many species *are* so very similar in appearance, while many isolated groups are not likely to come into contact to prove, or disprove, our theories by interbreeding. The complex *Otus* group, the scops owls, provides particular headaches and opportunities for the dedicated taxonomist, and subtle differences in their calls often provide the best distinguishing characteristic.

The Barn Owl is extremely widely distributed and has many different forms. These are recognizable by differences in size, colour or behaviour, yet all are still the same species, *Tyto alba*, and all could interbreed successfully if they were to meet. By moving around the world in one direction, the variation in such a species can be seen as a series of small, subtle changes of relatively little significance. But they add up to such a considerable difference that the two extremes could be taken for separate species. Knowing the extent of the gradation from one extreme to the other is therefore essential when deciding to classify the extreme forms as just races of one species.

In general, the list used in this book follows *A Complete Checklist of Birds of the World* by Howard and Moore, with amendments based on published research and specialist advice.

THE CHARACTERISTICS OF OWLS

Many owls live a wandering, nomadic life, travelling in search of food and settling wherever the conditions happen to be right for them. Others concentrate on learning their home ground, never leaving the immediate vicinity of their territory throughout adult life. While some species specialize in eating one particular kind of food, others are opportunistic, with a wide spectrum of

A brood of Barn Owl chicks of different ages; one is still to hatch out

prey. There are owls that lay just one or two eggs and those that have large but variable clutches, the number of eggs changing from year to year in response to changes in food supply.

While some are capable of catching and eating tiny insects in flight, and many capture small prey such as mice, voles and shrews, others are powerful predators well able to overpower strong, heavy prey. Even small species, like the American screech-owls, are sometimes ferocious in the extreme, taking birds larger and heavier than themselves. Tiny owls catch insects in the dripping wetness of hot, tropical forests, while big ones eat lemmings in the Arctic tundra and others plunge into icy rivers in pursuit of fish.

Popular belief holds that owls can see in the dark and hear far better than we do; it has even been said that they cannot see by day. Neither belief is true. Owls can see nothing if there is *no* light, of course, and many can see little better at low light levels than the average human. The range of sounds they hear may not be much different, if at all, from our own. This is not to say that their sight and hearing are not remarkably good — it is more a reflection of how refined our own senses are.

Species that live in defined territories all year round rely on an accumulation of knowledge. What, to us, may seem almost miraculous is, in reality, no more so than our own ability in certain circumstances. A comparison has been made with a person driving a motor car at

Eagle Owl catching a Norwegian lemming

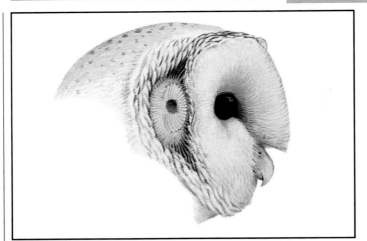

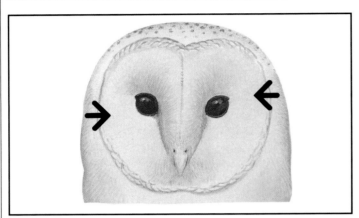

The Barn Owl's ear is covered by feathers, but here it has been exposed to show the skin flap (the operculum) and the ear aperture. The arrows indicate the asymmetrical placing of the ear openings

speed along a highway in the dark. We do this with a confidence and an ability that is not determined by the information we can actually *see*. We rely on prior knowledge and assumption (we 'know' that the road will not suddenly turn at right angles, cease to exist or degenerate into a dirt track). To an owl, this would doubtless appear as remarkable as its behaviour does to us. But it moves about in its own wood with the confidence and agility that comes through intimate knowledge of its territory.

Owls' eyes are in many cases large and specialized, nevertheless. They have little independence of movement, being so wide and so deep, or tube-like. The longest tubes are the eyes of the Snowy Owl, showing specialization for long-distance vision. Owls' eyes face forwards to give binocular vision, which is important in judging precise distances (using the characteristics of stereoscopic vision and parallax just as we do). Owls' eyes have large corneas and large, rounded lenses with short focal length which enable a greater light intake without the necessity for enormously long cylindrical structures. Their retinas have a preponderance of rods rather than cones, whereas daytime animals have more cones than rods. Cones deal with high light levels, sharp detail and colour, while rods take over at lower light levels. The concentration of rods produces greater senstivity in poor light. In humans the rods are more concentrated at the sides, and we see better in the dark 'out of the corners of our eyes', but cannot then discern much detail, partly because our visual concentration is better at the centre of our vision. Owls have retained better appreciation of detail along with increased sensitivity at low light levels.

Owls of open spaces, and daylight hunters, have less acute vision than those of dark, dense forest. Of the North American owls, the Burrowing Owl has the least ability to locate prey in poor light, seeing about as well as man. The Little Owl, often abroad by day, has eyes that are little different from those of daytime birds, and its colour vision — of no use at night — is good. An owl's iris is very sensitive, contracting in bright light to give a tiny, pinpoint pupil, but expanding in the dark until almost no iris colour is visible. An owl in daylight, with sunshine on one eye but the other in shade, will show a marked difference in its pupil sizes.

Owls' ears are equally variable in their performance, and in nocturnal species it is hearing, rather than sight, that enables them to catch prey in the dark. Owls of tropical rain-forest, which is a very noisy nocturnal environment, have less sensitive ears than those of temperate regions. Not only are owls' ears acutely sensitive, but they have special adaptations which allow the owl to pinpoint the source of a sound, which is equally vital. Often they are asymmetrical — one ear being larger than the other and also differently positioned on the side of the face. This gives them the ability to judge position with amazing accuracy, using the fractional differences in sound reaching the brain from each ear.

The ear openings of the Long-eared Owl are slits about 1½ inches (38mm) long which can extend to 2 inches (50mm). Each ear opening has a large flap of skin, edged by stiff feathers, in front and a smaller flap behind. The structure of the left and right ears is such that the precise orientation of the ear openings differs, one pointing higher than the other. The right ear opening is about 13 per cent larger than the left, while the flap in front of the ear is wider on the left, and that behind the ear is 50 per cent wider on the right. Long-eared Owls hear much the same range of sound as humans do, but hear low- and medium-pitched sounds about ten times better than we do. Their greatest sensitivity is actually at a higher pitch than ours and higher than most other birds. The Long-eared Owl can pinpoint the source of a sound to within one degree, which some humans can equal. The Barn Owl, also with extremely complicated ears, can pinpoint sound to within two degrees, and its ears are not only asymmetrical, but differ in sensitivity to high- and low-pitched sounds.

These remarkable adaptations allow an owl to listen for prey in the dark (or to locate prey beneath fresh snow) and, following the sound of squeaks and rustles, to swoop down and grasp the prey in its feet with

Short-eared Owl in flight

unerring accuracy. Owls often bob and twist their heads, and this is to get still more information on what they can see and hear by 'taking a reading' from several different positions.

Owls have other adaptations to assist their hunting, apart from eyes and ears. Their plumage is soft and, except in the case of fish-eating species and a few diurnal species, the flight feathers have fine, comb-like fringes which deaden the sound made by the movement of the wings through air. Not only does this mean that prey cannot hear the approach of the owl, but the owl can still use its own hearing while airborne, without interference from the rush of air through its feathers.

The fishing owls, which no doubt rely less on hearing and need not be so silent when approaching a fish, have their own special features, including unfeathered, scaly legs with sharp, spiny scales on the soles of their feet, enabling them to grip slippery fish more securely.

THE STUDY OF OWLS
Owls have one hugely helpful characteristic for those who wish to study them. Most species establish breeding territories and advertise them by calling. It is possible, therefore, to locate and even census breeding owls by listening for their distinctive calls.

In some cases it has been found that more owls have been present in an area than previously thought when tape-recordings of owl songs have been played in suitable habitats (or even habitats hitherto considered marginal). Owls tend to react very strongly to the voices of supposed intruders into their territories. This, however, is a disruptive and potentially damaging method of study which must be carried out with care and restraint.

Tape-recordings of owls have also proved of immense benefit in taxonomic studies. The analysis of sonograms has enabled specialists to separate species of *Otus*, for example, on the basis of their vocalizations.

Another method of counting owls involves the location of suitable nest sites. For many species this is very difficult, but in some areas some species have such a limited choice that inspection of nesting or roosting places is valuable in determining the local owl population. Barn Owls seem not only to be restricted by nest sites but also to be very dependent on roost sites within their hunting territory; in areas of intense agriculture, for example, the number of hollow trees or old barns is very small. Visits to such sites can establish

breeding numbers but care must be taken as the birds are easily disturbed and, in the United Kingdom at least, it is illegal to visit a nest site without a licence.

Nesting studies may be facilitated by the provision of artificial sites, and a surprising variety of owls will use 'nest boxes' of some sort. Barn Owls respond well to large boxes in suitable buildings, but boxes can equally well simulate broken branches or hollow trees (for Tawny and Ural Owls) and old woodpecker holes (for pygmy-owls).

The diet of many owls is well-known. This is because owls produce pellets. These are roughly oval or cylindrical masses of undigested material — fur, bones, beetle wing cases, feather shafts, even earthworm remains — which are regurgitated by an owl, either while it is perched in its territory or while it is at its roost or nest site. Species like the Barn Owl and Long-eared Owl produce pellets regularly in certain sites and literally scores may be gathered from beneath a tree or ledge. Others, like the Tawny Owl, produce them more randomly throughout their territory, making collection less easy. The pellets have a characteristic appearance for some species. They are easily broken down, usually in a shallow dish of water, and the prey remains can be isolated, identified and counted. By applying knowledge of which items are under- or over-represented in pellets, it is possible to gain a very good idea of the diet of the birds being studied.

Past studies relied heavily on the collection of specimens — simply shooting owls for museums. Owls are still collected, but improved techniques of live-trapping and release (which have been used in Peru where new species of owls have been discovered in nets) have made collection by gun largely a thing of the past. The owl can now be caught, weighed, measured, photographed and individually marked, then released unharmed within minutes. Nevertheless, the collections of museum specimens remain of great value, not least in the accurate production of the illustrations for this book. Those in the major museums, such as the American Museum of Natural History and the British Museum, are of immense value. Collections of eggshells, on the other hand, are of far more limited use – after all, most owls' eggs are rounded and white!

THREATS TO OWLS

It is evident from the species' accounts in this book that rather a lot of species are already rare and many are declining. Those that require large tracts of ancient forest, with undisturbed hunting and nesting areas and nest sites such as broken stumps of ancient, rotten trees, are facing problems as the great boreal forests are increasingly 'tamed' by foresters. The north-western race of the Spotted Owl faces an uncertain future as developers haggle over the fate of its remaining home woods, and the Great Grey and Ural Owls may be limited by lack of nest sites. Still worse are the problems faced by those owls restricted to specialized tropical forest habitat. The rapid and seemingly uncontrollable destruction of tropical rain-forests severely threatens many species and there are no easy answers.

Other threats are connected with the loss of habitat on small, isolated islands where owls have evolved into distinct species. Island forms of birds, mammals and other wildlife have always been susceptible to damage by man and to introduced predators or competitors.

Owls have attracted more than their share of folklore and tradition, and much of this has been to their detriment. Any bird whose presence is thought to foretell death, or in some other way is considered an ill omen, is likely to suffer persecution. Some species, including the Eagle Owl, have suffered because of their perceived role as a predator. Even the Little Owl, which eats mostly insects, was subject to a campaign to exterminate it from Britain (where it had, in any case, been introduced by man) because it was thought to be damaging small bird (and gamebird) populations.

Such attitudes are hard to change. Tawny Owls are still shot and trapped close to gamebird rearing pens in Britain. In Africa, owls are still killed to rid the area of evil spirits. But these threats are of little consequence when measured against the real problem of habitat loss.

GAPS IN OUR KNOWLEDGE

Owls are popular and, in a general sense, 'well known'. They have captured the imagination of writers, sound-recordists and film-makers alike, with their spine-tingling nocturnal screeches and the purest, most beautiful hoots. Most people like owls, yet most rarely, if ever, actually see one. At least in the western world, where few people now experience real darkness or roam around at night far from towns, owls are known by reputation, not from personal experience. It is the specialist researcher, or at least the keen birdwatcher, who sees more than one or two species of common owls in real life. The rest of us enjoy them in books, on Christmas cards or in films or on the television.

For birds that are so elusive, even the specialist has to admit that little is known of the biology of many species. For some, even a nest with eggs has never been found, almost nothing is known of their population dynamics, little about their everyday behaviour, and their food preferences are barely sketched out. Where, in this book, there is a simple statement – perhaps that the owl concerned lays four eggs in a tree hole, or prefers to eat small voles, or beetles – it can reflect hundreds of hours and thousands of observations which have been necessary to prove it. This book, indeed, relies heavily on the published researches of hundreds of dedicated ornithologists around the world. Without their work it would not have been possible.

It follows that there are still many facts to discover about most owls of the world. Few owls other than the commoner species in well-watched areas have been thoroughly studied. Some of the species' texts in this book are very short simply because little has yet been learned about the birds concerned.

THE VISUAL APPEAL OF OWLS

Owls have wonderful voices, but their appeal is essentially visual. Most people who buy this book will do so for the magnificent paintings by Trevor Boyer. So they should. Trevor was persuaded to illustrate every species himself, and I am very pleased that he did so. He has, where possible, used studies from live birds. His travels have taken him to exciting places in search of owls, and he has watched wild owls ranging from Blakiston's Fish Owl in Japan to the Burrowing Owls of the western USA. If wild birds were not co-operative, he has made use of captive birds for his studies. His White-faced Scops Owl painting was based on a single bird that looked emaciated and grotesque when alarmed, but softened to a rounder, more comfortable appearance when relaxed.

Trevor's incomparable painting technique and attention to accurate detail make the plates themselves a feast. It is all the better that the owls offer so much variety and such intricate beauty for Trevor to work his magic on. It is to them that this book is really dedicated.

White-faced Scops Owl

BARN AND BAY OWLS

THIRTEEN SPECIES IN TWO GENERA

BARN OWLS

ELEVEN SPECIES

MADAGASCAR GRASS OWL
Tyto soumagnei

LENGTH: *270 mm*   MAP NUMBER: 1
DESCRIPTION: *Small barn owl type, overall rufous-brown or ochre-red*
DISTRIBUTION: *Madagascar*
HABITAT: *Humid rain-forest*
STATUS: *Rare/endangered*

This ochre-red bird, also known as the Madagascar Red Owl (*Tyto alba*) in form. It has a typically heart-shaped face, a large, rounded head, rather tapered body and slender legs and toes. But its ruddy plumage and rufous claws set it apart.

It is found only on Madagascar and is now considered so rare as to be endangered. It is the Madagascar equivalent of the widespread grass owls but favours humid rain-forests rather than grasslands. Though its precise requirements are poorly understood, the loss of forest cover on Madagascar will have contributed to the decline and present scarcity of this bird, of which little is known. Many of the island's forests have been felled and replaced by plantations of introduced eucalyptus and other trees unsuitable for this owl. This process has decimated many indigenous species, including the Madagascar Serpent Eagle (*Eutriorchis astur*) and the unique varieties of lemur.

The Madagascar Grass Owl probably survives in the eastern forests, such as the Sihanaka Forest, but it has not been encountered in recent years. It was even thought to be extinct earlier this century, but a report in 1973 (the first sighting since 1934) revived a slender hope of its survival. Like many tropical species, it is all but unknown to western ornithologists yet the passing of such a handsome owl would be a great loss.

BARN OWL
Tyto alba

LENGTH: *330 to 430 mm*   MAP NUMBER: 2
DESCRIPTION: *Heart-shaped face, dark eyes, spindly legs; pale golden-buff and white to darker, greyer forms*
DISTRIBUTION: *North, Central and South America, Europe, Africa, southern and South-East Asia, Australasia*
HABITAT: *Grasslands, cultivation, scrub, forest edge*
EGGS: *3—11. Nest in hole or on ledge*
STATUS: *Widespread, locally threatened*

The ghostly Barn Owl is lovely to watch as it flies low over some rough field or along the rides of a young plantation, searching the grass tussocks for mice or voles. The Barn Owl of Britain, France and Spain, with its glowing golden-buff back and pristine white underparts, is perhaps the finest of all. In many other regions it looks less ethereal, as only its face is spotlessly white and it has greyer upperparts and darker underparts.

The Barn Owl is typical of the *Tyto* group. It has a heart-shaped face with a clearly-defined disc lined with short, stiff, slightly rippled feathers. Its eyes are small, dark and close-set, and separated by a long, V-shaped ridge which reaches a point over the deeply-hooked bill. From the front, this ridge of feathers can make the pink or yellow bill look small and harmless. This is misleading, however,

Barn Owl (*Tyto alba*)

since only the tip of the upper mandible is visible. A side view, with the feathers brushed back, would reveal a strong, down-tilted beak quite capable of dealing with a decent-sized rat.

The body of the Barn Owl is cylindrical, sitting fairly upright and tapering down from the broad, flat-topped head to a short tail. Its legs are thin, white-feathered and often extremely knock-kneed. Its feet are unfeathered and equipped with needle-sharp claws.

Barn Owls are found across vast areas of the world. They live on the tips of the southern continents at Cape Horn, the Cape of Good Hope and the South East Cape of Tasmania. They are found across most of Europe as far north as Scotland and Denmark and eastwards to the Black Sea. Barn Owls live in Australia, on tiny islands in the south Pacific, and are widely dispersed in South, Central and North America as far north as the Great Lakes. In Africa they occur everywhere, except in the Sahara and in the Congo basin rain-forests. In Asia, however, the birds are found only in India and the Indo-Chinese countries.

In both the northern and southern hemispheres, the Barn Owl is essentially a tropical creature, though its range extends into temperate regions. It cannot cope with the extreme cold experienced in parts of Asia and Canada. Barn Owls prefer dry rather than moist places and in many regions are suited to near-desert conditions. They can be seen flying at dusk from the great temples of Egypt after a searingly hot day.

They roost in rock fissures and huge trees, such as the African baobabs and giant Asian fig trees, but mostly choose undisturbed airy spaces in the roofs of church towers, barns, castles and even modest cattle byres. They will enter mines and wells and in Israel and the Galapagos, for instance, have been found deep underground on ledges in shafts.

A feature for which the Barn Owl is renowned is its unearthly spine-tingling screech. Curiously, few birdwatchers hear it. More commonly heard are the distinctive snores or hissing noises of young birds in the nest, or the sharp "*yip-yip*" of a Barn Owl flying past.

This bird does, in fact, have a varied vocabulary. Because of its internal structure, it does not make the hoot common among owls. Instead, it purrs, hisses, yells or screeches. The territorial call is the famous screech, actually a loud, hissing "*shrrreeee*". Males make a similar sound when chasing females, who reply with a wail. Aggression is accompanied by hissing and a loud clicking of the bill or tongue. Young birds snore and hiss when they want food or attention. This ploy usually succeeds, since the parents sense that prolonged hissing could attract a predator to the nest.

The ear of the Barn Owl has a large, square, pink flap in front of the opening, hidden behind feathers of the facial disc. The left and right flaps are asymmetrical and the two ears are positioned differently. They are also of differing sensitivity to high and low pitch, and receive slightly divergent ranges of sound. Although a fairly small head means that the ears are quite close, their contrasting faculties give the Barn Owl an acute ability to pinpoint the source of sound.

The facial disc, in effect, collects sound and concentrates it in the ears, allowing the owl to gauge precisely the direction and distance of a squeaking mouse or a rat rustling in the grass. The nervous system connected to the ears and the structure of the auditory area of the brain are the most complex and advanced of any owl.

A hunting Barn Owl rests for long periods on a low perch, such as a fence-post, and then flies over a suitable area in a free, wheeling flight until it hears or spots prey. It then launches itself into a headlong dive towards the grass, appearing to go face-first but swinging its feet downwards at the last moment both to strike and clutch the prey in a tight grip. Though less elegant in flight than the Short-eared Owl (*Asio flammeus*), the Barn Owl has less wing-loading — the weight per square centimetre of wing — than either the Short-eared, Long-eared (*Asio otus*) or the Tawny Owl (*Stix aluco*). It floats and twists with a freedom denied to heavier, smaller-winged birds and can react to movement with an instantaneous stall-turn, a twirl through 180 degrees or a dramatic tilt into a steep dive.

Barn Owls are nocturnal creatures but will hunt by day when necessary. Such a need arises during summer in northern countries when there are young to feed but only short nights in which to hunt, or during winter when food is scarce. So Barn Owls can be observed with some ease in Britain and north-west mainland Europe.

Despite its wide geographical range, the Barn Owl finds survival difficult in the modern world. In Britain, its numbers are in decline. This is unlikely to have been the result of persecution, as the Barn Owl is accepted as a farmer's friend, a useful ratter. Accidental poisoning is one hazard, as Barn Owls may feed on prey that consumes pesticides. Cold winters with deep snow make hunting difficult and reduce the population, though the numbers have also fallen during periods with mild winter weather.

The chief problem is the loss of habitat, and this has reduced potential nest sites and the number of hunting grounds. The Barn Owl, as its English name suggests, likes weathered old barns to nest in. It also uses ageing trees with deep hollows in their boles. But countless numbers of old trees have been torn up, along with many miles of hedgerow and small woods. Many trees have been toppled in gales. Old barns are eventually repaired, converted or knocked down and the new buildings which replace them offer less scope for an owl to enter.

In the Friesland region of the Netherlands, for example, there are many old barns with triangular boards at the top of the gable end. These were once owl windows, left open for the Barn Owl, but are now boarded up. Artificial nest boxes can be built in certain types of building, or slung beneath a large branch on a tree, and may be adopted by Barn Owls. But they are not a true substitute and do not halt the decline in numbers. Experiments with boxes in young conifer plantations, however, have shown that the owl population can be restored when sites are provided. Owls have occupied these boxes in large numbers.

The loss of feeding areas for the Barn Owl is a more difficult problem to correct. Under intensive farming, field edges have been ploughed to the limits and many strips of old grassland have gone for good. The traditional band of rough ground alongside woodland has also disappeared. Many grass strips are now tidily green but lack disorderly clumps and tufts, tall enough for mice and voles to hide in but short enough for the Barn Owls to catch them.

Barn Owls will fly long distances from their roosts and nests for good hunting, but that means that the density of owls in an intensively farmed landscape must be very low. To make do, Barn Owls hunt alongside roads and railways and many are killed after being swept into traffic by the currents of air generated by moving lorries. There are other, less obvious causes of death. Some Barn Owls, as the recovery of ringed birds has shown, drown in cattle drinking troughs, water butts and wells. They try to drink and bathe, become waterlogged and are unable to clamber out from the smooth-sided vessels.

The Barn Owl is basically a rodent-eater. In Colorado and other parts of North America, many feed almost entirely on mammals such as meadow and prairie voles, white-footed mice and least shrews. In Europe, Barn Owls mainly feed on small voles, mice and shrews, but may also catch birds, bats and other prey.

In California, Barn Owls catch and eat fish; in central Europe, they select prey as large as Moorhens (*Gallinula chloropus*), woodpeckers and jackdaws. In Asia, Barn Owls may catch snakes and frogs. On oceanic islands, they will feed heavily on petrels when these small, sea-going birds return by night to their nests in burrows. In short, although the Barn Owl survives mainly on voles, mice and rats, it will eat anything it can catch.

The availability of prey directly influences the breeding of Barn Owls, whose strategy ensures that at least one or two young are reared, even if the rest die. It is better to do this than attempt to rear a complete brood which fails completely due to the lack of food. The size of a clutch varies but it can be large, averaging between five and six eggs in many parts of the world. In extreme cases, between 10 and 20 eggs may be laid, the latter figure being among the largest clutches of any bird in the world.

The supply of food affects the number of eggs and the number of broods in a year. In the tropics, a plague of small rodents may help Barn Owls breed in profusion. In Zimbabwe, for example, a pair of Barn Owls laid four clutches in a little over eight months and fledged 32 young in 11 months. In Malaysia, Barn Owls have been found to produce clutches of six or seven eggs, or even up to 20, at an annual rate of three clutches, year after year.

Little can threaten owl chicks except a scarcity of food. But in poor hunting years, many die. The eggs are laid at intervals of one or two days and incubation begins with the first egg. As a result, the size of the young in a nest varies. The oldest may be eight times heavier than the smallest and, when food is scarce, the largest is fed and the weaker ones are allowed to starve. Once dead, they will be eaten by the others and, in this way, the fittest survive.

Young Barn Owls develop slowly and may be a month old before they begin to explore the surrounds of the nest, and 9–12 weeks old before they fly from it. Should they survive, they enter a world which, in many parts, is harsh and exacting. They will have to eke out an existence, often in poor habitat, learning to hunt and hopefully finding suitable terrain before the rigours of winter. Barn Owls need the support and sympathetic land management of all who work in the modern countryside.

There is one special case in which a localized race of the Barn Owl may best be considered a species in its own right. This is the Ashy-faced Owl (*Tyto (alba) glaucops*) of Hispaniola in the Caribbean. The American Ornithologists' Union (AOU) has 'split' this from the Barn Owl on the grounds that the two are now found side by side without evidence of interbreeding. In other words, they behave and reproduce quite separately, as different species.

The Dutch taxonomist and owl expert, Dr K H Voous, however, wrote in 1988 that the Barn Owl is exceptionally varied, with extremes in appearance that would scarcely seem to belong to the same species, produced by a multitude of different selection forces in widely differing conditions. He noted that, in Hispaniola, the large, white-faced American or Bahamian form, *Tyto alba pratincola*, has appeared alongside the indigenous small, relatively dark form, *glaucops*, probably as a result of changes in the environment caused by man, and interbreeding has not yet occurred. A similar situation exists on Lord Howe Island, between Australia and New Zealand, where Barn Owls from different places have been introduced, probably also without interbreeding. Voous concludes that it is not compulsory to separate *glaucops* as a separate species in its own right, although it is likely that more authors will eventually follow the AOU.

CELEBES BARN OWL
Tyto rosenbergii

LENGTH: *410 to 510 mm*   MAP NUMBER: *3*
DESCRIPTION: *Large, brownish barn owl with dark edge to facial disc, spotted underparts*
DISTRIBUTION: *Sulawesi*
HABITAT: *Rain-forest*
STATUS: *Probably rare*

This large, rather heavily-marked bird clearly belongs to the barn owl (*Tyto*) family but its overall form resembles that of the Masked Owl (*Tyto novaehollandiae*). It lives in the rain-forests of a number of the Sulawesi (Celebes) islands in the Indonesian archipelago, but is also associated with lowland habitats which have been eroded by deforestation programmes. Fortunately, the Celebes Barn Owl can adapt readily to the often inferior habitats created by the clearance of the rain-forest. On the northern peninsula of the island of Sulawesi, its range overlaps that of the smaller, redder Minahassa Barn Owl (*Tyto inexspectata*). But the adaptability of the Celebes Barn Owl

has prevented the common Barn Owl (*Tyto alba*) colonizing the island and establishing a niche there. The Celebes Barn Owl remains practically unknown. Details of its lifestyle and breeding biology have been little studied.

SULA ISLANDS BARN OWL
Tyto nigrobrunnea

LENGTH: *310 mm*   MAP NUMBER: 4
DESCRIPTION: *Dark barn owl type with little or no white*
DISTRIBUTION: *Sula Islands*
STATUS: *Known from one specimen only — extinct?*

This owl, also known as the Black-brown Owl or the Taliabu Owl, after the larger of the Sula Islands, is unknown from the wild. A single female collected on the Sula Islands, which lie in the Moluccas, Indonesia, remains the sole source of what scant knowledge exists of this bird. It is a matter of speculation whether these owls survive or are extinct. Their biology and behaviour in the wild is a field ripe for research. Indeed, the first task is to establish whether or not they still exist and, if so, the size of the population and its distribution.

MINAHASSA BARN OWL
Tyto inexspectata

LENGTH: *270 to 310 mm*   MAP NUMBER: 5
DESCRIPTION: *Small, dark with orange-yellow patches*
DISTRIBUTION: *Northern Sulawesi*
STATUS: *Rare/endangered*

The islands of Indonesia and New Guinea have groups of grass owls and barn owls which survive the rigours of heat and humidity in this demanding region. The Minahassa Barn Owl inhabits only the northern peninsula of Sulawesi, where the Grass Owl (*Tyto capensis*) and the Celebes Barn Owl (*Tyto rosenbergii*) are also found. The annual rainfall is over 120″ (300cm) and the temperature is always between 20° and 30° centigrade. The natural vegetation of this region is rich tropical rain-forest, abounding in lianas, palms, ferns and parasitic plants of all sorts on magnificent trees.

This is a relatively small owl with an attractive pattern of rusty-red and pale orange, an echo of the ruddy hues of several other related species in the region. The reason for such colours, which do not blend in with the all-pervading green foliage of the forest, is hard to explain. They may, perhaps, play a part in courtship rituals.

This owl is also known as the Unexpected Owl. The scientific version of this — *inexspectata* — includes the single 's' adopted when the bird was first described in 1879. Little is known of its behaviour, specific habitat requirements or status. It is believed to nest early in April, but even casual sightings of live birds are rarely reported.

MASKED OWL
Tyto novaehollandiae

LENGTH: *490 to 530 mm*   MAP NUMBER: 6
DESCRIPTION: *Large; dark, spotted barn owl*
DISTRIBUTION: *Australasia, New Guinea*
HABITAT: *Forest, open woodland, clearings*
EGGS: *2–4. Nest in hole*
STATUS: *Uncommon, declining*

This is very similar to a large, powerful Barn Owl (*Tyto alba*), and is the largest of the *Tyto* group. It has strongly-marked underparts and upperparts heavily peppered with grey, and a varying amount of rufous around the eyes and facial disc. When alarmed, it assumes the menacing pose typical of so many owls. This display includes a deep, forward-leaning crouch with wings half-spread, creating a broad, rounded shape from the front, accompanied by loud, resonant bill-snapping.

The species is found in Australia, Tasmania and the extreme south of New Guinea. Its strong relationships to the barn owls and the grass owls are quickly apparent. Up to seven races of the Masked Owl are found on different islands of the region or on the Australian mainland. But two of these may be separated as forms of another species, the Lesser Masked Owl (*Tyto sororcula*). Even within a race, there is considerable variation. That found on Tasmania is the largest and darkest of all, and in this and other respects is sufficiently distinct to be regarded by some authorities as a separate species. It is also the only race which can be described as common. Females are noticeably larger and darker than males.

The Masked Owl lives in forest and open woodland with clearings, or with adjacent open country over which it can hunt. But it is never very common. This is a shy, secretive bird; by day it hides in dense foliage or deep inside hollow trees and is a difficult creature to track down. *The Atlas of Australian Birds* recognized that its recently compiled distribution map for this species was very incomplete, as the bird is rarely observed and its call frequently passes unrecognized on the Australian mainland. In Tasmania, though, its range was more fully recorded. Some authorities believe the Masked Owl has declined and has disappeared from certain areas, but its resemblance to the Barn Owl makes early records unreliable.

In the Nullarbor Plain, astride the border of South and Western Australia, Masked Owls roost and nest in underground caves in the limestone landscape, but little information on the bird has been collected in this region. Since the 1920s, it has been reported only in 1962 and 1980, rare sightings which may be due to the remoteness of the region and the difficulty in finding this owl.

The Masked Owl usually lives in eucalypt forest and other woodland with clearings or woodland edge so that it can emerge into clearer spaces to hunt. It hunts at night, preying on rabbits and other small mammals, lizards and small birds. In Tasmania, at least, it feeds extensively on bandicoots, sugar gliders, possums and rabbits. Its decline elsewhere may be linked to the fall in numbers of native mammals since alien species were introduced by European settlers. It regurgitates large pellets of undigested material – bones, fur and scales – up to 3½″ (90mm) in length.

The nest is a bare scrape, which quickly becomes untidily padded with debris and the remains of prey, inside a cavity of some tall tree. In a eucalyptus, the nest will often be at a height of up to 65 feet (20m). Nests are also found on bare rock in the caves of Nullarbor. Two to four eggs are laid; they are rather dull, white and elongated in shape, unlike the shiny white spheres of most species. It is at the nest that loud, drawn-out, rasping snores and hissing sounds are most likely to be heard, but this is generally a very quiet owl in most circumstances.

LESSER MASKED OWL
Tyto sororcula

LENGTH: *490 mm*   MAP NUMBER: 7
DESCRIPTION: *Small, dark barn owl*
DISTRIBUTION: *Tanimbar Island in the Lesser Sundas,
Indonesia*
HABITAT: *Forest and scrub*
STATUS: *Uncommon or rare*

Often treated as a race of the Masked Owl (*Tyto
novaehollandiae*), this form is again regarded as a distinct
species, as it was considered to be when first described in
1826. At the same time, another race of the Masked Owl,
that from Buru Island in the Moluccas, Indonesia, has been
linked with the Lesser Masked Owl of Tanimbar Island in
one dimorphic species — that is, a species with two
different forms. These owls were once thought to be a race
of the Barn Owl (*Tyto alba*), a fact which illustrates the
uncertain links between groups of owls, especially when
several forms are found on separate islands. While its place
in the classification (taxonomy) of owls can be debated,
practically nothing is known of the lifestyle of the Lesser
Masked Owl.

NEW BRITAIN BARN OWL
Tyto aurantia

LENGTH: *270 to 330 mm*   MAP NUMBER: 8
DESCRIPTION: *Small barn owl, pale orange-rufous*
DISTRIBUTION: *New Britain Island off New Guinea*
HABITAT: *Forest and clearings*
STATUS: *Rare, little known*

The island of New Britain, off the east coast of New Guinea,
is the only one inhabited by this handsome owl. The
climate is typically hot and humid, reaching 30° centigrade
in January and scarcely falling throughout the year, with an
annual 120″ (300cm) of rain. The result is dense rain-forest
with tree ferns, palms, and an abundance of colourful
flowers. This is a small barn owl, predominantly pale
orange-rufous with delicate marbling and spotting of dark
brown. Little is known of its biology.

SOOTY OWL
Tyto tenebricosa

LENGTH: *330 to 380 mm*   MAP NUMBER: 9
DESCRIPTION: *Very dark, black-brown barn owl with
white flecks*
DISTRIBUTION: *New Guinea, Australia*
HABITAT: *Forest*
EGGS: *2. Nest in hole*
STATUS: *Probably rare but elusive*

Huge black eyes give a unique expression to the heart-
shaped face of this small, dark barn owl. A gawky bird, it
has a large head tapering abruptly into a thin body, with
gangly legs, outsized feet and a very short tail. The female
is much bigger than the male, a feature shared with
daylight birds of prey such as sparrowhawks and falcons. It
is among the more distinctive of the barn owls, but one of
the least documented.

The Australian population has recently been separated
into two species, the Sooty Owl and the Lesser Sooty Owl

(*Tyto multipunctata*), which has an isolated distribution in the Atherton region of north-east Queensland. Formerly regarded as just a race of the Sooty Owl, the Lesser Sooty Owl is similarly dark but smaller and much more heavily-spotted, as its scientific name implies. Both inhabit patches of rain-forest and wet eucalypt forests containing old trees with hollow trunks suitable for nesting and roosting. The Lesser Sooty Owl tends to favour extensive tracts of rain-forest, roosting in a variety of crevices, beneath over-hanging banks and in the tangles of aerial roots that swathe the giant forest trees. Since tree-felling has altered this habitat, both owls have adopted roadsides and clearings as hunting grounds and can be observed more frequently as a result.

In Australia, the Sooty Owl is considered rare; but the problems of locating it in dense forest make its exact status uncertain. It is found also in New Guinea and on the nearby island of Yapen. If disturbed by day, it may sit quietly, looking half asleep and disinclined to react, or it may flap out from the dense vegetation or tree hollow in which it sleeps and fly clumsily away with heavy, inelegant wingbeats.

The presence of this mysterious bird is best ascertained by its strange, exciting calls. These have an unearthly quality which penetrates far into the tropical and subtropical rain-forests, and across the densely vegetated gullies in which this owl lives. One of these calls, a strident, descending whistle, has been likened to the sound of a falling bomb. Other calls include duets between a pair in the form of rolling, chirruping, cricket-like trills.

Through these calls, the Sooty Owl has been located in many unexpected areas of Australia. Sooty Owls appear to require a territory of 500 to 2,000 acres (200–800 hectares) or more, whereas a breeding pair of Lesser Sooty Owls needs only 125 to 150 acres (50–60ha).

The varied prey includes some arboreal mammals such as possums and gliders, but consists mostly of ground-living creatures such as rats and bandicoots, which are

caught by a sudden pounce from a perch. The nest is often in the hollow of an ancient eucalyptus, sometimes as high as 100 feet (30 metres) above ground. One or two oval, white eggs are laid on a mat of debris and bones of the small mammal prey. It is common for only one of a clutch of two eggs to hatch, in contrast to the larger clutch and brood sizes that typical barn owls produce in response to the available supply of food.

GRASS OWL
Tyto capensis

LENGTH: *380 to 420 mm*   MAP NUMBER: 10
DESCRIPTION: *Dark-backed barn owl type with long, unfeathered legs*
DISTRIBUTION: *Africa*
HABITAT: *Moist grassland and open savanna*
EGGS: *4–6. Nest on ground*
STATUS: *Fairly frequent*

Grass Owls have broad, heart-shaped faces, dark eyes and spindly, knock-kneed legs. Like Barn Owls (*Tyto alba*), their upperparts have a beautiful pattern of salt-and-pepper grey flecks and dark-ringed small white spots against a warm brown background. However, Grass Owls are larger and heavier, with longer wings and shorter tails. Their behaviour resembles that of African Marsh Owls (*Asio capensis*), whose habitat they often share, although the longer-legged Grass Owls are more specialized in their habitat requirements.

Grass Owls vary in appearance, according to the region they inhabit. Opinion is divided about the number of species which should be recognized. There may be only one species (with at least 10 races), or possibly two if the African races are regarded as a separate species from the birds of southern Asia and Australasia. It is probable that consensus will be reached on one species, rather than on two that have evolved separately yet have produced a remarkably similar bird. But there are interesting contrasts which, given further study, may justify a continued separation. At present, birds of the African races are known as the Grass Owl (*Tyto capensis*), while those of Asia and Australasia are described as a separate species, the Eastern Grass Owl (*Tyto longimembris*).

In Africa, the birds are found as an isolated group in Cameroon, and also occur in Kenya and Zaire southwards to the Cape. Grass Owls are rare in the south and are limited to the eastern third of South Africa. They are more terrestrial than Barn Owls, as their longer, almost unfeathered legs suggest. They hide during the day in 'tunnels' in long grass, where they might also nest, and hunt over open, grassy spaces.

In southern Africa, this is a bird of moist grassland, bracken and heath, and is resident there unless driven out by drought, overgrazing or fire. If the land recovers, it promptly returns to its old haunts. Grass Owls prefer grassland areas near water, but will occupy dry habitats. This is especially so in years when large numbers of voles lead to an expansion of the owl population. Surplus birds then move into the dry, grassy vleis or bushveld.

Roosts are occupied for long periods and can be easily recognized by the trampling of the grass and deposits of white droppings and big, dark pellets. Sometimes the roost is a more sophisticated structure. It can include a feeding area backed by a tunnel several metres in length, leading to a comfortable roosting chamber. A pair may roost together or have separate sites and it is likely that a pair will begin to roost together shortly before nesting, then make a nest at one of the old, favourite roosting places.

The Grass Owl usually hunts at night, but can be seen flying in the early morning or late afternoon when food is scarce or when there are young to feed. It usually searches the ground in a low, wavering flight, like that of the Short-eared Owl (*Asio flammeus*), but will also hunt by waiting and watching from a perch.

Daytime hunting involves flights at up to 35 feet (10m) above the ground on regular, steady beats of the bowed wings. The Grass Owl's large head turns from side to side, scanning for prey. A dive to the ground is made about every ten minutes, but nine out of ten strikes yield nothing and the Grass Owl is quickly back into the air. A successful strike results in a lengthy spell on the ground as the owl prepares and swallows its prey. Some bats, birds and large insects may be caught in mid-air.

The bulk of the prey consists of rodents up to about 3½ ounces (100g) in weight, such as the large, aggressive vlei rats which the Grass Owl snatches and overpowers with its strong feet. Groove-toothed rats and water rats are also common prey, as are the climbing mice which can abound in the grasslands.

Grass Owls are usually quiet birds. However, their high, thin, insignificant calls can sometimes be heard at night.

When hunting, Grass Owls make clicking sounds, probably with the tongue. This may be to provoke rodents into betraying their positions by moving in alarm. It has also been suggested that the clicking is a form of echolocation. A female or her chicks will make wheezing, hissing sounds when the male visits the nest with prey.

The nest is generally built in the longest clump of grass available. It is simply a flat pad of grass at the end of a tunnel of vegetation. African Marsh Owls (*Asio capensis*) and African Marsh Harriers (*Circus ranivorus*) may nest within a few metres without aggression breaking out. Despite their names, it is the Grass Owl which selects the wetter places for nesting and the Marsh Owl which chooses drier spots. The Grass Owl, being the stronger, longer-legged bird, takes larger prey than the Marsh Owl.

Eggs are laid when the grass is thickest, in late summer and autumn, and the chicks leave the nest when vlei rats are most numerous. A single brood is reared to coincide with this seasonal abundance. Up to six eggs may be laid, at intervals of two to three days, but the female starts incubating only when the last egg is laid, so they all hatch together. This is one of the differences between the African Grass Owl and the Australasian birds, the Eastern Grass Owls. Even when the eggs are not hatched simultaneously, Grass Owl chicks never vary in size to the degree that young Barn Owls do.

This may assist vulnerable chicks by making a shorter period of fledgling for the whole family. Nevertheless, one chick in an average brood of three is often slow to develop and dies before fledging. Incubation lasts 32 days and the chicks begin to leave the nest after 35 days, although it is some time before they can fly.

EASTERN GRASS OWL
Tyto longimembris

LENGTH: *380 to 420 mm*   MAP NUMBER: 11
DESCRIPTION: *Long-legged, variable grass owl*
DISTRIBUTION: *Southern Asia, Australasia*
HABITAT: *Grassland*
EGGS: *4—8. Nest on ground*
STATUS: *Uncommon to frequent*

This owl is found in India and areas to the east, eastern China, certain islands of the Philippines and New Guinea, and eastern Australia. Its uncertain geographical range has raised doubts as to whether it is a collection of Grass Owl (*Tyto capensis*) races, or a separate, distinct species, the Eastern Grass Owl.

It has been claimed that there are two separate populations in Australia. One is found along the north-east coast from Cape York to Harrington. The other is based in the Rolling Downs and Lake Eyre and, in years of high numbers, disperses north-west towards the Top End and Kimberley. The Eastern Grass Owl is nomadic, in contrast to the African Grass Owl, which tends to be sedentary unless driven out by fire or drought.

Eastern Grass Owls from inland habitats have been known to follow plagues of long-haired rats and dusky field rats, and at these times have bred abundantly. They have then dispersed and, in many cases, have died when the supply of rats declined. The coastal population seems to be more sedentary.

Eastern Grass Owls may be semi-colonial but the pairs are separated by several hundred metres when nesting or roosting. However, hunting over concentrations of rodents brings many owls together. Up to 30 have been seen in the air at once. In one case, an area of 100 acres (40 hectares) of fallow rice was occupied by up to 100 Eastern Grass Owls in pursuit of abundant prey.

In India, this is a bird of tall, rank grass and wet grassland on floodplains, from the Himalayan foothills to the plains of Assam. If disturbed from its roost by day, it flies only a short distance before dropping back into the grass and out of sight. It feeds on field mice, and also on birds, reptiles and a variety of insects.

The breeding habits of this owl are very similar to those of the Grass Owl. However, the Eastern Grass Owl may lay a larger clutch, although the usual clutch size is only four, and is more likely to begin incubating from the first egg, and so have young of staggered age and size. These factors suggest a greater adaptability to irregular food supplies; in poor years the older, larger chicks will probably survive, while the younger ones succumb to starvation.

The eggs of Grass Owls in Africa are 24% bigger than those of Barn Owls (*Tyto alba*), but in Asia the eggs of the two species are of equal size. This indicates that interrelationships between grass owls and Barn Owls have followed different routes in each continent. It adds weight to the argument for separating Grass Owl and Eastern Grass Owl as two distinct species.

BAY OWLS

TWO SPECIES

BAY OWL
Phodilus badius

LENGTH: *230 to 330 mm*   MAP NUMBER: 12
DESCRIPTION: *Dark-backed, pale-faced with angular head, dark facial stripes*
DISTRIBUTION: *Northern India, Sri Lanka, southern South-East Asia, Sumatra, Java, Borneo, Samar*
HABITAT: *Forests*
EGGS: *3–5. Nest in hole*
STATUS: *Frequent but elusive*

Strictly nocturnal, the Bay Owl lives in dense forest and, for this reason, is less well understood than might be expected for a bird of its numbers and range. Known also as the Oriental Bay Owl, it is found from northern India eastwards to Thailand, Malaysia and Borneo, with some isolated outposts on islands ranging from Sri Lanka and Bali to Samar in the Philippines.

Bay Owls enjoy the vicinity of water. They eat frogs and probably catch and eat fish. The bulk of their diet is made up of small mammals, lizards, insects and forest birds caught while roosting. This species has a variety of call notes, including a whistle, a low hoot and a ringing chatter. The most common call is reported to be a series of loud whistles.

Though similar to a Barn Owl (*Tyto alba*) in appearance, the Bay Owl has more pronounced, angular upper edges to the facial disc. Its shorter wings are thought to be a natural adaptation for hunting in forests. These wings provide an easy passage between branches and a greater ability to twist and turn, when avoiding trees or pursuing prey.

There are five races of the Bay Owl, varying from the small, eastern variety to a distinctly larger bird found in India. One race, found on Bunguran Island in the Indonesian archipelago, is known only from a single specimen and has never been observed in the wild.

Bay Owl nestlings differ in size, indicating that incubation begins with the laying of the first egg. The full clutch is three to five eggs. The Bay Owl lays them in a hole in a tree over several days. As each egg takes the same time to incubate, the chicks hatch at intervals.

AFRICAN BAY OWL
Phodilus prigoginei

LENGTH: *300 mm* MAP NUMBER: 13
DESCRIPTION: *Dark, small-footed bay owl*
DISTRIBUTION: *Congo basin, Africa*
HABITAT: *Forest*
STATUS: *Rare, perhaps threatened/endangered*

In March 1951, an owl previously unknown to science was killed in the forested mountains of Zaire. Its features marked it out as a relative of the Oriental Bay Owl (*Phodilus badius*). This was the first recorded sign that a bay owl of any kind inhabited Africa. Birds new to science have often been discovered since, mostly in South America, but such finds are few and far between in Africa.

The African Bay Owl has smaller feet, shorter claws and a thinner bill than the Oriental Bay Owl. It is darker in colour, being more rufous and less golden-buff. It is also known as the Tanzanian or the Congo Bay Owl. In the world of owls, some classifications are unresolved and certain English names are far from settled.

With the exception of a single, unconfirmed report in the mid-1970s, the species has not been observed since 1951. It is assumed that some African Bay Owls survive inside the threatened forests of Zaire but this species might easily disappear before it becomes better known to ornithologists. African forests have not been ravaged to the same degree as those in South-East Asia and South America, but are increasingly affected by commercial projects. The true status of the owl is unknown.

Family STRIGIDAE

SCOPS OWLS TO FOREST OWLS

ONE HUNDRED AND THIRTY EIGHT SPECIES IN TWENTY FOUR GENERA

SCOPS OWLS

WHITE-FRONTED SCOPS OWL
Otus sagittatus

LENGTH: *250 to 280 mm*   MAP NUMBER: 14
DESCRIPTION: *Large, long-tailed, rusty-orange scops owl with yellow eyes*
DISTRIBUTION: *South-East Asia*
HABITAT: *Forest*
STATUS: *Rare, declining, elusive*

This is the largest of the world's scops owls, mainly because of its unusually long tail. It is found in a long, narrow strip of forest that runs from extreme southern Burma, through Thailand and along the spine of Malaysia. It may also live in the adjacent uplands of northern Sumatra, although only a single specimen has been collected on the island.

The genus *Otus*, which includes scops owls and screech-owls, is large and complicated. Identification is difficult as there are only slight variations in plumage. Much depends on the differences in calls. Good tape-recordings of all the calls of each species do not yet exist and, therefore, classification of the numerous species is still a matter of great debate.

Screech-owls are the representatives of the genus in the New World. But the White-fronted Scops Owl is one of three species in Oriental Asia that lie between the scops owl and screech-owl groups. Too little is known of their calls and behaviour to classify them with certainty.

Oriental Asia has numerous different scops owls. The variety of species includes some which can be grouped as 'superspecies', while many of the species have been split into a number of races. They form a complex cluster of small owls whose taxonomic relationships have yet to be fully worked out. The White-fronted Scops Owl is one of the species which remains little known. As a rare bird of mountainous rain-forest, it is, understandably, a difficult species to study. It presents an interesting challenge.

RUFOUS SCOPS OWL
Otus rufescens

LENGTH: *150 to 180 mm*   MAP NUMBER: 15
DESCRIPTION: *Small, red-brown, orange-eyed*
DISTRIBUTION: *Malaysia, Sumatra, Java, Borneo, Philippines*
HABITAT: *Lowland rain-forest*
STATUS: *Probably rare and declining*

A small, rounded owl found in the lowland forests of Malaysia, Sumatra, Java, Borneo and the Philippines, the Rufous Scops Owl may be limited to primary rain-forest, the habitat most threatened by clearances. But there is some hope that it will occupy re-grown forest when the felling is completed. The Rufous Scops Owl has a close equivalent in the Tropical Screech-Owl (*Otus choliba*), which lives in comparable surroundings in the Amazon rain-forest. In other types of South-East Asian woodland the Rufous Scops Owl is replaced by the Collared Scops Owl (*Otus bakkamoena*), which lives in more open, drier woodland, and by the Spotted Scops Owl (*Otus spilocephalus*), which prefers dense woodlands in mountainous regions. The Rufous Scops Owl is, therefore, neatly restricted to the tropical forests below altitudes of about 3,300 feet (1,000m).

The bird's call is a low, hollow hoot, repeated at intervals. This species is not believed to be endangered but the loss of habitat must cause concern. This almost unknown owl, at home among virgin forest fauna, may have to survive in degraded fragments of woodland.

SANDY SCOPS OWL
Otus icterorhynchus

LENGTH: *180 to 200 mm*   MAP NUMBER: 16
DESCRIPTION: *Small, rufous, white-spotted scops with yellow eyes*
DISTRIBUTION: *West Africa*
HABITAT: *Lowland rain-forest*
STATUS: *Probably rare and declining*

A peachy-buff owl, with piercing yellow eyes beneath a neatly 'eared' crown, the Sandy Scops Owl is an eyecatching African species. Its range extends from Liberia eastwards to Ghana, Cameroon and eastern Zaire, but it has a very restricted, disjointed distribution within this large region. It is a rare bird of lowland, primary rain-forest. The scarcity of the species and the unwelcoming terrain make the Sandy Scops Owl difficult to locate.

The rich forests within its range abound in epiphytic

plants, tree-ferns and bamboos. The humid climate of the rain-forests reaches 30° centigrade, with 120″ (300cm) or more of rain each year. In these conditions, plentiful food exists on the ground and in the foliage for insect-eating birds such as the small Sandy Scops Owl.

It feeds on grasshoppers and crickets, probably using the typical technique of scops owls of watching from a perch and dropping onto unsuspecting prey in near darkness. It has excellent powers of hearing and its eyesight is good at low light intensities. Its voice is a descending whistle, lasting about one second and uttered every three or four seconds. This call distinguishes the Sandy Scops Owl from the common Scops Owl (*Otus scops*). Little is known about the bird's biology or behaviour.

SOKOKE SCOPS OWL
Otus ireneae

LENGTH: *160 to 180 mm*   MAP NUMBER: 17
DESCRIPTION: *Dull brown scops, short-tailed, yellow-eyed*
DISTRIBUTION: *Kenya*
HABITAT: *Forest*
STATUS: *Rare and endangered but perhaps stable*

Only in the Sokoke-Arabuku Forest on the coast of Kenya can this small owl be found. The forested area in this region was halved between 1956 and 1966 but 135 square miles (350 square kilometres) remain. Up to 1,500 pairs of Sokoke Scops Owls live in this area but further deforestation poses a threat to their survival. One reserve has been established covering 15 square miles (40 sq km). It remains to be seen whether this will provide adequate protection, or whether more reserves will be needed to safeguard this rare and threatened bird.

Inside this open forest on the red magarini sands, the characteristic series of five to nine "*who*" notes, just under a second apart, can be heard after dark. The owls are not found in locations where the forest is lower than 10—13 feet (3—4 metres) in height, or where it grows on different soils. Much remains to be discovered about the reasons for such a narrowly-defined habitat.

SPOTTED SCOPS OWL
Otus spilocephalus

LENGTH: *180 mm*   MAP NUMBER: 18
DESCRIPTION: *Pale rufous scops owl, spotted white above, barred below*
DISTRIBUTION: *Himalyas, China, South-East Asia*
HABITAT: *Dense forest in uplands*
EGGS: *2—5. Nest in hole*
STATUS: *Widespread but declining*

This owl, which is also known as the Mountain Scops Owl, is found in a long, narrow strip along the Himalayas, more widely across southern China, Thailand and Malaysia, and in the highlands of Borneo and northern Sumatra. In the Himalayas, it occupies oak, rhododendron, blue pine and deodar forest at a height of 2,000—8,500 feet or more (600—2,600m), but descends to the warmer valleys in winter. In Sumatra, it occupies dense rain-forest in the mountains.

The Spotted Scops Owl lays its clutch of two to five pure white eggs in a cavity in a tree growing on a steep slope or on the side of a deep, shaded gully. Frequently it selects a woodpecker's hole. It is one of the most nocturnal of owls and is hardly seen by day at all. This helps distinguish it from the Collared Pygmy-Owl (*Glaucidium brodiei*), a bird of similar size which shares its woodland habitat but often hunts by day.

The ringing call of the Spotted Scops Owl, echoing through forests, has been compared to the sound of a hammer striking an anvil and led to the name 'Himalayan Bellbird'. Patience is required to trace these calls back to this tiny, round-headed owl. Its calls begin an hour or so before full darkness and continue in bursts throughout the night. A Spotted Scops Owl can be lured by imitated calls and this method provides almost the only hope of seeing one in the wild.

The Spotted Scops Owl has a distinctive row of black-edged, white scapular feathers but the purpose of this pattern is obscure. However, it is obvious that the long, fine plumes or bristles that surround the bill and sweep across the face have some sensory function, like the whiskers of a cat. The face is pinched into a central ridge with a strong, protruding bill and wispy plumes which create a central tuft.

The food of this elusive owl is not fully known. Though clearly capable of taking small rodents, lizards and small birds, it may be more dependent on beetles, cicadas, mantids and other large insects. The stomach contents of dead individuals have contained predominantly insects. The Spotted Scops Owl seems to hunt in or beneath the main canopy of the forest rather than venturing out, like most species of scops owl, into more open areas.

On certain Asian islands, the Spotted Scops Owl is

replaced by closely-related species. The owls of Taiwan and the Andaman Islands have been placed by some ornithologists in the same species. The Javan race *angelinae*, a dark-plumaged bird of mountain forest, is sometimes considered a separate species. This bird, which has been called the Javan Scops Owl, seems to be a much more silent owl. The only known vocalization is a hissing call given by fledged young, which have been found in dense forest in February.

The races of Spotted Scops Owl, which may in fact be separate species, all live on separate islands and never meet, so it remains unknown if they are capable of interbreeding, which would establish whether they belong to the same species. In any event, the isolation of these separate populations means that, in the long term, they are likely to develop into separate species.

ANDAMAN SCOPS OWL
Otus balli

LENGTH: *180 mm*   MAP NUMBER: 19
DESCRIPTION: *Rusty scops owl with distinct dark and light spots*
DISTRIBUTION: *Andaman Islands in the Indian Ocean*
HABITAT: *Forest, gardens*
EGGS: *2−3. Nest in hole*
STATUS: *Frequent*

Strictly nocturnal and rarely seen, the Andaman Scops Owl has a strong call of "*hoot! hoot-curroo*" with a characteristically rolled 'r'. This sound enables the owl to be tracked down in and around the settlements of the Andaman Islands, a remote island chain south of the Bay of Bengal and Burma. It broadly resembles the Spotted Scops Owl (*Otus spilocephalus*), but their relationship is disputed and the owl of the Andaman Islands has been isolated long enough for superficial differences to have evolved. The Andaman Scops Owl is more rufous and less barred, with a charming pattern of spots on its underside. It frequents the neighbourhood of buildings and villages, and was long ago noted as partial to entering bungalows. This bird is confiding and, if left alone, is happy to live alongside mankind and may be seen perched on houses.

The Andaman Scops Owl eats insects, particularly caterpillars, which it finds by sidling, parrot-like, along the boughs of small trees. This is a trait not usually associated with owls. From mid-February to mid-April, two or three pure white eggs are laid in a small cavity, which may be a deserted woodpecker hole or barbet nest hole.

FLORES SCOPS OWL
Otus alfredi

LENGTH: *190 mm*   MAP NUMBER: 20
DESCRIPTION: *Densely barred and streaked, rusty-brown scops owl*
DISTRIBUTION: *Flores Island near Java*
HABITAT: *Mountain forest and clearings*
STATUS: *Probably rare, little known*

This owl, also known as Everett's Scops Owl, has a densely-marked pattern on a rather dark, rufous ground colour that is shared by many of the Oriental owls. It replaces the Spotted Scops Owl (*Otus spilocephalus*) on Flores Island, east of Java, where it inhabits forests in the mountains above 3,300 feet (1,000m). There, the lofty altitude tempers the stifling heat and humidity.

What little is known about this owl is derived largely, and perhaps entirely, from the original specimens collected by Everett. The owl has had a chequered history in textbooks and has even been wrongly illustrated. The Flores Scops Owl is uniformly foxy-cinnamon above, with white spots on the scapular feathers, a dark facial disc, and yellow bill and eyes. The important details of its life — what it eats, where it nests and so on — are unknown.

STRIATED SCOPS OWL
Otus brucei

LENGTH: *160 mm*   MAP NUMBER: 21
DESCRIPTION: *Small, grey, streaked scops owl*
DISTRIBUTION: *Middle East, Central and Western Asia*
HABITAT: *Desert, semi-desert, oases*
EGGS: *3–6. Nest in hole*
STATUS: *Frequent but status uncertain*

Tucked up close to the trunk of a gnarled tree in a desert wadi, this owl looks pale and grey. Its markings resemble a piece of flaking bark or a crumbling slice of cork and it sits perfectly still to complete the illusion. It usually waits until dark before moving out to hunt for moths, beetles or crickets. Occasionally it searches by day. It has remarkable agility and may even catch small bats in the air. Its insect prey can be picked from foliage or caught in mid-air, as well as trapped on the ground.

In the Middle East, the Striated Scops Owl, also known as Bruce's Scops Owl, is a bird of semi-desert regions. In the Soviet Union, it is even known as the Yellow or Desert Scops Owl. It may be a form of the common Scops Owl (*Otus scops*) adapted to the harsh demands of the desert or, more likely, a form of the Oriental Scops Owl (*Otus sunia*). Its place in the large, complex family of scops owls has never been precisely understood.

The voice and neater, blacker streakings of this owl have usually led to its identification as a separate species. Its legs are more feathered than those of the Scops Owl, and its long wings are a fraction more rounded.

The Striated Scops Owl lives in arid foothills, close to cliffs and rocky gorges with scattered trees. But it also inhabits gardens in towns. This has raised doubts about whether it is a true desert bird. Its typical habitats are riverine forests of tamarisk, poplar and willow, as well as orchards, vineyards, citrus plantations and date palms. The open desert in regions of China, India and Pakistan may be the habitat of only a fraction of its population. Striated Scops Owls are present all year in Iran but are summer migrants to Iraq and Oman, spending the winter in the Indus Valley and around Bombay. Those from central Asia are also migratory, flying south to avoid the bitterly cold continental winters, but they travel only half the distance covered by the Scops Owls of Europe.

The Striated Scops Owl has two distinct calls, both soft, dove-like and carrying only short distances. The male on territory gives a hollow "*whoo*", which has been noted as being repeated about eight times in five seconds, or at a rate of 67 each minute. This contrasts with the 22–26 notes per minute produced by the Scops Owl. There is another hollow, resonant note, more drawn out and repeated at longer, less regular intervals. This may be a contact note or the call of the female. It also utters barking notes of alarm and a fierce rattling sound.

Though largely nocturnal, the Striated Scops Owl can be seen flying before dusk and, in Baluchistan, has been reported as hunting in daylight. Its behaviour has much in common with that of the Little Owl (*Athene noctua*), though that is a larger, stronger and more diurnal bird.

Nests have been found in woodpecker holes in poplars, willows, mulberries and date palms. They have also been found in cavities in river banks, in old stone walls and in the domed nests of magpies. In one study, younger birds occupied magpie nests while older pairs nested in old walls. This indicates that wall nests are the preferred, more successful sites. Magpie eggs were sometimes found in the owl's clutches of eggs, suggesting that the owls could take over from a pair of magpies even after they had begun to breed. The Striated Scops Owl nests earlier than the Scops Owl, which returns from Africa later in the spring.

SCOPS OWL
Otus scops

LENGTH: *160 to 190 mm*   MAP NUMBER: 22
DESCRIPTION: *Small, eared owl, complex grey-buff markings, pale eyes*
DISTRIBUTION: *Eurasia*
HABITAT: *Woodland, cultivation, forest edge*
EGGS: *3–6. Nest in hole*
STATUS: *Common, locally declining*

One penetrating call reveals the presence of a Scops Owl wherever it breeds, from south-west Europe across to eastern Siberia. The Scops Owl of these regions gives a short, piping "*chew*" or "*kiup*" sound, neither just one syllable nor quite two, and repeats it mechanically every two seconds for minutes on end. The African race, which breeds everywhere south of the Sahara, has a more vibrant, purring note, but is equally persistent.

A good view of this small owl, with its rich, intricate plumage, is rare however. They form elusive, tiny shapes in the gloom and are skilled at retreating into darkness. When tracked down, Scops Owls are often mere silhouettes on a chimney pot, or shapes on a wire beside a lamp post. In these situations, they look dumpy, sometimes longer-tailed and slimmer than Little Owls (*Athene noctua*), with slight, angular 'corners' to the head. Now and then, the ear tufts are raised.

The Scops Owl will fly away suddenly, with a quick, fluttering action. In flight, the tail looks short and the overall motion does not suggest a bird that undertakes long migratory journeys from Europe or Asia to Africa. By day, the owl may give a few calls from the depths of a thicket or high in a tree. But most vocal activity is after dark and increases as the breeding season approaches. During the day, the owls hide high up in thick foliage and, when approached, stretch upwards with the feathers of the body pressed flat, ear tufts erect and eyes closed to upright slits. Standing motionless, or swaying gently from side to side, the Scops Owl displays one of the finest examples of camouflage in the bird world.

For such a common, widespread member of the scops owl family, it is unsurprising that many races have been recognized. But the categories are unresolved and some authorities lump the Oriental races with Scops Owl, while others regard them as a separate species, the Oriental Scops Owl (*Otus sunia*). The dozen African races may likewise be separated into a species of their own. The best solution may be to accept them as three species. It is strongly argued that the Oriental birds, at least, are distinct from the common Scops Owl. The name, scops, derives from the Greek word for look, or watch. It was originally applied to owls of any form before being limited to the scops owl family in the genus *Otus*.

Scops Owl (*Otus scops*)

In September, migrant birds from Europe begin to reach Africa, spreading south into the savannas, though not the dense forests. They return northwards in April. Birds from Asia move to Ethiopia, flying a distance of up to 5,000 miles (8,000 kilometres). The Sahara crossing can be too exacting for some and they perish in the desert. African residents have shorter wings, as is to be expected in races which do not migrate. They prefer scrub and lowland woods, where they are often quite common, and feed on grasshoppers, beetles, moths, cockroaches and scorpions.

Scops Owls are territorial when nesting, though up to five may roost in a single tree in winter, and males defend their area by calling. But the Scops Owl is a relatively weak, inoffensive bird, less than three-quarters of the weight of the Little Owl, which may drive it from likely nest holes. Scops Owls are often moved from their nest sites, and even killed, by Tawny Owls (*Strix aluco*). Eagle Owls (*Bubo bubo*), and probably Barn Owls (*Tyto alba*), also attack and kill the Scops Owl. Contact with the Little Owl is kept to a minimum because the Scops Owl is significantly more nocturnal in its habits.

In Europe, Scops Owls prefer open woodland, parkland and trees around villages, but also occupy birch and conifer forest in the north. They are birds of cultivated countryside with plenty of trees, and have probably expanded in range and numbers with the clearances of European forests. The provision of good habitat — city parks are ideal — and hunting perches on telephone wires and lamp-posts has enabled them to spread to many towns and suburbs. Only the growth of vineyards, which has reduced the number of old trees, has hindered them.

The breeding area of Scops Owls may be more or less wooded and set in a variety of landscapes. Nests are made in hollows in old roofs, rocks, stone walls and in trees. Woodpecker holes are sometimes used and nest boxes will be readily accepted. After inspecting possible holes, the female begins to roost in the chosen nest site. It is often a half-open hole. Up to five white eggs, rarely more, are laid. Fed by the male while she sits, the female incubates them for 24 days. The chicks fledge in three to four weeks, leaving the nest site earlier than other owl chicks of similar size that nest deep inside safer cavities. They are fed on prey hunted by the male for the first 18 days and by both parents until they are about nine weeks old. Families may migrate as a group in autumn, facing together the rigours of a long, difficult journey to Africa.

ORIENTAL SCOPS OWL
Otus sunia

LENGTH: *160 to 180 mm*   MAP NUMBER: *23*
DESCRIPTION: *Pale, streaked, short-tailed scops owl*
DISTRIBUTION: *Southern and Eastern Asia*
HABITAT: *Forest and woodland*
EGGS: *3–6?*
STATUS: *Frequent to common*

The Oriental Scops Owl, like the common Scops Owl (*Otus scops*), lives in open woodlands, dry savannas and parks, and riverside belts of trees. The two birds share so many features that some authorities question whether the eastern group is a separate species. The Striated Scops Owl (*Otus brucei*), found from the Middle East to India, may be a third species or a race of one of the others.

To the east, the Oriental Scops Owl occupies much of southern mainland Asia, Sri Lanka, some islands in the Indonesian archipelago and Japan. In parts of this range, birds classified as Oriental Scops Owls live beside those deemed to be common Scops Owls, and behave separately. The Oriental Scops Owl prefers river valleys while the common Scops Owl lives in the higher woods. This difference in habitat supports the argument that they are indeed separate species. For clarity of study and documentation, it is surely useful to separate the three groups, which are more or less clearly identifiable.

Recent studies of the voices of these owls in Pakistan, published in 1986, suggest that they are genuinely separate species. Spotted Scops Owls (*Otus spilocephalus*), Scops Owls, Striated Scops Owls, Oriental Scops Owls and Collared Scops Owls (*Otus bakkamoena*) were tape-recorded and their songs were analyzed. They were also trapped, and their wing formulae were studied. These are the relative lengths of their primary feathers — the long, outer feathers on the wing — measurements which are remarkably constant within a species but often show distinct differences from one species to another.

Such factors are useful in identifying many of the small, difficult warblers, for example. These tests with scops owls supported the view that the species are indeed valid. In Pakistan, at the same time, Scops Owls and Striated Scops Owls were found breeding in the same region, while Striated Scops Owls and Oriental Scops Owls were also found breeding alongside one another. There was no evidence at all of interbreeding. They behaved quite separately, as would be expected of good species.

If they were simply races, it would be expected that mixed pairs and intermediate types would be found. On the other hand, Scops Owls and Oriental Scop Owls did not overlap. They are, in fact, mutually exclusive, which is further good evidence that they are separate, competing species which have no zone of overlap or intergradation.

These studies in Pakistan did, however, complicate matters, as the calls of the Collared Scops Owl there were found to be quite unlike the calls of Collared Scops Owls of eastern Asia. It was recommended that two species should be recognized: the Collared Scops Owl *Otus lempiji* and the Indian Scops Owl *Otus bakkamoena*. African Scops Owls were separated on the basis of their calls as *Otus senegalensis*.

Oriental Scops Owls from north-east Siberia and Japan migrate to China and India for the winter. On their return journey in spring, stray migrants have reached the Aleutian Islands of Alaska. In India they occupy both deciduous and evergreen forests, orchards and a variety of cultivated land with groves of trees which provide the dense foliage in which these birds delight to hide themselves away.

The voice is likened to a barbet's call, a monotonous three-note song described as "*kurook-took*" or "*wuk-tuk-tah*". Its rhythm, which has a great regularity over very long periods, has been compared to a giant pendulum or the working of a pump engine. The sound can be clearly heard over several hundred yards.

For its nest, the Oriental Scops Owl chooses a hole in a wall or in a tree trunk. It lays a small clutch of three or four small, white eggs. Little is known about the behaviour at the nest although it is assumed to differ from other scops owls in its general biology.

As a hunter, the Oriental Scops is much like its European counterpart. It takes a wide range of prey, including moths, beetles, locusts, small mice and shrews, caterpillars and spiders. It has been recorded eating great numbers of spiders when they are abundant in low bushes. Although it takes prey from the tree canopy, the Oriental Scops Owl also feeds on the ground and is less a forest hunter than a bird of open glades and woodland edge.

MENTAUR SCOPS OWL
Otus umbra

LENGTH: *160 mm*   MAP NUMBER: 24
DESCRIPTION: *Very dark brown scops owl, pale face, yellow eyes*
DISTRIBUTION: *Simeulue Island near Sumatra*
HABITAT: *Forest edges*
STATUS: *Local, perhaps rare, little known*

The Mentaur Scops Owl lives on the steep slopes of the island of Simeulue, off the north-west coast of Sumatra. Also known as the Simeulue Scops Owl, it is found at the edges of the forest and in areas of the forest that have been cleared and planted with cloves. It may be the same species as the Enggano Scops Owl (*Otus enganensis*), but has a noticeably different song which, fortunately, has been recorded on tape. The two birds are currently regarded as separate species but the individuality of the Mentaur Scops Owl has often been challenged. In the past it has been regarded at different times as a form of the common Scops Owl (*Otus scops*) and the Oriental Scops Owl (*Otus sunia*). Details of its biology are unknown.

ENGGANO SCOPS OWL
Otus enganensis

LENGTH: *160 mm*   MAP NUMBER: 25
DISTRIBUTION: *Enggano Island near Sumatra*
STATUS: *Local, probably rare*

Enggano is a tiny island off the south-west tip of Sumatra which has its own form of scops owl. Current research tends to support the view that it is a separate species and not an island form of the Oriental Scops Owl (*Otus sunia*). Though very similar to the Mentaur Scops Owl (*Otus umbra*), which lives on an island at the other end of Sumatra, 700 miles (1100km) to the north-west, their true relationship remains unclear. Island species, such as these, are adapted to life in their particular habitats and it is a matter of speculation whether they could survive conditions on the mainland. The survival of birds such as the Enggano Scops Owl is an example of exclusion by competition. If two owls eat similar prey and require the same habitat, then only the best adapted species will exist in any one place. Due to a lack of adequate reference, this species has not been illustrated.

AFRICAN SCOPS OWL
Otus senegalensis

LENGTH: *190 mm*   MAP NUMBER: 26
DESCRIPTION: *Small, streaked, grey-brown, eared owl with yellow eyes; best separated by voice*
DISTRIBUTION: *Africa south of the Sahara*
HABITAT: *Woodland, dry bush*
EGGS: *3–6. Nest in hole*
STATUS: *Frequent*

This bird lives in woodland and dry bush throughout its range, which stretches across much of Africa, south of the Sahara. It avoids desert and the thickest tropical forest and is not found in the southern, forested edge of West Africa, the Congo basin and parts of Ethiopia. In the south, the African Scops Owl is a bird of the bushveld, but is unable to survive in the treeless Karoo, the grassy upland plateaux or mountains. For this reason, it is absent from much of central and western South Africa and the coast of Namibia.

The African Scops Owl strongly resembles the Scops Owl (*Otus scops*) which migrates to Africa during the European winter. Some authorities have described it as a race of the European bird but, given the small differences that have been used to separate the South-East Asian scops owls, it seems sensible also to treat the African Scops Owl as a separate species.

It has the typical scops form with a rather angular head 'eared' at the corners. The ears may be laid back, flat and almost invisible, or raised as broad, blunt lobes or as longer, freer, pointed horns. The substantial look of these tufts when seen from the front, typical of eared owls, belies a thin, blade-like form. From the side, they are slender and weak-looking.

This bird is beautifully patterned, with intricate and delicate pencilling and bars of buff against a grey and brown background. Some birds are more rufous than others but are still essentially quite dark with a sombre hue. The underparts are broadly streaked with deep brown across the middle, with heavier markings than those of the European bird. The face is marked by two broad pale crescents between the eyes in the 'back to back' formation usual in scops owls. These help to give the African Scops Owl a mobile face, as the pale markings can be drawn up into two, almost vertical lines, or relaxed into a pair of mirror-image curves. The facial disc is greyish, ringed with subtle barring, visible only at close range, and edged with a narrow line of black.

The eyes of the African Scops Owl are pale yellow and round, with the clear corneas bulging like glass marbles. Like those of many birds of prey, these eyes are striking when seen from the front, but only from a close side view can their almost hemispherical shape be appreciated.

This owl adapts its appearance to its needs. When wishing to stay hidden, it stretches upwards, appearing long and thin. To examine an intruder it may turn its head through almost 180 degrees to look over its shoulder. In this position, the eyes are half-closed, the edges of the facial disc are scarcely visible and the ear tufts are raised. In more relaxed mood, the owl is rounder and dumpier, its head often sunk into its shoulders and its facial disc looking rather more distinct.

African Scops Owls, like other scops owls, are best detected by their calls. The territorial call differs markedly from that of the European bird. The monotonous, trilling call, a common enough night sound in the African bush, can provoke a small chorus of voices echoing in the darkness. As many as six or eight birds may be heard together, each asserting a territorial right.

The call is a "*kruup*" sound with a vibrant, purring effect quite distinct from the clear, liquid note of the Scops Owl so familiar around the Mediterranean. It is repeated every five to eight seconds, whereas the common Scops calls every two seconds. Calling starts soon after dark, when the owl leaves its concealed daytime roost. The female has a higher and softer call, and there also several other calls, especially at or near the nest.

The roost may be used regularly over long periods and gradually a mess of white droppings, pellets and bits of food accumulates beneath it. The bird itself may settle only a few feet (a metre or so) above the ground, but is always well-hidden in foliage or a tangle of creepers and roots. If approached, it stays still but under real pressure may sway from side to side before breaking cover and flying off into another thicket close by. It dislikes being in the open by day, as it is likely to be mobbed by other birds or attacked by predators. Like certain small North American owls, it may be so reluctant to fly that it can be picked up by hand.

Like other scops owls, it is strictly nocturnal unless disturbed. At night, it moves to a perch and sits, hunched and bent over, scanning the ground for prey. Being a small owl, lacking large feet and bill, it is not a powerful hunter, and is content with tiny prey. This consists largely of woodlice, millipedes, centipedes, beetles, grasshoppers, moths, cockroaches and spiders, which usually abound on its territory. It will sometimes kill a small rodent or small bird, or perhaps a gecko or a lizard, but it is basically insectivorous.

Its favoured habitat is acacia and mopane woodlands, which are full of old, gnarled trees, often with broken branches as a result of elephant damage. Such woodlands provide abundant cavities for roosting, open branches from which to scan the ground and holes for nesting. The nest may be in a natural cavity in a trunk, an abandoned woodpecker hole or, occasionally, in a hole at the end of a broken branch. One was even discovered in the base of a Lappet-faced Vulture's (*Torgos tracheliotus*) nest. They will also use nest boxes.

The clutch of eggs is small, four at most, and the eggs are incubated for 22 days. The chicks fly 25 to 28 days after hatching, but how long they continue to depend on their parents for food after that is not known. The female broods the chicks, rarely leaving them for the first 10 days, but gradually helping to supplement the food brought by the male. His hunting efforts increase when the chicks hatch and there is a rapid reduction in his calling during the night. To feed large chicks he will bring some 40 to 50 items of food to the nest each night, while the female will bring perhaps half as many.

The chicks are at risk from predators of all kinds — birds, lizards, monkeys and snakes — and therefore leave the nest as early as possible, though many are killed before they have a chance to fly. Despite this heavy predation, and the small size of clutches, the population is not declining and the African Scops Owl looks likely to remain a widespread, successful species for a long time yet.

FLAMMULATED OWL
Otus flammeolus

LENGTH: *160 to 170 mm*   MAP NUMBER: 27
DESCRIPTION: *Small, eared owl, with complex pattern of rufous, brown and buff, dark eyes*
DISTRIBUTION: *Western North America, Central America*
HABITAT: *Mountain conifer forests*
EGGS: *3–4. Nest in hole*
STATUS: *Frequent*

This is the North American equivalent of the European Scops Owl (*Otus scops*). The Flammulated Owl is found in mountain conifer forests above the western deserts of the United States, along the ridges of the Rocky Mountains from British Colombia south into Central America. Its favoured habitat is forests of ponderosa and yellow pine, often mixed with oak or aspen, with bushy undergrowth. It also thrives in woods of bristlecone, lodgepole and sugar pines with Douglas firs. It is a summer visitor to the northern parts of its range, migrating to Central America to escape the intense cold of winter in the Rocky Mountains.

The Flammulated Owl is the smallest and lightest of the North American *Otus* owls. The name means 'ruddy' or flame-coloured. The streaks of reddish feathering on its back resemble the shafts of sunlight that may penetrate the dense foliage of the tree in which it roosts by day. Its plumage has one of the most cryptic patterns of any owl, with cross-bars, points and arrows of dark brown on a background of greys, cool buff and ochre. The face and scapulars have rusty-coloured areas. This detailed patterning is reminiscent of the Scops Owl in Europe, which it resembles in many ways, although it differs in having dark brown eyes. It exploits its camouflage by leaning against the trunk of a pine. If disturbed, it stretches upwards with its plumage tightly sleeked. In this pose, its outline is difficult to discern and it resembles a piece of broken branch.

This bird has a delicate, lightweight physique, similar to that of the Elf Owl (*Micrathene whitneyi*). The bill is small and narrow and the long, thin toes have very fine claws. Its ear tufts are small and inconspicuous, and only erect if the owl is disturbed during the day.

In some parts of its range, the Flammulated Owl lives in unusual clusters. Several pairs occupy territories so close together that they may even overlap, yet there are large, vacant spaces between the groups. It is probable, though, that this elusive species is overlooked in places where it is actually present — in many areas it is known to be present throughout suitable habitat. In regions where it is scarce,

the Flammulated Owl is best detected by playing recordings of its voice in the evenings between May and July. Real birds will often call back and unexpected numbers have been found in this way.

The voice of this owl is perhaps its most curious feature. The call is a soft "*hoo*", repeated every few seconds. The sound is remarkably deep, with a ventriloquial effect, and seems to be the call of a much larger bird farther away. It is as if the small Flammulated Owl was simulating a more dangerous species. The structure of the vocal organs has been shown to facilitate the deep sound. This feature indicates that the owl has no close relationship with any other owl species.

Nests are usually in tree holes, often old flicker's holes in aspen. The eggs are laid on a scattering of loose, dry material. Some pairs nest in boxes, whether erected especially for owls or intended for American Kestrels (*Falco sparverius*). They lay only three or four eggs, a mark of a species that enjoys a fairly stable life, without fluctuating numbers caused by unpredictable changes in food availability.

The Flammulated Owl eats mainly nocturnal insects and spiders. It is primarily a moth-eater and flies with great agility from tree to tree or above the woodland canopy, capturing its prey in its bill. It is active mostly just after sunset and at dawn, with a lesser peak of activity in the middle of the night, a pattern resembling that of nightjars and, indeed, the moths which it eats.

RAJAH'S SCOPS OWL
Otus brookii

LENGTH: *230 mm*   MAP NUMBER: 28
DESCRIPTION: *Large, bright, eared scops owl, boldly patterned rusty-brown, black and cream*
DISTRIBUTION: *Sumatra, Java, Borneo*
HABITAT: *Mountain forest*
STATUS: *Probably declining*

The mountains of Java, Sumatra and Borneo are home to this owl, which resembles the larger Collared Scops Owl (*Otus bakkamoena*) of China. However, like many island owls, it has stronger, brighter colours. The Rajah's Scops Owl inhabits forests 4,000 to 8,000 feet (1,200–2,400m) above sea level. It is believed to be quite widespread, but reports are rare and no nest has yet been found. The call has been described as a clear note, repeated monotonously. This is one of many birds of the tropical forests which have never been comprehensively studied. Forest clearances on these islands must pose a threat to the future of this colourful owl.

MADAGASCAR SCOPS OWL
Otus rutilus

LENGTH: *190 to 230 mm*   MAP NUMBER: 29
DESCRIPTION: *Pale, brown scops owl, marked with white and streaked below*
DISTRIBUTION: *Madagascar, Pemba Island*
HABITAT: *Forest, brush and plantations*
EGGS: *4–5. Nest in tree hole or on the ground.*
STATUS: *Probably declining but locally common*

Over a period of several millennia, isolated populations of the Collared Scops Owl (*Otus bakkamoena*) are thought to have evolved into two distinct new species, the Madagascar Scops Owl and Indonesia's Magic Scops Owl (*Otus manadensis*). The Madagascar Scops Owl itself, which is also known as the Ruddy Scops Owl, has two geographically separated populations on islands off the coast of East Africa. It occurs on Madagascar and on Pemba Island off the Tanzanian coast. The Pemba Island birds are sometimes recognized as a separate species, the Pemba Scops Owl *Otus pembaensis*.

In Madagascar, scattered records imply a wide but sparse distribution. Unexpectedly, perhaps, in this island of many threatened rarities, it has been reported as common in places and even abundant. It is common in the forested area between Betsileo and Tanala, in the forest of Ankafana and around Zahamena. It is quite widely spread in woodland habitats away from the high plateau, and is found between sea level and 6,000 feet (1,800m). The Madagascar Scops Owl is also able to occupy sparser brush and remnants of partially exploited forest as well as the primary forest habitat.

The owls of Pemba nest in heaps of dead branches and leaves on the ground, in plantations of exotic trees such as cloves and mangoes as well as in the native forest. However, this species usually nests in tree cavities, laying four to five eggs.

Pemba Island birds, completely confident of their camouflage, sit so tightly when disturbed at the roost that they can be picked up by hand. On Madagascar, the call is a series of five to seven rapid, short hoots. They call as the sun sets, though less so after nightfall, with a short "*uh*" note uttered every half a second or so. This may, indeed, be both birds of a pair calling alternately. They also call in flight as they move from tree to tree, pausing as they drop down to snatch an insect from the ground, or to catch a moth in mid-air. They are certainly among the most delightful of small owls to watch but few birdwatchers have had the opportunity to see them.

MAGIC SCOPS OWL
Otus manadensis

LENGTH: *190 to 230 mm*   MAP NUMBER: 30
DESCRIPTION: *Bright rusty-red scops owl, boldly chequered*
DISTRIBUTION: *Sulawesi and South-East Asian islands*
HABITAT: *Forest, forest clearing*
STATUS: *Widespread but probably declining*

The Magic Scops Owl is a small, nocturnal bird with piercing eyes and angled ear tufts. It is widespread and relatively well-known among the oceanic islands of eastern Indonesia. There are further isolated populations on the Mentawai Islands off western Sumatra and, to the north, in the Philippines and the Japanese Ryukyu Islands. It lives in beautiful but demanding regions where 100 inches (250cm) of rain fall each year and the temperature often exceeds 30° centigrade.

A single, gentle call note from the darkness reveals the presence of this owl, but it can be difficult to get a good view of it. The Magic Scops Owl is divided into several island forms, variously known as the Celebes or Sulawesi Scops Owl, the Mentawai or Sipora Scops Owl and the Moluccan Scops Owl. There is no consensus on whether they form different species. The Magic Scops Owl group replaces the Collared Scops Owl (*Otus bakkamoena*) of the Asian mainland on many of the oceanic islands,

occupying roughly the same ecological niche.

The birds from the Mentawai Islands off Sumatra are geographically isolated and differ in appearance from other Magic Scops Owls. They have been named *Otus mentawi*. In Sulawesi (Celebes), the owls live in a variety of forest habitats from sea-level up to around 8,200 feet (2,500m) and are the basic, greyish *manadensis* group, which does not vary in colour. In other islands, yet another species has been split off. This is the *magicus* group, which includes a variety of more or less red, brown and grey types with calls recognizably different from *manadensis* and from each other.

Biak Island, off the northern coast of Irian Jaya (New Guinea) has a related owl, the rare Biak Island Scops Owl (*Otus beccarii*). Extensive surveys carried out in 1973 found just one pair, which was living in the only patch of forest left undisturbed on the island. Whether they survive is a matter of speculation. These small owls may be another separate species, or yet another link in the complex chain of Magic Scops Owls on the islands. The birdwatcher's best plan with these frustratingly difficult owls is to leave the taxonomic arguments to the museum specialists, get a list of which type is on each island and stick to the simple principle: 'If it is on Buru, it must be *magicus*'.

LESSER SUNDA SCOPS OWL
Otus silvicolus

LENGTH: *230 mm*   MAP NUMBER: 31
DESCRIPTION: *Dull, pale, uniform scops owl, lightly barred*
DISTRIBUTION: *Flores and Sumbawa Islands*
HABITAT: *Mountain forest, bamboo thickets*
STATUS: *Very local, probably rare*

This bird, one of the larger Asian *Otus* owls, occurs only on the islands of Sumbawa and Flores in the Lesser Sunda Islands, an Indonesian archipelago situated south of Sulawesi, between Java and New Guinea. The Lesser Sunda Scops Owl is found alongside the Magic Scops Owl (*Otus manadensis*) on Sumbawa and Flores; and, on Flores, there is a third species, the Flores Scops Owl (*Otus alfredi*). There must be distinct differences in the ecology of these three species to allow them to co-exist on these relatively small islands without competition.

The Lesser Sunda Scops Owl, also known as Wallace's Scops Owl, is found in bamboo thickets in the lowlands and in forest up to a height of 5,250 feet (1,600m). The bird also occurs around farms and even in the town of Ruteng on Flores. It breeds in May. This is a more olive, less rufous bird than the other owls on the islands. Its ability to live close to human settlements and in a variety of habitats indicates a degree of adaptability that augurs well for its future survival. In common with many other insular or remote species, its biology has yet to be fully studied in the field by ornithologists.

Trevor Boyer's painting illustrates the type specimen of this species, which is an immature female. The very few barred feathers on the underside are presumably new, adult-type feathers, beginning to displace the plainer feathers of the juvenile plumage.

WHITEHEAD'S SCOPS OWL
Otus megalotis

LENGTH: *230 mm*   MAP NUMBER: 32
DISTRIBUTION: *Luzon Island in the Philippines*
EGGS: *3−4.*
STATUS: *Local and probably endangered*

Found only on northern Luzon, the main island in the Philippines, Whitehead's Scops Owl may perhaps be simply a large, brown race of the Collared Scops Owl (*Otus bakkamoena*), or a race of the Spotted Scops Owl (*Otus spilocephalus*). But its isolated situation suggests that it is a true species, like other localized forms in the region.

The bird is named after its discoverer, John Whitehead, a Victorian ornithologist. Although in poor health, he left England in 1884 on a four-year expedition to Borneo. In December 1893, he returned to Asia, this time to Luzon. Whitehead complained that the hunters who acquired specimens for him were 'worse than useless', damaging the birds so badly that even he was unable to do much with them. He discarded most of the skins.

Struggling on in harsh conditions, Whitehead made nine expeditions, returning between each of them to Manila, where he prepared specimens and sent them to England. On one occasion, a batch of specimens was destroyed by fire and Whitehead returned to an island to replace them. In doing so, he discovered a new species of eagle, the spectacular Philippine or Monkey-eating Eagle (*Pithecophaga jefferyi*).

These were exciting times with much to discover and collectors had few scruples about using a gun to achieve their ends. In 1899, aged just 38, Whitehead died from dysentery and fever on Hainan Island off southern China.

Whitehead's Scops Owl lays three or four eggs, in the period of maximum rainfall, but little more is known about the species today than was known in the late 19th century. As with so many obscure species, which modern ornithologists can locate only with great difficulty, it is perhaps remarkable that it was ever discovered.

COLLARED SCOPS OWL
Otus bakkamoena

LENGTH: *190 to 230 mm*   MAP NUMBER: 33
DESCRIPTION: *Small, dark scops owl, heavily spotted*
DISTRIBUTION: *South and East Asia, Indonesia, Japan*
HABITAT: *Light woodland, forest edge*
EGGS: *3–5. Nest in hole*
STATUS: *Widespread and frequent*

This owl's range covers a huge, diverse area of Asia and it is one of the most widespread of scops owls. As a result, it has become the standard owl against which other owls in the region are generally judged and described. Its range overlaps with those of Rufous Scops Owl (*Otus rufescens*) and Spotted Scops Owl (*Otus spilocephalus*). It is, though, absent from many islands, where it is replaced by closely related species that seem better adapted to island life.

The Collared Scops Owl is found from the tropics of Java and the Philippines to temperate Siberia, and from Pakistan eastwards to Japan. There are over 20 races; they are generally brown birds without the grey and rufous shades evident in races of many other species. Recent studies have led some experts to split this species. Birds in India, the Himalayas and westwards to Arabia have been christened the Indian Scops Owl but have retained the scientific name *Otus bakkamoena*, while the eastern races have retained the common name Collared Scops Owl and been given a new scientific name, *Otus lempiji*. This is confusing, to say the least. The bird is therefore treated here as one species, under its long-standing name, Collared Scops Owl (*Otus bakkamoena*).

In South-East Asia it inhabits coastal mangrove swamps and areas of grassland with scattered trees. As the forest has been gradually replaced by mixed farmland, scrub and gardens, the Collared Scops Owl has increased in numbers and spread at the expense of more specialized forest owls. It is rarely found in areas over 3,300 feet (1,000m) above sea level. At higher altitudes, it is replaced by the Spotted Scops Owl.

One of the larger Asian *Otus* owls, it has the rounded wings typical of forest-living scops owls which do not migrate far. It is a characteristic scops owl in shape and appearance, with a large head and wide chest, tapering down to a narrow rear end and short tail. The ear tufts at the corners of the head add to the triangular effect.

Asleep, this owl can look dumpy and rounded but, when active and alert, it is more angular, adopting a variety of postures with attractive twists and turns of the head and body. The plumage of the head has a 'frosted' look, with whitish bands from the inner edges of the ear tufts running down over the eyes to the 'moustache' beside the bill. There are speckled white sides to the head around a browner facial disc. The colour of the eyes varies from brown to hazel to golden-yellow.

This owl is rarely seen by day. When roosting it looks like a broken branch, adopting an upright, still posture in the shade of a branch covered with creepers. In the evening, it reveals its presence. The calls begin at dusk and continue intermittently all night long. The sound is a monotonous "*whut?*" in an unhurried, questioning tone, delivered every three seconds for spells of 10 or 15 minutes. After a while, the calls stop, but then start again from a different tree, as if the bird had paused to snatch prey from the ground. Both sexes call for long periods but only rarely have there been reports of duetting pairs.

This is a slightly larger bird than the Oriental Scops Owl (*Otus sunia*), which can often be found nearby, and it eats proportionately more mammalian prey, though its main food is insects. This probably allows the two to live side by side with little aggression. The Brown Hawk Owl (*Ninox scutulata*) may also occupy the same areas but it is larger and eats insects caught in flight, and so avoids direct competition. The Collared Scops Owl eats chiefly beetles, cockroaches, grasshoppers and moths, but it varies its diet with rodents and small birds, geckos and even bats.

The breeding season and clutch size vary throughout its range. In the south, the Collared Scops Owl breeds in the wettest period of the year, laying three or four smooth, rounded white eggs. In the north, it lays four or five eggs in the spring. In India, it lays three to five eggs and generally nests in a tree cavity. In many regions this is the commonest owl and it will nest in abandoned buildings near towns and villages. Those in Sri Lanka nest at the edges of tea or rubber plantations, a choice which demonstrates its ability to adapt to large-scale changes of habitat. Though large numbers are killed in China and Korea for their reputed medicinal powers, the owl is respected and feared elsewhere in its range as a bird of ill-omen. It is one owl whose future seems assured.

GRAND COMORO SCOPS OWL
Otus pauliani

LENGTH: *200mm*   MAP NUMBER: 34
DESCRIPTION: *Small scops owl*
DISTRIBUTION: *Grand Comoro Island in the West Indian Ocean*
HABITAT: *Forest/upland heath intergrade*
STATUS: *Rare and endangered*

When this small owl was first discovered in 1958, the ornithologist involved considered it to be a new species, on the basis of its distinct form and voice, but was persuaded that it was merely a race of the Madagascar Scops Owl (*Otus rutilus*). Not really satisfied, however, C W Benson went on to study the Madagascar species, and this further convinced him of the validity of his initial suspicions; he had, indeed, found a new species.

The Grand Comoro Scops Owl was initially discovered when birds were heard calling. A specimen was then collected at La Convalescence, in the upper reaches of forest on the west side of Mount Karthala on the island of Grand Comoro off East Africa. Despite searches elsewhere, it was not found in any other forest tracts. Then it was heard again in the same area in 1981 and, in 1983, several were calling on the south side of the same mountain.

It is now thought to be present throughout the forest/heathland intergradation zone around the mountain, but it must be extremely rare. It was believed initially to be restricted to the evergreen forest of the mountains, but the edge of the forest and its transition into the strange, high-mountain heath is now more clearly established as its favoured habitat. This unusual montane habitat is markedly different from the lowland habitat of the Madagascar Scops Owl.

The single specimen collected had a few beetle remains in it stomach, but there is no other evidence as to its diet. Other details of its life are largely unknown.

The habitat of the bird has not yet been destroyed but a worrying development is the construction of a hiking track up to the open heath at the top of the mountain. This track may one day be upgraded into a road, encouraging more people to visit a small and fragile ecosystem. Damage and disturbance could prove disastrous for the birds. There are other excessively rare species in the mountain forest – the Grand Comoro Flycatcher (*Humblotia flavirostris*), the Grand Comoro Drongo (*Dicrurus fuscipennis*) and the Mount Karthala White-eye (*Zosterops mouroniensis*). Unfortunately, the whole region is unprotected and the Comoro Islands are not party to international agreements on the trade in endangered species. Prompt action is needed if these birds are to survive.

SEYCHELLES SCOPS OWL
Otus insularis

LENGTH: *200mm* MAP NUMBER: 35
DESCRIPTION: *Small scops owl*
DISTRIBUTION: *Mahé in the Seychelles*
HABITAT: *Forest*
EGGS: *1? Nest in ground cavities?*
STATUS: *Rare and endangered*

Although discovered in 1880, this owl was not seen again for so long that it was thought to be extinct. The major account of Seychelles' birds, written in 1940, did not include it and the owl was formally pronounced extinct in 1958. One had, however, been killed in 1940, but only in 1960 was this specimen re-examined and its identity realized. Here was an 'extinct' bird, proved still to exist 60 years after its first report.

It was assumed that very few still survived. In 1969 it was estimated, on very little real evidence, that a population of 20 birds was the likely maximum. Studies in 1975–76, however, revealed at least 12 pairs in the Mission area. These were identified by small but constant differences in their voices. The pairs were found to be regularly spaced at around 1,100 yards (1,000m) apart. On the basis of this even distribution, and the extent of the available habitat in the known historical range of the species, the estimate was revised to at least 80 pairs, and possibly twice that number. It is even possible that the numbers have risen somewhat as secondary forest has matured.

It is still an extremely elusive bird, confined to the small island of Mahé, where it lives in the forest that covers about a third of the island. It occupies the regrowth after felling from 800 to 2,000 feet (250–600m) above sea level. Presumably, it once occupied highland and lowland forest all over Mahé before the cover was destroyed. There have been persistent local reports from Praslin, but visiting ornithologists, even armed with tape recordings of the species' call, have failed to find it there. However, calls like those heard on Mahé were heard in the Vallée de Mai in August 1976. There have also been reports from the island of Félicité. The call is described as "*tock, tock*".

The forest where the owl lives is remote, high, frequently shrouded in mist and occurs mainly at the head of valleys that taper upwards into the mountains. The owl itself seems to be strictly nocturnal in its habits. The stomachs of collected specimens have contained remains of grasshoppers, beetles, lizards and vegetation. Insects, tree-frogs and lizards probably form the bulk of the diet. Also known as the Bare-legged Scops Owl, it was at one time thought to be an island race of the Madagascar Scops Owl (*Otus rutilus*).

This owl spends a lot of time on the ground in boulder-strewn areas within the forest and, although the nest is unknown, it may nest in ground cavities. High-pitched whistling calls have been heard from mating birds from October to April. It is thought that only a single egg is laid. Fledged young have been found in November and June, which could indicate a twice-yearly breeding cycle.

The upper valley woodlands have been free from logging until recently, when new forestry extraction techniques have opened them up to the foresters who have already cleared practically all the forest cover elsewhere. The Morne Seychellois National Park is the only hope for the species' survival, as elsewhere it seems inevitable that it will disappear.

EASTERN SCREECH-OWL
Otus asio

LENGTH: *190 to 230 mm* MAP NUMBER: 36
DESCRIPTION: *Fierce, yellow-eyed, eared owl, boldly marked*
DISTRIBUTION: *Eastern North America*
HABITAT: *Forest and scrub*
EGGS: *3–7. Nest in hole*
STATUS: *Frequent*

From the Great Lakes of North America south to the Gulf of Mexico, the Eastern Screech-Owl is common and is found widely in woods, parks, gardens and orchards. It occurs both in cities and remote forests. This is one of the most nocturnal of North American owls, roosting by day in a hidden cavity. It may, though, be seen in the evening, as it flits down to a stream to bathe. So fond are Eastern Screech-Owls of bathing that many are found drowned in steep-sided water butts, a fate also suffered by the Barn Owl (*Tyto alba*) in Europe.

Like many nocturnal owls, the Eastern Screech-Owl is traced most easily by its calls. A single, long trill on one pitch is often heard in duets and is the contact call used by a pair while hunting. A typical territorial song of the Eastern Screech-Owl is a mellow, tremulous whinny, a series of quavering whistles on a slight downward scale. A different whinnying note can be heard in autumn.

In the backwoods of North America, the Eastern Screech-Owl is often still regarded as a bird of ill-omen. Its mournful wail is said to foretell disaster and death. Those woken by the calls once undertook various odd rituals, such as turning a shoe upside down, to silence the bird.

There are three distinctly coloured forms, two of which, grey and red, overlap. Grey birds are the commonest form in the north and, oddly, in southern Texas, while redder birds are the commonest form in the south. A third form, a very pale, greyish bird, is found in the north-west. Where grey and red owls are found together, mixed pairs can occur and they may produce both grey and red young. The

Eastern Screech-Owl (*Otus asio*)

red form is a dominant colour genetically, and intermediate colours are generally rare. However, in Florida and a few other regions, the population is evenly divided between red, grey and intermediate birds.

Experiments have shown that red owls have a higher rate of metabolism than grey owls. Field study has established that red birds are more likely than grey ones to die during heavy snowfalls and they also seek more sheltered places to roost. It seems that the colours of Eastern Screech-Owls bear some relationship to temperature, grey birds being better adapted to colder northern regions.

All forms have feathered ear tufts, which are raised when alarmed, vivid yellow eyes, white spots on the 'shoulders' and complex bars and streaks on their underparts. Roosting owls have such confidence in their camouflage – their raised ear tufts enhance their resemblance to a broken branch – that they remain still even when closely approached. In such circumstances, it is possible to lift one off its perch. It may spit and snap its bill but rarely strikes with its needle-sharp claws.

Male Screech-Owls are territorial for most of the year and their territories tend to be separated by a vacant buffer zone. After a solitary winter, males call each night after sunset from February onwards to attract a mate and advertise their territorial claims. Females may not appear until March; courtship calls cease when they are paired.

One of the male's winter roosts is usually chosen for the nest site. The nest may be in a suitable hole in a tree, in an owl nest box, or perhaps in a dovecot or a Purple Martin nest box. Occasionally a pair of owls and a pair of martins successfully nest in separate chambers of a bird house. At other times, the owls will kill and eat the martins.

Three to seven eggs are incubated by the female for 26 days, the male doing all the hunting for the pair. The young are fed by both parents for four weeks in the nest and for a further five to six weeks after leaving it. During this time they make a variety of hoarse wailing and squealing noises. If the chicks are approached too closely by an observer, the parents will swoop silently and unnervingly again and again at the intruder's head.

Nocturnal insects make up much of the owl's diet. It is a surprisingly agile bird, despite its rather dumpy, short-tailed shape, and catches many insects in flight, snapping them up with a loud click of its bill. It also pounces on larger insects on the ground, taking them in its tightly feathered feet. Short, rounded wings give it great manoeuvrability in tight spaces among trees. Its varied diet includes flying squirrels, rats, moles, shrews, bats and birds ranging from pigeons and quails to waxwings, swallows and American Robins. Its ability to kill birds much larger than itself has led to it being described as 'a feathered wildcat, a savage little brute'.

Though it moves off the high ground to less harsh lowland areas in winter, this is a resident rather than a migrant species, and it therefore struggles to find suitable food in severe weather conditions. Eastern Screech-Owls can put on large amounts of fat in the autumn and will hide food in caches. They survive winters by remaining inactive during the harshest weather, feeding on the stores of hidden prey when the weather permits. On dry, calm winter nights they will hunt successfully for small birds and rodents. Many forage on or beside roads at this time and are killed by traffic. Winter poses a further hazard: when food is short, Eastern Screech-Owls are often caught and eaten by larger owls.

WESTERN SCREECH-OWL
Otus kennicotti

LENGTH: *200 mm*   MAP NUMBER: 37
DESCRIPTION: *Like Eastern Screech-Owl; best separated by voice*
DISTRIBUTION: *Western North America, Mexico*
HABITAT: *Forest and scrub*
EGGS: *2 – 7. Nest in hole*
STATUS: *Frequent*

The strange world of the cactus desert, mesquite bush and scrubby woodlands west of the Rocky Mountains is home to this species. It also occupies a variety of wooded regions and open, scrubby ground, from humid conifer forests near the coast to tropical deciduous woods. On the Mexican plateau, the Western Screech-Owl breeds at up to 8,200 feet (2,500m) above sea level.

This bird is a close relative of the Eastern Screech-Owl (*Otus asio*). The two screech-owls occasionally interbreed in the border area between Mexico and the United States. Such breeding is a rare event, however, and it is generally believed that there is no zone of regular hybridization.

The Western, Eastern and Pacific Screech-Owl (*Otus cooperi*) form a 'superspecies' group to which may be added a fourth form, the Balsas Screech-Owl. This has been separated as a species, *Otus seductus*, or treated as a race of the Western Screech-Owl. Balsas Screech-Owls are resident in the lowlands of Colima and the Rio Balsas valley in Michoacán and Western Guerrero in Mexico.

The Western Screech-Owl has two distinctive calls. One is a short, mellow, tremulous whistle, rather than a screech, repeated in a long, even series of notes which starts slowly but accelerates until the notes run together, ending in a roll, rather than the shriek or whinny of the eastern bird. A different call is used when a pair are duetting: a short trill followed quickly by a longer one, unlike the single trill of the Eastern Screech-Owl, which also has a whinnying call that this species lacks.

The Western Screech-Owl varies in colour from region

to region. It is richly reddish in the humid north-west, duller brown in California, grey in the deserts and blackish on the high Mexican plateau. In general, it is darker in the wetter areas of its range. The intricate plumage pattern also varies geographically. The bill is black, in contrast to the greenish or yellow bill of the eastern species.

A hunting Western Screech-Owl usually selects an open perch, often below the canopy of a tree or perhaps on a bare, protruding branch, where it has a clear view of open ground. It feeds mainly on insects and spiders, and will take large centipedes and scorpions. Grasshoppers, crickets, Jerusalem crickets, stick insects, moths, caterpillars and beetles are frequent prey. It will also take crayfish, geckos and small mammals such as pocket gophers, kangaroo rats, mice and voles. Birds as large as pigeons, domestic hens and pheasants are often successfully tackled. In summer, this owl hunts around street lamps, catching the insects attracted by the light. In winter, in certain regions, it becomes a suburban bird, preying on mice and sparrows.

Two to five eggs are laid in a woodpecker hole in a saguaro cactus or in a tree cavity; the birds will also use nest boxes. The owls defend their nest vigorously. Indeed, an unsuspected pair may be discovered if, by chance, the nest is closely approached and an enraged owl sweeps silently past — or even delivers a smack to the head.

WHISKERED SCREECH-OWL
Otus trichopsis

LENGTH: *190 mm*   MAP NUMBER: 38
DESCRIPTION: *Well-marked rufous owl, small ears, yellow eyes*
DISTRIBUTION: *Arizona, Central America*
HABITAT: *Mountain forest*
EGGS: *3–4. Nest in tree hole*
STATUS: *Restricted, probably scarce*

This small owl is a resident species in dry forest in the mountains of Central America, from Arizona in the US south to Guatemala and northern Nicaragua. It occupies mixed pine and oak woods above 4,000 feet (1,200m), and sometimes pure oak or pine, and even coffee plantations. The range of this species overlaps extensively with those of the Flammulated Owl (*Otus flammeolus*) and the Western Screech-Owl (*Otus kennicotti*). In places, all three species can be found together.

This owl looks like a small version of a grey Western Screech-Owl, with pointed, streaky 'horns', large yellow eyes and a broad, pale, greyish area across the lower face. It has slightly ringed facial discs and long, markedly wispy 'whiskers'. The wing feathers are strongly marked with bands of dark grey-brown and cold off-white. There is geographical variation in colour, the birds tending to be greyer in the north and browner in the south; redder individuals occur more frequently in the south. Plumage patterns, overall size and the amount of feathering on the feet also vary across the range.

The Whiskered Screech-Owl is brilliantly camouflaged and is rarely seen by day. It sits very still, hidden away close to the trunk of a tree, and is well concealed and reluctant to move. Its voice may be a series of short whistles, which have been described as a 'slowed down and syncopated trill', or an unusual, irregular burst of short hoots, like a passage of Morse code. If the song is imitated, the owl becomes increasingly irritated and may pursue the imaginary intruder, walking recklessly along the ground to the imitator's feet.

Whiskered Screech-Owls are territorial throughout the year and regularly show aggression if their nests are approached by birds of other species. It is curious that a small, relatively weak owl, mainly an insect-eater, should so fearlessly defend its territory.

These owls nest in old woodpecker holes or natural cavities in trees, laying three or four white eggs. They hunt in the lower branches of dense woods, only occasionally dropping to the ground in pursuit of some small mammal or insect. Instead of perching and pouncing, they adopt livelier methods, pursuing flying insects through the foliage. These are usually crickets, grasshoppers, locusts or praying mantises. Assorted beetles, butterflies, moths and big, hairy caterpillars are also snapped up.

BEARDED SCREECH-OWL
Otus barbarus

LENGTH: *200 to 230 mm*   MAP NUMBER: 39
DESCRIPTION: *Small screech-owl, plain-faced but boldly marked below*
DISTRIBUTION: *Guatemala, southern Mexico*
HABITAT: *High mountain forest*
STATUS: *Local and scarce*

This small, dainty, crisply-marked species is found in open, wet mountain forest in Guatemala and in central Chiapas in southern Mexico. Its range is adjacent to that of the Whiskered Screech-Owl (*Otus trichopsis*), which prefers the drier forest to the south of the mountain spine. The Vermiculated Screech-Owl (*Otus guatemalae*) occupies forests at lower altitudes. All three species therefore appear to live separately in their preferred habitats, in a neatly interlocking pattern which is not obvious on small-scale distribution maps. This is a typical screech-owl in its behaviour and feeds mainly on insects. Its voice is a very soft trill.

VERMICULATED SCREECH-OWL
Otus guatemalae

LENGTH: *200 mm*   MAP NUMBER: 40
DESCRIPTION: *Rufous, eared owl, marked with white spots on scapulars, streaks below*
DISTRIBUTION: *Mexico to north-west Argentina*
HABITAT: *Woodland and forest*
STATUS: *Common but declining*

This bird is found from Mexico southwards to northern Brazil and north-west Argentina. The Vermiculated Screech-Owl is a variable species in colour, occupying a broad range of habitats. It occurs principally in rain- and cloud-forests on the lower mountain slopes, but there are races in the higher forests of Veracruz and the semi-deserts of western Mexico. It is found widely in Panama, on both sides of the mountain divide, but is never common there. This owl survives quite well in areas of new forest growth after the primary forest has been felled.

Where the Vermiculated Screech-Owl comes into contact with other species, they neither compete nor overlap, but have a neatly-interlocking distribution. This species occupies the more open spaces when other owls are present in the forest. If there are no other owls, it will move into the denser cover of the forest itself.

The ground colour of the plumage varies from rufous to dark brown, marked with intricate and beautiful patterns, with large white spots on the outer scapulars and some wing coverts. The ear tufts are barred, and the upperparts are neatly and finely streaked and cross-barred with brown. The facial discs are ill-defined, which suggests that the owl makes little use of specialized hearing when hunting. And, though the bill is immersed in a tuft of feathers, there are no specialized 'whiskers' that would indicate a particular adaptation for hunting insects in flight or among foliage. This owl, like other *Otus* species, is an engaging bird, which can take on a wide range of expressive shapes and postures.

Its song is a long, whinnying whistle with little change of emphasis, which sounds remarkably like the song of the Marine Toad (*Bufo marinus*). As so often with screech-owls and scops owls, it is most readily located by its vocalizations. In Panama, the song is described as a short, quavering trill, while a longer song is given by birds in Belize. In Mexico, the songs are long trills on a single pitch, swelling to a penetrating sound that abruptly stops. The song of the female is noticeably higher than that of the male. Up to 140 notes have been recorded in a nine-second trill. Part of this variation in voices may be due to there being two species.

Little has been learned of the Vermiculated Screech-Owl's behaviour. In southern Mexico, it is often heard calling after sunrise in dense cloud-forest, and may even come in to imitations at that hour. It is thought, however, to be mainly nocturnal. This owl can be assumed to encounter other owls because it shares its range and habitat with around 11 other species. Its habitat has already declined in extent and is still threatened. The population of the Vermiculated Screech-Owl may have declined as a result, but it adapts readily to life in secondary forest. Though not often seen, it is not really a scarce species.

PERUVIAN SCREECH-OWL
Otus roboratus

LENGTH: *200 to 230 mm*   MAP NUMBER: *41*
DESCRIPTION: *Small, eared, rusty-brown with black streaks and bars, yellow eyes*
DISTRIBUTION: *Ecuador, Peru*
HABITAT: *Scrub and high open woodland*
STATUS: *Rare, perhaps endangered*

Found only in south-west Ecuador and north-west Peru, this owl is little known to the outside world and seems destined to remain a mystery for some time to come. It is found in the scrubby steppe of the upper Maranon Valley in Peru, and may perhaps be only a race of the Tropical Screech-Owl (*Otus choliba*). Contemporary scientific study of this owl has proved difficult in a region noted for its extreme political instability.

PACIFIC SCREECH-OWL
Otus cooperi

LENGTH: *230 mm*   MAP NUMBER: *42*
DESCRIPTION: *Large scops owl, facial disc edged dark, crown and ear tufts barred*
DISTRIBUTION: *Western Central America*
HABITAT: *Low scrub, coastal mangrove*
STATUS: *Restricted, uncommon*

Low scrub and mangroves on the Pacific coast of Central America are favoured by this attractive, contrastingly plumaged owl. Its range stretches from southern Mexico to El Salvador and Costa Rica. This is a relatively large New World screech-owl, with a deeper voice than many other species found in the Americas.

TROPICAL SCREECH-OWL
Otus choliba

LENGTH: *190 to 230 mm*   MAP NUMBER: *43*
DESCRIPTION: *Small, eared greyish scops owl, closely barred and streaked*
DISTRIBUTION: *Central and South America*
HABITAT: *Savanna woodland*
EGGS: *1–3. Nest in tree hole*
STATUS: *Frequent to common*

The Tropical Screech-Owl is the standard small owl of South America. It is a common and widespread bird at the centre of a group of rarer Central and South American screech-owls. The Tropical Screech-Owl replaces the screech-owls of North America on the savannas and in the dry woods from Costa Rica through South America as far south as northern Argentina.

This is the most adaptable of the South American screech-owls, and the most successful. Its distribution overlaps those of more specialized screech-owls, which occupy more limited ecological and geographical ranges. It is distinguished from other species by its combination of ear tufts, a dirty white face outlined in black and a prominent pattern of dusky streaks with angled, or V-shaped, bars which give a herring-bone pattern to the underparts. Most birds are grey-brown, but there is also a much rarer rufous phase.

In Panama, the Tropical Screech-Owl has been little studied but is described as fairly common. It is found in open woodland, especially near the edge, and along the edges of forest clearings. It also occurs where scattered tall trees remain in cultivated or developed areas. This is the commonest owl on the Pacific side of the country.

Deforestation has benefited the Tropical Screech-Owl, opening up new clearings and areas of secondary growth which provide the open spaces and lightly wooded habitat it prefers. It lives in parks and residential areas in Panama City and other large towns. It is strictly nocturnal and is not easy to track down, even in the cities. Like many of the more common owls, it is numerous and widespread, but its breeding biology and behaviour have not been comprehensively studied. This species mainly eats insects and spiders, although captive individuals take readily to a regular diet of mice.

The call is a dry, purring trill or bubbling note, usually ending in an abrupt, questioning "*ook?*" or "*ook-ook?*". The call is most frequently given just after dark and again before dawn. Birds can be most easily located at these times, either against the light night sky in the suburbs or against a pale, moonlit sky in remote wilderness areas.

The species has been split into several races, but this is largely based on the study of museum specimens rather than on fieldwork. It lays its eggs in almost any kind of cavity, from a low tree hole to an abandoned bird nest or even a rotten fence post. Up to three white eggs are laid. A small clutch like this is a common feature among the smaller screech-owls and scops owls.

BLACK-CAPPED SCREECH-OWL
Otus atricapillus

LENGTH: *230 mm*   MAP NUMBER: 44
DESCRIPTION: *Large scops, rufous, dark-capped*
DISTRIBUTION: *Eastern South America*
HABITAT: *Lowland tropical and subtropical forest*
STATUS: *Scarce, declining*

This owl, previously treated as the same species as the Long-tufted Screech-Owl (*Otus santaecatharinae*), is one of several closely-related species. The Black-capped Screech-Owl occupies tropical dry and deciduous forest in Brazil, where it is separated by range and habitat from the Tawny-bellied Screech-Owl (*Otus watsonii*) of the Amazonian forest, and from the elusive and less distinct Long-tufted Screech-Owl of the south-eastern Brazilian mountains. There are two races of the Black-capped Screech-Owl, one in central and southern Brazil, the other restricted to the south. Very little is known about any of these owls, which keep to the dwindling forests, where they are extremely well concealed by day and almost impossible to find by night.

RUFESCENT SCREECH-OWL
Otus ingens

LENGTH: *200 to 230 mm*   MAP NUMBER: *45*
DESCRIPTION: *Pale scops with short, blunt ear tufts; complex crossed streaks below*
DISTRIBUTION: *Venezuela to Bolivia*
HABITAT: *Andean forest and scrub*
STATUS: *Uncertain, little known*

Along a narrow strip of the eastern Andes, from Venezuela south through Colombia and Ecuador to Peru and Bolivia, the Rufescent Screech-Owl lives in the humid cloud-forest at altitudes between 5,900 and 8,200 feet (1,800–2,500m). It is a typically 'short-eared' screech-owl, with rusty-brown colouring and barbed-arrow markings on its underparts. The facial disc and ear tufts are less developed than those of the Black-capped Screech-Owl (*Otus atricapillus*), but more so than those of the Bare-shanked Screech-Owl (*Otus clarkii*), to which it is closely related. The White-throated Screech-Owl (*Otus albogularis*), which has no obvious tufts or disc at all, takes this trend further, a sign of its greater evolution away from the common screech-owl stock.

The Rufescent Screech-Owl is a bird of forest on the spectacular slopes of the Andes above the Amazon floodplain. The song is a fast series of about 50 notes given in a burst lasting some 10 seconds. This species has a longer tail, especially in females, than other *Otus* species in the region, and has powerful, fully-feathered legs.

CINNAMON SCREECH-OWL
Otus petersoni

LENGTH: *210mm*   MAP NUMBER: *46*
DESCRIPTION: *Small, buff-brown scops with brown eyes*
DISTRIBUTION: *Ecuador, Peru*
HABITAT: *High cloud-forest*
STATUS: *Probably rare/endangered*

The high forests of Peru have yielded several surprises to visiting ornithologists in recent years. Species of birds new to science have been discovered there with surprising regularity, and in 1976 a small owl was found on a mountain ridge in the extreme north of the country. It was described as a new species and named in honour of Roger Tory Peterson, American bird artist and identification expert, and inventor of the modern field guide.

A party from the universities of Princeton and Louisiana State visited the Cordillera del Condor a year after two other previously undescribed birds had been discovered. The ridge is isolated and rises to 8,200 feet (2,500m) above sea level, forming the border between Peru and Ecuador. Above 6,200 feet (1,900m) it is almost always shrouded by cloud, which wets the subtropical forest. Exposed ridges have stunted trees with few birds. Other ridges associated with this cordillera also have mossy cloud-forest, and the same small owl has since been discovered on them, too. It ranges from the Cordillera del Cutucu in southern Ecuador southwards to the region of La Peca in Peru and perhaps into Colombia, also.

The closely related Rufescent Screech-Owl (*Otus ingens*) was found to inhabit the same forests in two places in Peru and one in Ecuador, but it is suspected that this species lives rather lower down in the mountain forests than does the Cinnamon Screech-Owl. The latter is very much like the Cloud-forest Screech-Owl (*Otus marshalli*) of the departments of Pasco and Cuzco, Peru, in this respect. The Rufescent Screech-Owl also extends much farther south along the Andes, while to the north lives another species, the Colombian Screech-Owl (*Otus colombianus*). The latter bird is the closest relative of the Cinnamon Screech-Owl and was considered a race of the Rufescent Screech-Owl until recently, when it was given species status.

The Cinnamon Screech-Owl is a small, warm buff-brown owl with medium-length feathery ear tufts, a narrow, pale buff collar, almost fully-feathered legs and brown eyes. It is very like the Colombian Screech-Owl, but much smaller and with shorter, more slender, more extensively feathered legs. Its facial disc is rather darker, with more defined blackish rims. Compared with the Rufescent Screech-Owl, it is much smaller, less barred beneath and more buff-coloured above and less dark brown. It also lacks all white marks on the wings and body, its palest areas being bright buff, which separates it from all other *Otus* owls but the Colombian. Compared with the Tawny-bellied Screech-Owl (*Otus watsonii*) of lowland Amazon forests it has sparser leg feathering, shorter, buffy-brown (rather than long, pointed and blackish) ear tufts and less black on the edge of the facial disc.

Although there appears to be little or no difference in appearance between the sexes, there is individual variation in the detailed pattern of the plumage, as with most *Otus* owls. Some appear browner and others are redder in general hue, but a rich cinnamon background colour is shared by all known specimens.

The voice of this owl has been recorded and its song is distinctive, as would be expected for an *Otus* owl. It is a simple series of notes, rapidly repeated at 0.15 second intervals, rising slightly until steadying for about 20 notes, and then subsiding. The song can last for six seconds.

COLOMBIAN SCREECH-OWL
Otus colombianus

LENGTH: *230mm*   MAP NUMBER: 47
DESCRIPTION: *Reddish or brownish scops, short tail, long legs, brown eyes*
DISTRIBUTION: *Colombia, Ecuador*
HABITAT: *Cloud-forest*
STATUS: *Probably rare/endangered*

There is a small group of dark-eyed *Otus* owls in South America which are clearly closely-related, but have been separated into species by American scientists. One is the newly-discovered Cinnamon Screech-Owl (*Otus petersoni*), and this is the most closely-related to the Colombian Screech-Owl which has been elevated to a full species rather than a race of the Rufescent Screech-Owl (*Otus ingens*), as was previously thought. The other brown-eyed species from the high Andes is the Cloud-forest Screech-Owl (*Otus marshalli*) of Peru, while the Tawny-bellied Screech-Owl (*Otus watsonii*) is a lowland bird. All are rather buff or tawny in their basic background and down-feathering coloration, rather than white as in other *Otus* species.

In the Colombian Screech-Owl, all the paler areas are cinnamon-buff, as on the Cinnamon Screech-Owl. This separates it from all other *Otus* species which have white markings. The Colombian Screech-Owl has reddish and brownish forms, but always has tawny under-feathering. It has rather less feathering on the legs than all the other brown-eyed species, except the Cinnamon Screech-Owl.

The Colombian Screech-Owl is about 15 per cent larger than the Cinnamon Screech-Owl, and its proportions are rather different. The Colombian is a shorter-tailed and longer-legged bird. Its legs and feet are unusually large for an *Otus* species. It also has longer, broader ear tufts, a less conspicuously defined facial disc and more cross-bars on the underside.

Both species live in the mysterious, damp, gloomy cloud-forest of the Andes, the Colombian in the west, the Cinnamon in the east. Their precise relationships, behaviour and ecology are still little-known and are subject to speculation rather than hard information based on observed facts. It may be that future studies will link them more closely with lowland species, or perhaps separate yet more groups, currently referred to as races, as new species of *Otus* owls. The *Otus* genus is undoubtedly the most complicated and difficult of the owl groups.

TAWNY-BELLIED SCREECH-OWL
Otus watsonii

LENGTH: *190 to 230 mm*   MAP NUMBER: 48
DESCRIPTION: *Dull, greyish scops type, orange eyes*
DISTRIBUTION: *Northern South America in Amazon basin*
HABITAT: *Tropical rain-forest*
STATUS: *Uncertain, probably declining*

Dense rain-forest in South America is the dark retreat of this small, elusive and little-known owl. The Tawny-bellied Screech-Owl is found in Surinam, eastern Colombia and Bolivia. It also lives in the Amazon basin. In Venezuela, it is found up to altitudes of 6,900 feet (2,100m) in the Perija Mountains and north of the Orinoco and at lower levels to the south of that great, curving river. The forests, immense both in their range and the size of their trees, certainly provide a variety of different habitats for small owls. Such an environment offers much diversity within small areas, including the extensive range from ground-level to the high canopy of the forest. This species, however, seems almost always to be found low down, rarely more than 30 feet or so (10m) above the ground. It frequents the interior of the forest, rather than the edge, and can be found in mature secondary growth.

The Tawny-bellied Screech-Owl has slight ear tufts and is a darker bird than the Tropical Screech-Owl (*Otus choliba*), with more tawny coloured underparts. It also has a different voice, producing a series of mellow "*whoo*" notes at the rate of about two per second. These continue for up to 20 seconds at a time. The notes often start softly, then become louder only to fade away. This evocative call can sometimes be heard just before darkness falls.

PUERTO RICAN SCREECH-OWL
Otus nudipes

LENGTH: *220 mm*   MAP NUMBER: 49
DESCRIPTION: *Plain-faced, short-eared, rufous scops owl, rather plain above, barred below*
DISTRIBUTION: *Caribbean islands*
HABITAT: *High woodland and forest*
EGGS: *2—3. Nest in tree hole*
STATUS: *Restricted, scarce*

A bird of high tropical forest, this owl is found on Saint Thomas, Saint John and Saint Croix in the Virgin Islands and on the neighbouring island of Puerto Rico in the Caribbean. It has slight ear tufts above its ruddy face, and its yellow legs and feet are unfeathered. The bird's general appearance marks it out as a close relative of the Vermiculated Screech-Owl (*Otus guatemalae*) of Central America. It has a call like a Burrowing Owl (*Athene cunicularia*), a loud "*coo coo*", and is known locally as 'the cuckoo bird'. It also has a long, quivering trill. By day, the Puerto Rican Screech-Owl roosts in caves, trees and dense foliage, emerging at night to hunt insects. Its nest is usually located in a cave in a limestone cliff, or in a hollow tree, or even in the roof of a house. It lays two or three white eggs.

BARE-SHANKED SCREECH-OWL
Otus clarkii

LENGTH: *230 mm*   MAP NUMBER: 50
DESCRIPTION: *Small, greyish scops type, very small ear tufts, pale yellow eyes*
DISTRIBUTION: *Costa Rica, Panama, Colombia*
HABITAT: *High altitude forest*
STATUS: *Restricted, scarce*

The mountain forests of Costa Rica, Panama and north-western Colombia form the range of the Bare-shanked Screech-Owl. Such habitats are being reduced by clearances and this owl is almost certainly declining. A study is required of the degree to which this small owl can adapt and survive, but in its thickly wooded montane habitat the ornithologist needs determination even to see one. This is a rather large, big-headed, spotted bird with noticeable ear tufts and gleaming yellow eyes. The legs are mainly bare but are not easily seen in the wild. It has a cinnamon or tawny-brown face, reddish-brown upper-parts and a pattern of short, broken bars, streaks and square white bars or spots underneath.

It is the only screech-owl found in the mountain forests of Panama, where it lives at heights between 3,300 and 6,600 feet (1,000–2,000m). It is thought to be rare here but may well have been overlooked. In Colombia, there is one report of a Bare-shanked Screech-Owl in humid mountain forest, but elsewhere in that country and in other regions it also occurs along woodland borders and lines of trees. Its call is a high, musical note, followed by three notes in quick succession – "*coo, coo-coo-coo*".

WHITE-THROATED SCREECH-OWL
Otus albogularis

LENGTH: *190 to 230 mm*   MAP NUMBER: 51
DESCRIPTION: *Dark, round-headed scops owl, white 'moustache', orange eyes*
DISTRIBUTION: *Northern Andes*
HABITAT: *Cloud-forest*
STATUS: *Uncertain*

Occurring only in the high cloud-forest of the Andes, often above 8,200 feet (2,500m), the distribution of the White-throated Screech-Owl appears on the map as a thin, spidery line stretching from Venezuela and Colombia southwards to Ecuador, Peru and Bolivia. Its habitat is the most extreme of any of the South American screech-owls, and its facial appearance is also distinctive. It has a rounded head and neither the facial disc nor the feathery ear tufts are fully developed. It has occasionally been placed in its own genus, *Macabra*, but is now generally treated as an unusual *Otus* species.

The voice of this owl resembles that of the Black-capped Screech-Owl (*Otus atricapillus*) of the lowlands. It makes a long series of rapid, high-pitched whistles, uninterrupted for up to a minute at a time. Very little is known about this bird's behaviour but intriguing reports exist of one nest on the ground among ferns and another built in a 'cup nest' just above ground level. The latter may have been the nest of a small bird taken over by a pair of owls.

CLOUD-FOREST SCREECH-OWL
Otus marshalli

LENGTH: *200 mm*   MAP NUMBER: 52
DESCRIPTION: *Chestnut and black back, small ear tufts, dark eyes*
DISTRIBUTION: *Peru*
HABITAT: *Cloud-forest*
STATUS: *Uncertain, possibly endangered*

In 1967 a new owl was discovered in Peru – this time a tiny screech-owl. A full description of it was published in 1981. The bird was the Cloud-forest Screech-Owl, from the Andes of south-central Peru. Its nearest relatives are believed to be the Central American Bearded Screech-Owl (*Otus barbarus*) and the Bare-shanked Screech-Owl (*Otus clarkii*) which extends into Colombia.

It is one of four screech-owls which replace each other at different altitudes along a heavily-forested slope rising 9,800 feet (3,000m) from the valley floor to the crest of a cordillera. The lowest-occurring species is the Tawny-bellied Screech-Owl (*Otus watsonii*) of lowland dense forest. Above this the Rufescent Screech-Owl (*Otus ingens*) is found in the lower cloud-forest, then comes the Cloud-forest Screech-Owl in the mid-range cloud-forest, with the White-throated Screech-Owl (*Otus albogularis*) taking

over in the very highest montane forest.

The Cloud-forest Screech-Owl is found in a remote, high area where eerie hillsides disappear upwards into the persistent cold, clammy mist which keeps the forest dripping wet. It is a typical screech-owl in appearance, except that it has clear patterning all over the underparts, with transverse white spots separated by bold black and rufous bars and streaks. It has a well-defined, black-edged facial disc and big, dark eyes. The rather small, rounded ear tufts have very dark outer edges, while the inner ones are pale buff with brown bars. The inner edges continue downwards as a slight pale V above the eyes, outlining a darker, well-barred forehead. The upperparts are rich chestnut with black bars, neither streaked nor spotted. It is similar in size to the Bearded Screech-Owl but smaller than the Bare-shanked Screech-Owl.

First found in June 1967, it was one of three new owl discoveries in Peru in a few years, all caught with the aid of mist-nets. A male was caught and collected in the Provincia de la Convencion, Departamento de Cuzco. The species was named in honour of American ornithologist Joe Marshall, Jr, in recognition of his long-standing interest and expertise in the complex group of *Otus* owls.

WHITE-FACED SCOPS OWL
Otus (Ptilopsis) leucotis

LENGTH: *190 to 240 mm*   MAP NUMBER: 53
DESCRIPTION: *Large, grey scops with black-edged, white face, orange-red eyes*
DISTRIBUTION: *Africa south of the Sahara*
HABITAT: *Thorn scrub, savanna woods*
EGGS: *2–4. Nest in old bird of prey nest in tree*
STATUS: *Scarce*

The White-faced Scops Owl is a resident of virtually the whole of Africa south of the Sahara. It is absent only from the dense forests of Zaire and Cameroon, parts of the Horn of Africa and the Cape. It is found in savanna and woodland with sparse ground cover. Yet across this enormous range, it is generally uncommon.

Sometimes described as the most beautiful of all owls, it has a striking white face surrounded by black, and piercing orange eyes. The unusually large, feathery ear tufts can be raised, erect and well-apart, more prominently than those of any other scops owl. A pair of White-faced Scops Owls seems capable of communication in various ways, using eye and facial expressions, movements of the ear tufts, and bobbing and weaving movements of the body.

Like most owls, they also bob and roll their heads from side to side in their efforts to pinpoint the position of prey

and predators. The object they are focusing on appears to change position against the more stable, distant background. This use of parallax, which is facilitated by eyes and ears that are widely separated and facing forward, is one of the most distinctive features of the owl family. In total darkness they may use only the ears.

The White-faced Scops Owl is such a distinct species that it is given its own genus, *Ptilopsis*, by some specialists. The openings of its ears are twice as large as those of any comparable scops owl. The prey is frequently bigger than that caught by most scops owls in the Old World and includes larger animals, which it tears apart in the manner of Short-eared Owls (*Asio flammeus*).

The White-faced Scops Owl likes to perch in small,

thorny trees in savanna landscapes. In Kenya, it occupies bush and woodland to a height of 5,500 feet (1,700m) and is absent from the humid coastal strip and the most arid parts of the country. Further south, however, it is reported from the extensive bush on the dry Kalahari sands. In southern Africa, this owl is said to prefer thorny trees along the banks of dry water-courses.

A pair may be found close together, and the birds are usually not too well hidden. They rely instead on the cryptic pattern of their plumage and are difficult to see when leaning close to an upright branch. Though sometimes found by day, they hunt entirely at night. Their huge ears suggest they rely largely on hearing to detect small creatures in the darkness. From an open perch with a good view, they drop down onto prey that includes large insects, scorpions, small rodents and a few small birds.

The male calls to defend his territory, most often at dusk and dawn. Northern birds give a mellow, flute-like double note every few seconds. Southerly ones have a different call, a longer, bubbling series which begins as a stutter and ends on another flute-like sound, this time a rising "*wh-h-h-h-oo-oo*". It is only just discernible as disyllabic. There is also a lower contact call of "*to-whit-to-wheet*".

Territories may be quite small and nests have been found surprisingly close together. This is especially so when rodents abound. Nest sites may be in natural holes or on top of old nests of other birds, ranging from the spindly platforms of pigeons to the massive nest of an eagle or a colony of buffalo weavers. The nest is used for several years in succession.

Up to four shiny white eggs are laid and they are incubated from the first one so that the young hatch at intervals. From the date of laying, incubation takes about 30 days. The breeding season varies markedly throughout the range. In Zimbabwe, it is August to November. Further south, birds may breed at any time between July and February. The chicks move out of the nest onto nearby branches by the time they are four weeks old. A few days later they start to fly. Their hissing, exhaling notes, as they beg for food, may betray the family's location.

SAO THOMÉ SCOPS OWL
Otus hartlaubi

LENGTH: *180 mm*   MAP NUMBER: 54
DESCRIPTION: *Scops owl with very slight ear tufts, bare legs*
DISTRIBUTION: *Sao Thomé island*
HABITAT: *Forest*
STATUS: *Probably scarce*

The island of Sao Thomé, off the west coast of Africa, south of Nigeria, has an endemic scops owl. This is similar to the common Scops Owl (*Otus scops*) but has unfeathered feet, virtually no ear tufts and calls that are given at 15–20 second intervals. It can be found in forests to heights of 4,300 feet (1,300m), living in the dense foliage of low trees and occasionally dropping to the ground to pick up a beetle or lizard. This owl is possibly only a well-marked race of the common Scops Owl, long isolated on its tropical island, but the differences in calls and appearance are stronger than is often the case with island populations of the various *Otus* owls.

It is easy to imagine an owl reaching such an isolated island, but less easy to imagine a male and female reaching it independently at the same time. A pair must surely have flown in together. Such migrations open up a rich field of speculation. If more Scops Owls were to reach Sao Thomé, it is possible that, by adding genes from the parent population, they would slow down the evolution of the island species. But it remains unknown whether, if the original stock has changed significantly, new birds arriving from the mainland would breed together rather than with the earlier colonists, leading eventually to a second island species. Alternatively, they might be eliminated by competition with the more established island owls.

SPECIES ALLIED TO SCOPS OWLS

—————— FOUR SPECIES IN FOUR GENERA ——————

PALAU SCOPS OWL
Pyrroglaux podargina

LENGTH: *220 mm*   MAP NUMBER: 55
DISTRIBUTION: *Palau Islands*
HABITAT: *Forest, mangroves*
STATUS: *Uncertain*

East of the Philippines, separated from those islands by the vast depths of the Mindanao Trench, a far-flung string of tiny isles and atolls forms the Caroline Islands. The largest of these are the Palau Islands, which break the surface of the Pacific as the merest tips of an undersea ridge. However remote they may seem, these tiny isles have their own owl species and perhaps even their own genus. The Palau Scops Owl is abundant throughout the islands, occurring in all types of forest. It is found particularly in ravines but also frequents the thickets of mangroves growing from coastal swamps.

The birds are found in pairs or family groups all year and are active at dusk and at night. They feed on insects and earthworms. The voice is a long series of short hoots building to a peak, then a descending series of two-syllabled notes uttered in flight. The male and female sometimes call in duet.

Such isolated island species show that, on rare occasions, owls can and do move long distances. It is proof also that they can adapt to special circumstances and take advantage of any opportunity that presents itself. Once, in the distant past, owls must have dispersed, for some unknown reason, from their natal woods and reached the Palau Islands. This remarkable species is the result.

GIANT SCOPS OWL
Mimizuku gurneyi

LENGTH: *300 mm*   MAP NUMBER: 56
DESCRIPTION: *Large, boldly-streaked scops owl*
DISTRIBUTION: *Marinduque and Mindanao, Philippines*
HABITAT: *Highland forests*
STATUS: *Uncertain*

Though no giant among owls in general, this is the largest 'scops', although it is usually placed in a separate genus from the *Otus* owls, as it is so distinct from them. The Giant Scops Owl lives in highland forests on the southern Philippines, mainly on the island of Mindanao but it is also reported from Marinduque to the north. It may occur on islands in between where suitable habitat still exists.

This is a boldly patterned owl whose underparts have broad, drop-shaped streaks quite unlike anything found on typical scops owls. Little is known of its behaviour or even its calls and, like so many species isolated on difficult terrain, it remains something of a mystery.

MANED OWL
Jubula lettii

LENGTH: *440 mm*   MAP NUMBER: 57
DESCRIPTION: *Bushy ear tufts, yellow eyes in white-edged, blackish disc, rusty upperparts*
DISTRIBUTION: *West Africa*
HABITAT: *Tropical forest*
STATUS: *Probably rare and declining*

Tropical African lowland forest with an abundance of creepers is not an easy habitat in which to search for owls. For this reason, the literature on African birds takes the optimistic view that the Maned Owl may be more common than reports suggest. This owl lives in isolated places where the habitat continues to flourish, from Liberia and Ghana eastwards to Cameroon and Zaire. But within that large sweep of western Africa its range is disjointed and probably shrinking as timber companies start clearances.

The bushily-crested head and the yellow eyes and bill give it a striking appearance. It is sometimes known as the Akun Scops Owl, but is larger than any scops owl and may be a link between scops owls and wood owls, or a branch on the family tree leading to the eagle owls. The Maned Owl has also been linked with the Crested Owl (*Lophostrix cristata*) of South America (and therefore named *Lophostrix lettii*), but the connection is somewhat speculative. There are, of course, many ancient ties between the two continents, formed before the two continental plates drifted apart.

Three factors aid birdwatchers who are in search of the Maned Owl. It roosts in dense creepers but is sometimes found by groups of small birds which mob it, scolding it unremittingly with long, noisy calls. At dusk, the Maned Owl flies up to an open perch and may then be seen against the twilit sky. Finally, it has a distinctive call, a double hoot, the second note higher than the first, repeated every ten seconds or so. But threading a path through the jungle at night, trying to track a distant call, is not an easy way to locate any bird. Despite its relatively large size, this is not a particularly powerful owl and it feeds largely on insects.

CRESTED OWL
Lophostrix cristata

LENGTH: *400 mm*   MAP NUMBER: 58
DESCRIPTION: *Plain brown owl, with long, white-edged ear tufts, yellow eyes*
DISTRIBUTION: *Central America, northern South America*
HABITAT: *Tropical forest*
STATUS: *Probably threatened*

The Crested Owl of Central and South America may be related to the Maned Owl (*Jubula lettii*) of western Africa. However, it looks distinctly different, with a different plumage pattern and more separated ear tufts of long, snowy feathers. These flaring ear tufts make it perhaps the most spectacular of American owls. At times they are held straight up and slightly back, but they can also be spread out horizontally. It breeds in tropical forests from the Amazon basin northwards to Mexico.

This owl is strictly nocturnal, spending the day hidden away in dense foliage, often close to a stream. It sometimes roosts very low down, but by dusk it will be calling from the tops of tall trees. In Colombia and Venezuela it prefers lowland forests and areas of high trees with dense undergrowth. It is not found in mountainous areas nor in clear-cut forest but favours primary forest and clearings within the forest.

The Crested Owl gives a low, frog-like trill, accelerating from a stuttering start to a purring "*k, k, k-k-k-krrrrrr*" sound. The initial stuttering notes can be inaudible at a distance but the rest of the song carries a long way. This growl is repeated every few seconds. Nests are in hollow trees but there is an old report of a pair nesting in the loft of a large house.

EAGLE OWLS

TWELVE SPECIES

GREAT HORNED OWL
Bubo virginianus

LENGTH: *430 to 530 mm*   MAP NUMBER: 59
DESCRIPTION: *Very large eagle owl, heavily barred*
DISTRIBUTION: *North and South America*
HABITAT: *Woodland, parks, forest, desert*
EGGS: *1–6. Nest in deserted tree nest or on ledge*
STATUS: *Widespread and frequent*

The giant owls of Europe, Asia and Africa are separated into several species, each with its own distribution and preferred habitat. The Great Horned Owl, however, is the only species of eagle owl found in the Americas. Its range stretches from the western reaches of Alaska south to the tip of South America, and it is found in a greater variety of habitats than any other owl. It is a bird of northern forest, mixed and deciduous woodland, mountains, desert and even coastal mangrove swamps. On other continents each of these habitats would probably be occupied by separate large species.

The Great Horned Owl is a big bird. It looks heavy, solid and broad-chested with a large head. Its tufted horns of feathers are widely spaced; its expression can be menacing and fearsome. This is a soft-plumaged giant, but an aggressive predator whose power almost rivals the Eagle Owl (*Bubo bubo*) of Eurasia. Indeed, the Great Horned Owl so resembles the Eagle Owl that their separation rests largely on geographical grounds, a superficial difference in plumage and differences in their calls. It is probable that eagle owls originated in Africa and spread through the Old World over a long period of time, evolving in the process into ten or more species.

The spread from eastern Asia to western Alaska must have been relatively recent because the New World owl remains a single species, although separable into several races. In time, these races may diverge sufficiently to produce the same diversity of species in the Americas as is found in the Old World.

The Great Horned Owl is slightly smaller than the Eurasian Eagle Owl. It has narrower ear openings, but in other respects its structure is almost identical. It has similarly awesome feet and claws, with densely feathered toes and powerfully muscled legs. Like many owls, its legs seem very short in a perching position but reveal an unexpectedly long reach when striking for prey.

In comparison with human anatomy, the owl's feet are equivalent to human toes and its shin is a fusion of the foot bones. The bird's 'knee', which bends backwards, corresponds to the human ankle and its 'thigh', which is usually hidden, to the human shin. The owl's real knee-joint actually points upward, and its thigh is angled back and down to the pelvis. A bird striking with its feet extends all these joints and, for an instant, its legs become long and free of the body feathers. This is seen vividly on flashlit photogaphs taken at the moment of the kill, a sight scarcely observable in ordinary field conditions.

The plumage of a Great Horned Owl has bars across the underside rather than streaks along the body, as on the Eagle Owl. This feature is also seen on other American owls. The Great Horned Owl is a grey-brown bird, less bright than most eagle owls, with intricate, beautiful barring and pencilling on the upperparts. Its distinct facial disc can be almost clear white or orange-buff with rings of brown. Large, intensely yellow eyes dominate the face.

Great Horned Owls survive almost Arctic conditions in Alaska, at the far northern edge of woodland that grows stunted and short in the severe climate. A few wandering birds even venture onto the tundra. Further south, the owls live in extensive conifer forests up to altitudes of 11,000 feet (3,300m) in Colorado; in wide tracts of aspen; in rocky canyons, in deserts and prairies and in almost any clump of trees offering concealed shelter.

In the tropics, these owls avoid the densest rain-forest but survive well in all forms of evergreen and deciduous woods and open mangroves. In the Andes, they are found in treeless wastes in Ecuador at up to 14,000 feet (4,300m) and at close to such altitudes on the cold, remote mountains of Peru.

Over this great range and diversity of habitat there are considerable variations in size and colour. The Great Horned Owls of the far north are the largest of all, as is to be expected. The larger the size, the smaller the bird's surface area in comparison to its volume. This helps conserve heat. The prevalence of larger size in colder regions conforms to Bergman's rule and is shown by many birds and mammals. Gloger's rule is also followed, with owls from the warmest, wettest parts of the range being noticeably darker than owls from cooler, drier regions. Great Horned Owls of the desert are smaller than their counterparts in the forest to the north and south.

The Great Horned Owl does not usually become active until after sunset. In the desert, however, it may catch lizards that become slower and less alert in the cool of the afternoon, and the owl may hunt by day when food is scarce in severe weather. Otherwise, it remains holed up in a tree or among shaded rocks all day, assuming a tall, upright posture, akin to that of a Long-eared Owl (*Asio otus*), when disturbed. This is rarely seen in Eagle Owls.

The calls begin as the Great Horned Owl moves at dusk. The territorial song of the male is a deep, booming sound, soft but far-reaching, and is enough to send birds and mammals scampering for cover. The male utters four to five short, deep hoots, "*Hoo, hoo-oo, hoo hoo*", and the female responds with six to eight lower hoots, "*Hoo, hoo-hoo-hoo, hooo-oo, hoo-oo*". Females also have higher-pitched, two-syllable calls and often join in eerie duets with their mates. Courting owls break into weird choruses of cat-like noises, moaning sounds and laughing notes.

Great Horned Owls drive all other owls from their territories. Their presence also has an impact on daytime birds of prey, their rivals for food, such that a change of territory by this huge owl means a complete reshuffle of territories by diurnal raptors to maintain a safe distance from the owl and each other. Those birds of prey which do not compete for food, such as the carrion-eating Turkey Vulture (*Cathartes aura*), may be safe close to the owl's nest. Great Horned Owls have been known to kill a great variety of other owls, including Long-eared, Short-eared (*Asio flammeus*), Barred (*Strix varia*), Burrowing (*Athene cunicularia*) and Barn (*Tyto alba*) Owls, as well as screech-owls (*Otus spp*). Daytime raptors, ranging from American Kestrels (*Falco sparverius*) to harriers and several forms of buzzard, have also met untimely ends.

On the prairies, these owls eat chiefly jackrabbits and cottontails. Their numbers and breeding performance fluctuate with the abundance of their prey. Elsewhere, in more varied surroundings, a wider range of prey exists and almost any creature may be in danger from the fierce owl with the angled horns. Overall, three-quarters of its prey consists of mammals, with rather few birds but a large number of insects, spiders, scorpions and crabs. Hares, cottontail rabbits, meadow voles and white-footed mice make up the bulk of the food in most places. In Chile, these owls catch the black rats and rabbits introduced to the region, but gophers, prairie dogs, kangaroo rats, ground squirrels, woodchucks, and even porcupines and skunks are also taken. In South America, monkeys and various marsupials are added to the list.

The birds among its prey include ptarmigan, bobwhite, Mallard (*Anas platyrhynchos*) and other ducks, geese and even swans and herons. Over 50 bird species are recorded as prey of the Great Horned Owl. The Great Horned Owl catches a wider range of prey than any other bird in the New World and, where opportunity exists, a hungry owl can master remarkably large prey.

These owls are residents and pairs remain in their territory for many years. In the Rocky Mountains and the Andes, most make only minor, local shifts to lower, less snowbound areas in winter. On rare occasions, the owls make longer journeys if there are dramatic declines in the numbers of their prey. Great Horned Owls of large, pale northern races are then seen far south of their usual range.

Most Great Horned Owls select the old nest of a large bird of prey in which to lay their eggs. The Red-tailed Hawk (*Buteo jamaicensis*) most frequently supplies them with their future home, high in a big pine or aspen. Nests are commonly used alternately by the owls and two or three species of birds of prey. Red-tailed Hawks, Goshawks (*Accipiter gentilis*) and the owls may each use a nest in successive years. In parts of the range, the owls are likely to nest in big hollows in trees, or in depressions at the base of branches or where great limbs have fallen from ancient trees. Nests on cliff ledges or on the ground are much less common than is the case with the Eagle Owl. In Ohio, Great Horned Owls have been studied nesting in colonies of Great Blue Herons (*Ardea herodias*), using nests from previous years in the interior of the heronry. The herons preferred nests at the tops of trees whereas the owls tended to use nests in the middle of dead trees, sometimes as little as 7 feet (2m) from an active heron nest. Such use of colonial nests is widespread in North America.

In the north, Great Horned Owls are among the earliest birds to nest, sometimes being on eggs in January and regularly incubating at the start of March. The eggs are large and white and a typical clutch is of one or two. When food is abundant, the female may lay as many as six. They are incubated by the female for between 28 and 35 days and the chicks remain in the nest for up to seven weeks. The male often brings a surplus of food to his family, and the nest can be littered with heaps of rotting meat. The chicks cannot fly for 10 or 12 weeks and many fall to the ground before fledging. Around this time they are very noisy, making loud discordant screams. The parents may feed their young well into the autumn. More young survive when larger prey, such as rabbits and hares, are available, than in years when small mammals and birds are the staple diet. Adults with young are aggressive to intruders.

Among the American Indians, the Great Horned Owl was once wreathed in superstition and dread but was respected and left unmolested. The arrival of European settlers began a long history of persecution. The worst threat to the Great Horned Owl comes from habitat changes, whether the felling of woods or more subtle changes which reduce the numbers of their prey. Life in the modern world is perilous for a big owl such as this. Many are shot and trapped around game-shooting areas. Of more than 200 ringed in the nest and later recovered in North America, more than a quarter were shot and almost as many were trapped. Many others were killed by traffic or electrocuted by overhead wires. Despite this, the species is still common over much of North America.

Intriguing predictions have been made about this species by Dutch ornithologist and owl expert K H Voous. As open prairie land and forest have been cleared and ploughed, the larger animals preyed on by the Great Horned Owl have declined and the bird has turned to smaller creatures. In the distant future, the owl may well decline in size as it adapts to new conditions and, eventually, it will either die out or survive as a mere shadow of its former self.

Great Horned Owl (*Bubo virginianus*)

EAGLE OWL
Bubo bubo

LENGTH: *580 to 710 mm*   MAP NUMBER: 60
DESCRIPTION: *Very large, eared owl; complex warm to pale brown, barred and streaked; orange eyes*
DISTRIBUTION: *North Africa, Europe, Asia, Middle East*
HABITAT: *Mountainous forest, semi-desert, rocky slopes*
EGGS: *1–4. Nest on ledge or in deserted tree nest*
STATUS: *Widespread but everywhere scarce, locally endangered*

This is the most dramatic of all owls, a creature to match any bird in the world for sheer excitement and awesome power. Only the Snowy Owl (*Nyctea scandiaca*) and the huge Blakiston's Fish Owl (*Ketupa blakistoni*) equal it in bulk and weight. Verreaux's Eagle Owl (*Bubo lacteus*) of Africa rivals the Eagle Owl in wingspan but not weight, while the Great Horned Owl (*Bubo virginianus*) is big but is little more than half the weight of a European Eagle Owl. The Powerful Owl (*Ninox strenua*) of Australia is almost as long but has shorter wings and weighs considerably less.

Eagle Owls are elusive in the wild. Sightings may be disappointingly brief and frustrating. At dusk, as it sits on an earth bank above a dry wadi, surrounded by cereal fields, this bird may look like nothing more than a hessian sack until it stands up and flies away, disappearing swiftly from view. The fortunate birdwatcher may see an Eagle Owl on one of its favourite ledges, sitting deep in shade, immobile, more statue than living bird until it swings its great head to one side. In Yugoslavia, Eagle Owls can often be seen with other predators at night by roadsides, attracted by the rats that feed on refuse. But it is the patient birdwatcher who sees these great creatures at their best. Then, they are simply incomparable.

Eagle Owls range from Norway eastwards to Sakhalin Island in a huge sweep across Europe and Asia. But, apart from occasional stragglers, they are not found in Japan, nor the British Isles. They are absent from the broad belt of boreal forest to the north, where Great Grey Owls (*Strix nebulosa*) and Ural Owls (*Strix uralensis*) hold sway, but Eagle Owls do breed to the south, deep into the Sahara and possibly as far as Chad. They also breed in parts of Arabia and eastwards across southern Asia, including most of China, but are not found in the southernmost regions of South-East Asia. Despite their extensive range, they are never common and, across much of Europe, have become rare and endangered.

In this broad geographical range, these legendary owls encounter great diversity of climate and habitat and have proved adaptable and quick to seize opportunities. They seem equally at home in a northern pine forest or a hot, tangled gorge in the Mediterranean; in a broken desert rock face, or even on the artificial cliff of the stepped pyramid at Sakkara in Egypt. They are to be found in the pastures of Tibet at altitudes of 15,400 feet (4,700m) and in lush forests and flowery meadows above 6,500 feet (2,000m) in the Alps. In large, dense forests, however, the Eagle Owl is replaced by the Tawny Owl (*Strix aluco*).

This widespread distribution in a variety of different habitats suggests that the Eagle Owl was once a thriving species. But in the modern world it suffers relentless persecution. In many countries, it is shot, trapped and harried out of existence. Modern agriculture, tourism and urbanization have significantly changed the environment and reduced the amount of prey. When the countryside cannot support good numbers of medium-sized mammals and birds, the Eagle Owls leave, starve or turn to smaller fry. Like the Great Horned Owl, it is a bird best suited to a landscape that has largely gone, and it may be in the process of evolutionary decline. Big birds such as this need big country, extensive tracts of undisturbed wilderness with plentiful food.

The Eagle Owl is massively built and is all solid, weighty muscle compared to the lightweight owls around it. The Great Grey Owl may look magnificent but it is largely loose feathers around a small body and cannot match the strength of the Eagle Owls of central Europe. Female Eagle Owls are heavier than their mates and often darker in colour. In flight, Eagle Owls look obviously large and heavily-built, with barrel-shaped bodies and broad wings. Their flight action is like that of a Buzzard (*Buteo buteo*).

The glorious eyes are orange-yellow or a deeper, fiery orange. The face has a central area of white, finely peppered with grey and brown, above a whiter throat which serves as a recognition mark between members of a pair. Blackish, frowning brows continue into the long, pointed ear tufts which usually point sideways. They are rarely raised upright at the roost, unlike those of the Long-eared Owl (*Asio otus*), so seem to have little function in camouflaging. They are used mostly for communication and recognition at night. When raised in aggression, the tufts stand on end in a frightening display, sweeping up in an inward curve and twisted full-face to confront the intruder. At other times, they may be laid back and twisted flat against the sides of the head, or drooped in a curious, almost semi-circular shape.

The ear tufts are generally held in a more raised position in the male, and more horizontal or drooped in the female. A side view of the head shows that these apparently substantial ear tufts are in reality thin 'blades' attached to the front of the face, leaving the top of the head smooth and rounded.

Eagle Owls are separated into between 12 and 24 races, according to various authorities, and there may be a case for splitting some into separate species. West European birds have the richest colours and are darkest above and have the most orange-brown on the face and underparts. At times, especially in Scandinavia, their upperparts are almost solidly black with rusty markings. Central Siberian birds are enormous and have much more white and a frostier appearance but still show rufous-buff on the flight feathers. In flight, they show a contrastingly bright patch just beyond the bend of the wing. This is also seen on the Great Grey Owl and is akin to the bright, pale wing patches of Long-eared Owl and Short-eared Owl (*Asio flammeus*). In India, Eagle Owls live in humid, warmer conditions and are smaller and darker than other races.

An unusual group is found in the North African desert. Here the birds are small and pale and, in the northwest of the continent, may live alongside larger Eagle Owls but remain separate. There may also be a difference in voice, but this is unconfirmed. It is possible that these desert Eagle Owls are actually a different species, the Pharaoh Eagle Owl (*Bubo ascalaphus*). But, though there are no obvious intermediate birds in northwest Africa, there are such forms in the Middle East, so the case for this species is not yet proven. The Indian race, *bengalensis*, may also

Eagle Owl (*Bubo bubo*)

prove to be a distinct species.

Wherever they are found, Eagle Owls are not only the most dominant owl but they also dominate most daytime birds of prey. On very rare occasions, an Eagle Owl has been killed by a Golden Eagle (*Aquila chrysaetos*) or White-tailed Eagle (*Haliaeetus albicilla*), but it is far more common for an Eagle Owl to kill other birds of prey, including owls. They frequently kill Tawny Owls and will overcome buzzards with ease. Long-eared Owls are so commonly reported as their prey that they seem to be a regular source of food. Other prey includes such powerful adversaries as Goshawk (*Accipiter gentilis*), Peregrine (*Falco peregrinus*), Rough-legged Buzzard (*Buteo lagopus*) and Gyrfalcon (*Falco rusticolus*), as well as Raven (*Corvus corax*) and several smaller birds of prey. The Eagle Owl will also take young birds of prey. Even young White-tailed Eagles have reportedly been snatched from open, conspicuous nests at night.

Peregrines are always driven from any cliff where Eagle Owls settle, but Golden Eagles and Eagle Owls appear to co-exist, nesting well apart, as if carrying equal authority. Each acts more or less like the other when territorial spacing is determined. The Eagle Owl may almost be seen as a nocturnal Golden Eagle, though the latter is considerably larger and over twice as heavy.

Territories are advertised by frequent calls. These are mainly those of the male, a very deep, far-carrying "*ohoo*". The first part carries most emphasis. The female has longer, higher calls and the two may be heard in duet. A variety of calls has been described, including loud and impressive barks and an abrupt, fearsome "*hoo*" when threatening an intruder. Obvious topographic features, such as rocky pinnacles, stark ridges and mountain peaks, form regular song posts dotted around the outer limits of their territories. The owls visit them regularly, though they call only for a few minutes before moving on to another.

The nest is a mere scrape in some fissure or cave, or a site beneath a large overhanging rock on the least accessible part of a cliff. In forests, these owls may nest on the ground, but only rarely use the nest of another bird (unlike the Great Horned Owl, which prefers the old stick nest of a hawk or eagle). In parts of Europe it is believed to be dangerous to visit the nest of an Eagle Owl as they will attack any intruder. In the north, however, most observers have found them to be inoffensive and the birds generally withdraw to a safe distance. Indeed, they are often practically impossible to see at the nest. But females have been known to attack intruders and, in Finland, such reports are increasing, as if the behaviour of the owls there is undergoing change.

The female alone incubates the eggs, while the male hunts and brings her food. There are usually one or two eggs, and only rarely three or four. Once they hatch, after 32 to 35 days, the male has an even busier life until the female starts to hunt once again when the young are four or five weeks old. Even in successful nests, at least one chick usually dies before fledging, to be eaten by the remaining chicks. The young move from the immediate surroundings of the nest but cannot fly until seven or eight weeks old and still require feeding for some weeks after that. Like a number of other owl species, they are scarcely able to fend for themselves until late autumn. Then, they must compete with adult Eagle Owls for a place to settle, find good feeding, learn to hunt and master their habitat, all at the worst time of year. The first winter of an Eagle Owl's life is a time of great danger.

It is perhaps surprising, given these pressures, that the young Eagle Owl rarely moves far. Most pass their lives in the same territory; only in Siberia is there some regular movement, due to heavy snowfall and severe cold. Adult Eagle Owls can live for at least 20 years in their remote home ranges. To do so, they must find plentiful food. They feed chiefly on mammals, though they also take a wide range of birds. The list of bird prey includes ducks, grebes, Coot (*Fulica atra*), Capercaillie (*Tetrao urogallus*) and Black Grouse (*Tetrao tetrix*), pheasants and partridges, pigeons, woodpeckers, crows, doves and small birds, even Alpine Swift (*Apus melba*). But wherever rabbits and hares are numerous, they are preferred. The Eagle Owl will also catch roe deer fawns, chamois, young foxes, voles, mice, squirrels, moles, rats, hedgehogs, frogs, newts and crabs. Even farmyard cats fall prey to this owl.

The prey chosen by a pair of Eagle Owls reflects both the ease with which it can be caught and its local abundance. The commonest animal may not be the most easily caught and another species will then be the most frequent prey. Larger prey is preferred as it provides most nourishment. Food preferences change with prevailing circumstances. One pair may rely on voles but turn to rats on a rubbish tip when they are scarce; another pair may eat largely rabbits; and another, on the coast, may prey mainly on seabirds.

Eagle Owls can catch prey in the air or on the ground. They can hunt within forests but prefer more open spaces in which to search and chase. It has been said that the Eagle Owl is built to feed on medium-sized mammals but has to make do with lesser fare. The Eagle Owl requires quiet, undisturbed countryside and, though it does seem more and more able to tolerate man's presence, its retreats are under pressure from tourists and developers. All in all, its future may be bleak.

CAPE EAGLE OWL
Bubo capensis

LENGTH: *500 to 580 mm*   MAP NUMBER: 61
DESCRIPTION: *Very large, eared owl, spotted dark on cream underparts*
DISTRIBUTION: *East and Southern Africa*
HABITAT: *Mountains, high woodland*
EGGS: *1—3. Nest on ground or old nest in tree*
STATUS: *Widespread but scarce, locally threatened*

This is one of the most handsome eagle owls, a proud, strong predator with a look of staring intensity. Face to face, the Cape Eagle Owl reveals eyes that are unusually large and are clear amber or pale orange in colour. Like the Eagle Owl (*Bubo bubo*) of Europe, it is a deadly hunter with muscular legs, powerful feet and long, stiletto claws. Basically warm brown in colour, the Cape Eagle Owl is heavily mottled and barred on the back, wings and tail. It is spotted white in splashes across the wing coverts and finely barred on the chest above a clear white belly. The ear tufts are spread broadly above a white facial disc that is neatly edged with black.

Three races are usually recognized. One is found in the highlands of Ethiopia, where it overlaps with the smallest desert races of Eagle Owl. There is a larger, heavily-marked race, often known as Mackinder's Eagle Owl, in parts of Kenya and in a range south to Zimbabwe. The typical race is found south to the Cape and into Namibia; it is about three-quarters of the size of the East African bird.

The Cape Eagle Owl is a little-studied bird, except at a few nests, and is often difficult to watch. It lives in woodland from sea-level to the mountains of Ethiopia, and in much more arid areas with dry bush and kopjes — the characteristic rocky outcrops and hillocks of much of the African wilderness. Wooded gullies with running streams in hilly country, shady ravines and scrubby slopes with scattered boulders are typical habitats. More open country is visited during nocturnal hunting forays. More rarely, as in the flat Karoo landscape of the north-west Cape, this owl lives away from the mountains. Sometimes it will enter cities such as Johannesburg to prey on roosting pigeons.

Usually the Cape Eagle Owl roosts by day in deep shade on the ground or a rock ledge, and is not at all easy to locate. Even when closely approached, it is reluctant to fly and may be missed in daytime by all but persistent owl-watchers. Sometimes one will sidle into the light to sunbathe, and may even hunt by day, but generally this is a bird of dusk and dawn, the times when it moves to more open spaces to hunt. Bare, round-topped granite kopjes make ideal perches but any prominent place with a good view will do.

At dusk, the Cape Eagle Owl calls frequently with a variety of deep hooting calls. These are usually of two or three syllables, "*ho-hooooo*" or "*ho-hooooo-ho*", the first part being the strongest and highest. The female may call with the male, but not in a true duet. Her call is higher-pitched. There is also a quick, triple hoot of greeting and courtship and a loud, sharp bark of alarm, "*wak wak wak*".

This owl captures its prey with a long glide down from its perch. It takes a large variety of small and medium-sized creatures such as mole rats, hyraxes and hares, and will also catch springhares, young duikers and klipspringers, mongooses and even the occasional genet or civet. In Ethiopia, fruit bats are regularly caught. Nocturnal birds such as Barn Owls (*Tyto alba*) are taken, as well as daytime birds, including Kestrel (*Falco tinnunculus*) and even Lanner Falcon (*Falco biarmicus*), guineafowl, francolins, pigeons and starlings. It is recorded that the strange, heron-like Hammerkop (*Scopus umbretta*) has been killed and eaten by this strong owl. Lizards, frogs, scorpions, grasshoppers, beetles and crabs also feature in the bird's varied and opportunistic diet.

Individual owls nevertheless tend to be quite specialized in their diets. In Kenya, mole rats are favoured; in Zimbabwe, red hares, scrub hares and hyraxes. The abundance of the most-easily caught prey determines the numbers of owls. Their territories vary greatly in size in relation to available food. The owl must take large prey to survive most efficiently, and this limits its numbers. A substantial meal will satisfy its hunger for some time and will dispense with the need for further energetic hunting.

Cape Eagle Owls form lasting pairs which nest in large territories. The closest nests will be perhaps 1½ miles (2.5km) apart. The pair will usually roost together before the breeding season, often close to the eventual nest site. The nest is a shallow scoop on the ground with no lining added. It is usually on a rock, between clustered boulders or in a tangle of old roots. More rarely, a higher ledge or even a big tree fork will be selected. There is often a second scrape close to that eventually used by the female.

She lays two eggs, though sometimes one or three. Mackinder's Eagle Owl incubates them for 34 to 36 days, while birds in the south take 38 days. Not only do the eggs of the southern race take longer to hatch but the chicks of these smaller birds take longer to fledge than those of the big middle-African birds, which is the opposite of what may be expected. The chicks hatch at intervals, sometimes four days apart, so the differences in their sizes, develop-ment and abilities are marked.

It is six to eight days before these weak chicks, which can barely lift their heads to accept food, open their eyes. It is almost two weeks before much down appears on their skinny, bare bodies but, by then, they will hiss aggressively at intruders and be ready to struggle over a meal. After three weeks, their first feathers are growing well and by 32 days the facial disk is outlined and fully developed. After 55 days they wander from the nest but are unable to fly until around 75 days old.

For the chicks, the male will bring food just once each night, and sometimes not at all, but the female makes this last for six separate meals during the night. Large prey may be ripped apart and brought to the nest piece by piece over several nights. The female leaves the chicks after three or four weeks, returning only to feed them, but both adults stay close by. A combination of short, aggressive rushes and noisy distraction displays will see off most predators.

Some animals may be drawn to the vicinity of the nest by the remains of prey, pellets and bone. Genets can end up as prey themselves, but larger predators pose a threat to the chicks. Once on the wing the birds have few enemies, but hunting owls may be killed by road traffic in more populated areas, and collisions with fences or overhead wires are an increasing hazard. Commercial development in the African wilds is gradually hemming in this wonderful bird. Only time will tell how well it can survive in its changing environment.

SPOTTED EAGLE OWL
Bubo africanus

LENGTH: *450 mm*   MAP NUMBER: 62
DESCRIPTION: *Smallish eagle owl, dark above, pale below with fine bars, smudged spots*
DISTRIBUTION: *Africa south of the Sahara, Arabia*
HABITAT: *Savanna and light woodland*
EGGS: *2—4. Nest on ground or old tree nest*
STATUS: *Frequent to scarce*

This is the common 'horned' owl of much of Africa, south of the Sahara. The Spotted Eagle Owl is found in a variety of habitats ranging from desert to woodland. It is mainly insectivorous, and lacks the strength and size of the great eagle owls. Its bulk is barely a quarter of that of the Eagle Owl (*Bubo bubo*) of Europe, and Verreaux's Eagle Owl (*Bubo lacteus*) is more than three times heavier.

The plumage of a Spotted Eagle Owl is a rather deep,

cold brown, neatly spotted over the crown, neck and upper back. It is more coarsely marked on the wings and has broad bars over the flight feathers and tail. Underneath it has crosswise barring, and variable degrees of broad spots and blotches. The head is fairly small for an eagle owl, giving it a tight, alert expression, like an outsize Little Owl (*Athene noctua*), with frowning brows, white crescents between the eyes, black edges to the facial disc and sparkling yellow eyes. Its feet are proportionately smaller and weaker than those of other eagle owls. There are greyer birds and a northern race with brown eyes and fewer spots.

Spotted Eagle Owls are found in parts of Arabia and south of the Sahara, except in regions of dense tropical forest and the tip of the horn of Ethiopia. Its habitat varies from rocky hills in desert regions to woodland, and from sea level to altitudes of 6,900 feet (2,100m) in Kenya and even 7,500 feet (2,300m) in the mountains of Cameroon. In the south, these owls are most common in quite dry, even semi-arid areas, with broken rocky slopes and deep gullies. They are least common in the flat open bushveld or denser tracts of woodland. Road cuttings and cleared areas bring this species into the forest. Similarly, eroded gullies where trees have been washed away by rains also attract the Spotted Eagle Owl.

It spends the day concealed in a tree or on a rock ledge, or beneath a bush or even in the burrow of an antbear. If it feels close to discovery, it will stretch upwards, closing its eyes to inconspicuous slits, raising its ear tufts, keeping rigid and enhancing the natural camouflage of its plumage pattern. If flushed, it may move to a nearby rock and sit in the open, where it risks being dived upon and even injured by crows. Despite such inactivity, the Spotted Eagle Owl has been watched by daylight following a honey badger, hoping to benefit from the disturbance created by this surprisingly strong predator.

Once dusk approaches, the Spotted Eagle Owl emerges and its upright, eared form is well-known to many Africans. Unlike many owls, it is frequently seen because it hunts by roadsides and around street lights. Prey taken on the ground is killed in a steep swoop from a perch. At the last moment, the owl raises its wings and swivels its body forward, legs outstretched in a killing blow, eyes closed for protection. If the victim survives the strike, it will be dispatched neatly by the bill. When the owl is after larger prey, it will chase it in longer, more agile bursts of speed. Around street lamps it snatches flying insects, bats and even birds out of the air.

Its food consists chiefly of insects, small mammals and small birds, supplemented by reptiles, scorpions, crabs, snails, frogs and almost anything else it can find. In Nigeria, birds studied in woodland fed largely on gerbils but in areas where the woods had been cleared, scorpions, beetles and reptiles were eaten. The long list of bird prey includes such surprises as Lanner Falcon (*Falco biarmicus*), hornbills, sunbirds and terns. In general, the Spotted Eagle Owl takes advantage of concentrations of insects in towns, and small mammals along the grassy roadsides. When it eats a lot of small prey, this owl uses a great deal of energy in hunting flights, just to find and catch enough food to survive.

The calls are mellow, hooting sounds, including a typical "*boo-boo*" from the male, with the second note a little lower than the first. There is also a three-syllable version from the hen. Unlike the Cape Eagle Owl (*Bubo capensis*), the pair perform a genuine duet, the two calls following on so closely as to sound like one bird in a long sequence around dusk and dawn. Faster, softer "*bokok bokokokokok*" calls are given during courtship, and various chuckles, hisses and clucking noises can be heard from both parents and chicks in the nest.

As with many large owls, the pair is stable until one bird dies. Such lifelong devotion is undoubtedly of value to a large predator that stays on one territory all the year round. It needs a thorough knowledge of its surroundings to hunt efficiently. For breeding, it is helpful to have a strong bond that requires only a simple renewal each spring. The birds may not realize it, but they will have a sense of familiarity with each other. Among other large predators, such as the Osprey (*Pandion haliaetus*), a surviving member of a pair may have a poor season when mated to an inexperienced new partner; the same is probably true in owls.

The owls defend the area around the nest but it is unclear if they defend a larger hunting territory. Their defence is, in any case, basically vocal; frequent calling is usually enough to deter rivals. The pair will roost together, often touching bills and preening each other, but the details of their courtship are poorly studied. The nest is a mere scrape in some form of cover, whether on the ground or a ledge, or in a tree. These owls will use old Hammerkop (*Scopus umbretta*) nests, which are enormous mounds of sticks, or those of crows and Sociable Weavers (*Philetirus socius*). But the eggs may also be laid on a steep bank, among fallen boulders, or even on a window ledge of some large building. The same nest site may be used again and again, despite the apparent risk of disease and the accumulation of parasites. The area around the nest is said to have a distinctive smell, and heaps of pellets, droppings, bits of down, feathers and prey remains litter the site.

Usually two to four eggs are laid. They are incubated by the female, a tight sitter who leaves the nest two or three times a night for less than half an hour at a time, to feed on prey brought by her male. The eggs hatch after 30 to 32 days and the newly-born chicks are weak and helpless at first but quickly become competitive, gulping food down whole. The female sometimes raises her wings and snaps her bill in a ferocious display to repel intruders. Sometimes she performs distraction displays to lure predators from the nest; at other times, she presses home a direct aerial attack, flying intimidatingly at people or predators.

The young fly well after seven weeks. They follow their parents and beg loudly to be fed. For at least five more weeks, and probably longer, they depend on their parents for food but they soon begin to catch prey themselves. If prey is abundant, and if a nearby territory has been vacated, the young Spotted Eagle Owl may breed when less than a year old. If it survives its first winter and becomes established in a territory, its chances of living for another ten years or more are quite good.

Spotted Eagle Owls do not shun the vicinity of people and many die in accidents with traffic, fences and overhead wires. One bizarre report described an owl found dead after its foot had become trapped between the body and shell of a large tortoise. There are reports that the residues of pesticides used in Africa are increasing in owls. These seem mainly to be those banned in Europe and the United States, such as DDT. It is quite likely that these poisons will become the main threat to this species.

FRASER'S EAGLE OWL
Bubo poensis

LENGTH: *390 to 450 mm*   MAP NUMBER: 63
DESCRIPTION: *Large, eared, broadly-barred owl, dark eyes*
DISTRIBUTION: *West Africa*
HABITAT: *Lowland rain-forest*
STATUS: *Rare, perhaps endangered*

The lowland forests of West Africa, which are seriously threatened by logging activity, have three eagle owls — Fraser's, Shelley's (*Bubo shelleyi*) and the Akun Eagle Owl (*Bubo leucostictus*) — which can live successfully together in the same region, but relatively little is known about them. Fraser's Eagle Owl is a magnificent bird, large and upright, tapering down from its broad, square head and barred chest to a very short tail. Its ear tufts are wide and dark, its eyes large, dark and liquid with pale blue lids. The Nduk Eagle Owl, a rare form from Tanzania, is larger and darker with less regular bars beneath. It may best be seen as belonging to the same species as Fraser's Eagle Owl, a local race which may be evolving towards a new species.

From Mount Limba in Liberia eastwards to the extreme west of Uganda, Fraser's Eagle Owl lives in ancient, untouched evergreen forest. But it sometimes occupies disturbed areas and forest clearings and may prove capable of surviving even when most of the virgin jungle has been cleared. Like many tropical species, its survival depends on its capacity to adapt.

This owl emerges to hunt at dusk, watching and waiting on an open perch for insects, millipedes and frogs, then swooping down to kill. Now and then, it varies its food, catching a small bird, bat or squirrel. Despite its size and imposing looks, it is clearly not a ferocious predator.

The call of Fraser's Eagle Owl is a long *"twowooooot"*, repeated every three or four seconds. The second part of this hoot is higher and more of a whistle than the first. The bird has, however, a varied repertoire of moaning, purring and mewing notes. It nests in a tree cavity and the young are probably dependent on their parents for many months after leaving the nest.

FOREST EAGLE OWL
Bubo nipalensis

LENGTH: *510 to 610 mm*   MAP NUMBER: 64
DESCRIPTION: *Very large, long-eared, barred eagle owl, yellow eyes and bill*
DISTRIBUTION: *Himalayas, India, South-East Asia*
HABITAT: *Wet forest*
EGGS: *1. Nest in abandoned tree nest, on ledge or in cave*
STATUS: *Scarce/threatened*

There are magnificent owls, subtly beautiful owls, and boldly patterned owls but few are as handsome as this bird. The Forest Eagle Owl has strikingly long, outspread 'horns', big yellow eyes and splendid barred plumage. It is a large owl, too, and a powerful predator, truly one of the great eagle owls.

This bird occupies forests in areas of high rainfall and often high temperature in the Himalayas, India and much of South-East Asia. In the Himalayas, it lives in a variety of dense evergreen forests and mixed woods at altitudes up to 6,900 feet (2,100m). It sleeps by day in dense cover, but sometimes spreads fear among lesser forest birds by hunting during daylight. As dusk falls, it may move to the edge of a forest or the side of a clearing where it can watch for prey, though most of its hunting is within the forest. Other birds and small mammals of the forest should indeed be wary of this owl. It can catch and overpower peafowl and junglefowl (albeit at their roosts), pheasants, hares and occasionally even jackals and young barking deer. It has been well described as a 'feathered tiger'.

The main call of the Forest Eagle Owl is a low, deep, far-carrying hoot. Various shrieks, attributed to some unknown 'devil bird', may also be the work of this colourful forest character. The race found in Sri Lanka is more identifiable as the local 'devil bird', with a courtship performance involving dreadful shrieks and strangled cries. A hollow in a tree, or the abandoned nest of some large eagle, or even a deep, shady cave is used as a nest in which a single, smooth egg is laid. The breeding biology of the Forest Eagle Owl is not known in any detail but in the Himalayas it breeds in February and March and in Sri Lanka in April and May. It has a reputation for aggressive, fearless defence of its young and few people or predators would wish to tangle with this impressive bird.

MALAY EAGLE OWL
Bubo sumatrana

LENGTH: *400 to 460 mm*   MAP NUMBER: *65*
DESCRIPTION: *Smallish, long-eared eagle owl, large eyes*

DISTRIBUTION: *Burma, Malaysia, Sumatra, Java, Borneo*
HABITAT: *Mountain rain-forest*
EGGS: *1. Nest in tree hole or hollow*
STATUS: *Uncertain, probably rare and declining*

This is a smaller bird than the Forest Eagle Owl (*Bubo nipalensis*) and the two inhabit separate areas. The Malay Eagle Owls replaces the larger, more powerful species in the forests of Burma, Malaysia, Sumatra and Borneo. This is surprising, as they appear to differ sufficiently in size and hunting skills to be able to live side by side, in the manner of eagle owls in the jungles of Africa. In Sumatra, the Malay Eagle Owl is resident in woods from sea level to a height of 5,300 feet (1,600m) on Mount Singgalang. It lays a single egg in a tree hole, or at the base of an epiphyte which makes a suitable sheltered hollow against a large branch. In Borneo, the flight call is described as several hoots followed by a groan. In the local mythology of Java some of its loud calls are attributed to demons.

SHELLEY'S EAGLE OWL
Bubo shelleyi

LENGTH: *610 mm*   MAP NUMBER: 66
DESCRIPTION: *Large, dark, barred eagle owl*
DISTRIBUTION: *West Africa*
HABITAT: *Lowland rain-forest*
EGGS: *? Nest in tree cavity*
STATUS: *Uncertain, probably rare and declining*

This is the largest of the three eagle owls found in the African rain-forests, a formidable predator worthily compared to the Forest Eagle Owl (*Bubo nipalensis*) of Asia. This is a giant owl, powerfully built with broad shoulders and a large, heavy head curiously lacking in pattern or expression. This is largely due to the colour of the dark brown eyes.

Rare and unevenly distributed, Shelley's Eagle Owl is found in very small pockets in Guinea, Liberia, Ghana, Cameroon, Gabon and Zaire. Its call is a loud, wailing "*kooouw*". It sometimes spends its day quite low down in the dense forest but probably nests higher, in a tree cavity. Almost nothing is known about the food of this owl, except that it can catch flying squirrels. Its size and powerful build suggest that it feeds on large prey; the strong feet, which have a fierce grip and long, arched, needle-sharp claws, could well subdue and kill a substantial bird or mammal when need be.

VERREAUX'S EAGLE OWL
Bubo lacteus

LENGTH: *600 to 650 mm*   MAP NUMBER: 67
DESCRIPTION: *Very large, powerful, pale grey eagle owl, finely barred, black edges to facial disc*
DISTRIBUTION: *Africa south of the Sahara*
HABITAT: *Woodland, bushveld*
EGGS: *1–2. Nest in hole or abandoned tree nest*
STATUS: *Widespread but scarce, locally threatened*

Verreaux's Eagle Owls are widely distributed in Africa, south of the Sahara, except for the driest deserts and most dense forests. They are spread only patchily through West Africa from Senegal and Gambia to Nigeria and Cameroon but are commoner in the east. They favour rather dry woodland, though they often live in river valleys, and frequently occupy clumps of introduced conifers or eucalyptus, or acacias. In southern Africa, these owls are most common in woodland and bushveld to the east and become very rare towards the south or westwards onto the Kalahari sand.

This is a large, rather grey owl, neatly peppered with dark and light freckles, closely and finely barred over the head, and more broadly marked with wavy bars which are spread evenly over the underparts. The big, broad head has quite blunt ear tufts, which are often hardly visible. Its very pale facial disc is edged with broad, upright bands of black, seen most clearly on adult birds. The large eyes are dark brown, rimmed with pale pink.

This bird, also known as the Giant Eagle Owl, is named after Jules Pierre Verreaux, a member of a noted French family of collectors and taxidermists. Verreaux first travelled to Africa with his uncle in 1818, when he was 11, and returned before he was 20. He amassed a vast collection of birds and eggs but he and his brothers were none too accurate in their records and formal identification of specimens. Nevertheless, Verreaux's Eagle Owl (and his eagle, another of Africa's finest birds), commemorate a career which ended in London. Verreaux was a founder of the British Ornithologists' Union.

Verreaux's Eagle Owl is, in effect, a nocturnal equivalent of the large diurnal eagles whose habitat it shares. It is a powerful hunter and can take prey as large as vervet monkeys, springhares and even Secretary Birds (*Sagittarius serpentarius*). Its feeding is general rather than specialized; its hunting technique is flexible and its diet is catholic. This owl may drop from its roost onto a passing animal in the middle of the day, though it usually emerges from its hideaway only at dusk to fly to a favourite

T. BOYER

perch overlooking open space. After spotting prey, it will strike in a sudden lethal dive.

Like eagles, it kills larger prey by a combination of its immensely powerful grip, long sharp claws and the sheer power of its strike. The powerfully-muscled legs, backed by the weight and momentum of this great owl, pack a massive punch. At other times, the owls fly through the upper branches of trees and quite dense bush, crashing through the twigs and sending roosting guinea fowl and other terrified birds fleeing through the night. On such raids, it will catch a variety of birds, including a range of other owls and even the eagles that hunted in the same area by day. Almost nothing is safe from Verreaux's Eagle Owl.

The broad, soft, silent wings give the bird great manoeuvrability. It is capable of a delicacy of touch sufficient to capture flying moths and other insects, as well as lightning twists and turns that end the life of a passing bat or small bird. Among other prey, the South African hedgehog is regularly captured. Verreaux's Eagle Owl is the only predator of this spiny creature, whose neatly-peeled skin is often found beneath the owl's regular perch.

The males are lighter and smaller than females and it is likely that they eat different food. This would allow a pair to survive in a smaller territory than would be needed if they fed on the same prey. The resident owls build up knowledge of their surroundings and its available food over long years, and can adapt to changing conditions with relative ease.

If one type of prey becomes scarce, these owls will not be so reliant on it that they must move away. They turn to something else. In general, they prefer larger, more accessible prey from which they can gain nourishment most efficiently. Fluctuations in food may well affect their breeding efforts, as with most owls.

The territory of a pair of Verreaux's Eagle Owls is very large, as much as 17,000 acres (7,000ha). This will supply all the needs of the pair and their young, which stay with their parents for a long time after leaving the nest. The pair roosts together most of the time and their young will often be found in adjacent trees. These may well include young reared in a previous season, which are still fed by the male but assist the female to rear her new brood. Whole families, some with chicks from up to three years before, can be found clustered together, a remarkable trait for a large owl. Some pairs breed every year, or for several years in a row, but may miss a year if the most nutritious prey is scarce. Exactly how these variations are controlled is not known.

A territorial bird will regularly call at dusk and even in

the late afternoon, but the most intense vocal performances come just before dawn. The call is said to carry for more than three miles (5km) through calm air. It is a deep, grunting hoot, described as "*hook*", usually uttered in a series of up to five notes. The female has a lower voice than the male. Like Cape Eagle Owls (*Bubo capensis*), the two may often call together but their duet is not synchronized like that of Spotted Eagle Owls (*Bubo africanus*). The call may be linked with a visual signal. The throat pulsates with each note, revealing a white patch which must be easily visible to the bird's partner.

Courtship is attended by more rapid hooting and excited calling and whining as the pair bow to each other or preen one another's feathers. They seem to share a deep, lasting attachment and, like other large, eared owls, they exhibit an ability to communicate by facial expression. The nest is simply that of another large bird, such as the bulky pile of sticks heaped up by an eagle, crow or Hammerkop (*Scopus umbretta*). Sometimes a new nest may be taken over while still in use and the rightful owners forced out.

The usual clutch is of two eggs but only one chick normally survives long enough to fly. The eggs hatch after anything from 32 to 39 days and the chick is in the nest for up to ten weeks. The first chick will be up to a week old when the second hatches and, if fully fit, it will easily dominate the sibling and appropriate all or most of its food. Presumably the second chick is a safety measure in case of sickness or the loss of the first to a predator, but it is rarely required. The smaller one may survive for two or three weeks but almost always succumbs. The larger chick may attack and eat the smaller one.

Verreaux's Eagle Owl is the African counterpart to the Great Horned Owl (*Bubo virginianus*) of North America but is larger, and more akin to the Eagle Owl (*Bubo bubo*) of Europe in its size and predatory power. It faces similar problems, but in a less acute form. However, the constant rise in human population, and the changes this brings about, will threaten this owl's prospects of survival. It may be forced to live off smaller prey, in less than perfect habitats, or it may join many of the larger mammals in being confined to game parks. Whether a more sanguine outlook is justified will depend on this splendid owl's capacity to adapt to change in the African continent. Life for such a big predator may prove difficult.

DUSKY EAGLE OWL
Bubo coromandus

LENGTH: *430 to 480 mm*   MAP NUMBER: 68
DESCRIPTION: *Plain, dark brownish eagle owl, orange eyes*
DISTRIBUTION: *India and South-East Asia*
HABITAT: *Riverine forest and forest edge*
EGGS: *2. Nest in tree*
STATUS: *Uncertain, probably declining*

This bird is widespread in forests and in cultivated areas with plentiful trees in India and South-East Asia. It is a resident, and likes densely-foliaged trees, including old mangoes and tamarinds, close to water. It may live in the same clump or grove all the year round, usually in pairs. This is not one of the larger eagle owls. It has paler yellow eyes and a less fierce mien than the Eagle Owl (*Bubo bubo*); its narrow ear tufts often stand erect and close together, rather than spreading out sideways over the crown.

By day the Dusky Eagle Owl usually sits quietly, tucked away in dense foliage or in the shade of a branch, but it is not strictly nocturnal and may move around in daylight. It will hunt on dull, wet days, but usually the serious task of catching prey starts a little before dusk. Small mammals, small birds and lizards are typical prey and birds' nests are raided for their young. This owl can catch roosting parakeets, and House Crows (*Corvus splendens*) and Jungle Crows (*Corvus macrorhynchos*) are often taken. But anything from a small hawk such as the Shikra (*Accipiter badius*) to rollers, doves and pond herons will be caught from time to time. Large prey is decapitated before being swallowed or carried back to the nest.

A deep, resonant booming "*WO, wo, wo, wo-o-o-o-o*" is a frequent call, day and night, uttered with the quickening, fading pattern of a small ball bouncing freely to a standstill. Like many other owls, this creature also has the habit of making surprisingly loud clicking or snapping sounds with its bill when alarmed or annoyed.

Nests are in tall trees, such as peepul, kadam or sheesham, often based on nests left by kites or vultures, and are lined with a few bits of green foliage. Usually two white eggs are laid, the second several days after the first, leaving the second chick much the smaller and weaker. More often than not, only one survives. The breeding season varies according to locality, being December to January in northern India but somewhat later in the south.

AKUN EAGLE OWL
Bubo leucostictus

LENGTH: *400 to 460 mm*   MAP NUMBER: 69
DESCRIPTION: *Boldly barred, smallish eagle owl, bright yellow eyes*
DISTRIBUTION: *West Africa*
HABITAT: *Equatorial rain-forest*
EGGS: *? Nest in tree hole or perhaps on ground*
STATUS: *Uncertain, probably threatened/endangered*

This lightly-built bird completes the trio of eagle owls — alongside Shelley's (*Bubo shelleyi*) and Fraser's Eagle Owl (*Bubo poensis*) — found in the equatorial rain-forest of Africa. The Akun Eagle Owl is considerably less powerful than Shelley's Eagle Owl, the biggest of the three. While the eagle owls of the Asian forests live in exclusive territories, the three African species live side by side without undue competition.

With small feet, the Akun Eagle Owl is incapable of overpowering large birds or mammals. It may even be fully insectivorous. Little wonder that it hides by day and calls only rarely by night. It is an eagle owl largely restricted to eating beetles and cockroaches.

Like its fellow forest owls in West Africa, this bird is apparently·widely distributed from Guinea and Liberia to Zaire and northern Angola. But this disguises a very local, restricted pattern of occurrence. The Akun Eagle Owl is a rare resident in increasingly fragmented forests and on forested islands in rivers. Close study might well lead to its classification as endangered, a rarity facing further decline.

Its call is a low, accelerating rattle, "*tok tok tok-ok-ok-okok*", but this is not given very often. A high-pitched, rising "*heuuuw*" is made by the young when begging for food. This might prove useful to birdwatchers wishing to locate breeding Akun Eagle Owls, in the same way that the 'squeaky gate' call of young Long-eared Owls (*Asio otus*) is of value in tracing them in Europe. The nests of Akun Eagle Owls may be on the ground but there is only slight evidence for that; nothing of real substance is known about its breeding behaviour.

PHILIPPINE EAGLE OWL
Bubo philippensis

LENGTH: *400 mm*   MAP NUMBER: 70
DESCRIPTION: *Dark orange-brown eagle owl, boldly streaked*
DISTRIBUTION: *Philippines*
HABITAT: *Tropical rain-forest*
STATUS: *Uncertain, probably declining and perhaps threatened*

Sometimes separated from the eagle owls and called the Philippine Horned Owl (*Pseudoptynx philippensis*), this is a bird of similar size to the Malay Eagle Owl (*Bubo sumatrana*) but replaces it in Luzon and Mindanao. It is a strange eagle owl of tropical forests, with dark, orange-brown plumage on the head and upperparts. It is a far less powerful predator than the Forest Eagle Owl (*Bubo nipalensis*) which is found on the Asian mainland.

FISH OWLS

FOUR SPECIES

BLAKISTON'S FISH OWL
Ketupa blakistoni

LENGTH: *600 mm*　MAP NUMBER: 71
DESCRIPTION: *Huge, dark eagle/fish owl, feathered legs, yellow eyes*
DISTRIBUTION: *East Asia, Japan*
HABITAT: *Riverine forest*
EGGS: *1–2 (rarely 3). Nest in abandoned tree nest or box*
STATUS: *Endangered*

In extreme north-east Asia, Manchuria, on Sakhalin Island, the southernmost Kuriles and on Hokkaido, Japan, lives as formidable and extraordinary an owl as any in the world. Blakiston's Fish Owl is a giant bird, larger even than Siberian Eagle Owls (*Bubo bubo*) and with a wingspan close to 6 feet 6 inches (2m). It was once listed as a sub-species of the Brown Fish Owl (*Ketupa zeylonensis*) of southern Asia, then separated as *Bubo blakistoni* before being returned to the fish owl genus *Ketupa*.

Its structure, which includes fully-feathered legs, is very like that of an eagle owl although it has bristly toes like the other fish owls. The ear tufts are long, loose and rather ragged for an eagle owl and the long bill is more protruding and less angled downwards. The plumage, which is stiff and far less soft than in most owls, is typical of the fish owls. The flight feathers are smooth-edged without the fringe of tiny barbs along the leading edge that softens the margin and creates the silent flight characteristic of even the largest eagle owls. However, the flight of Blakiston's Fish Owl is nevertheless reported to be silent. And, whereas other Asian fish owls have small skeletal differences in relation to eagle owls, this owl has none. It is rather intermediate in character. Though generally placed in the *Ketupa* genus, it is closer in more respects to the *Bubo* species.

This is a bird of cold climates, often contending with severe winters even though it lives near fast-flowing rivers and deep wells that do not normally freeze. It is an owl of dense, dark, primeval forests, whether coniferous, deciduous or mixed, bordering lakes, rivers and even the ocean shore. It seems to be restricted to improbably cold, difficult places for a fish-eating bird. This places it at a grave disadvantage during a freeze. It has probably retreated to such areas due to competition with diurnal fish-eating birds of prey, such as the large East Asian sea eagles. But in southern regions, it is probably the pressure of dense human populations that has caused this owl to retreat to more remote locations.

In Japan, the common practice of channelling any river of moderate or greater size between artificial banks, making a canal of even the wildest stream, has ruined the majority of fish owl habitats. In its Soviet range, this fish owl may be found at a density of one pair to every 7½–9 miles (12–15km) of large river. In Hokkaido, however, all the untouched rivers now occupied are less than 6 miles (10km) in length. All the longer stretches of river have been canalized and are of no practical use to such a discriminating bird.

Blakiston's Fish Owl was once known as 'the god who defends the village' and, like the brown bear, was held in reverence in Japan. Later it suffered persecution, especially in winter when it was forced to live close to openings in the ice and was killed easily by hunters and fur trappers. Developments in the modern world leave this owl few places where it can thrive.

In Japan, Blakiston's Fish Owls are seriously endangered and confined to relict areas of undisturbed forest. Under Japan's conservation laws, the owl is fully protected but the tree in which it lives can be chopped down, more or less with impunity. In 1983, less than 30 birds were recorded but, by 1984, the survey workers had gained the confidence of more of those guarding secret nests and some 50 birds were located. Only two pairs, however, were known to have bred successfully. Others live in captivity but some of these are isolated in zoos or private collections which keep only one bird each. A potential captive breeding stock is going to waste. In the Soviet Far East, a few hundred may still survive. Their continued existence is dependent on the remoteness of their environment and the lack of human interference.

Japanese birds have suffered also from the attentions of photographers and other enthusiasts. Some are ignorant of the damage they cause; others are indifferent to it. Recent efforts to discourage them have included trapping the birds and placing highly-coloured reflective rings on their legs to make them less attractive in flashlit photographs. It is a matter of concern to ornithologists that such last-ditch methods are needed to protect a bird on the verge of extinction in Japan.

Other developments have had happier results. Special nest box schemes in the forests of Hokkaido have helped enormously as a lack of suitable nesting sites was limiting the numbers of Blakiston's Fish Owls. Most there now nest in boxes and their productivity has improved. These great owls seem unable to breed every year but many pairs in boxes succeed in two years out of three. Increasing numbers are able to rear two chicks successfully rather

Blakiston's Fish Owl (*Ketupa blakistoni*)

than the single juvenile that for so long seemed normal.

The owls are active throughout the night, around dusk and even in daylight during the long summer days in north-east Asia, when they must hunt to feed their young. In the winter, they are much more nocturnal, emerging at dusk, often with a flurry of calls. The territorial song is deep and resonant, a sequence of quick, short notes such as "*boo-bu*" or "*boo-boo-buo*", though it lacks the carrying power of the Eagle Owl's song. Male and female may call together in complicated duets.

Whatever its place in taxonomy, Blakiston's Fish Owl devours a great deal of fish, crayfish and frogs. Pike, catfish, burbot and salmon, all species that can achieve considerable size, are caught regularly and the owl's preference depends on supply. These owls eat the trout which abound in late summer in Japan, before turning to salmon in the autumn. By the spring, they live largely on swarms of frogs that spawn in the riverside marshes. Small mammals, hares, martens and even cats and dogs are also killed and eaten, as well as the occasional duck, hazelhen or smaller bird. On the Kuriles, the owls fish on the rocky sea coast and, though their prey will vary from inland locations, the bulk of it will still be fish. Where they exist in sufficient numbers, these owls may gather in small groups by the openings in the river ice in winter.

Hunting often involves walking into the shallows, perhaps crossing ice, snow or rocks, or passing along regular tracks worn down through long vegetation at the water's edge. An owl may sit motionless for long periods on a favoured perch overlooking water, perhaps hunched on a low branch or standing on a spit of sand. When prey is spotted, it will leap with half-open wings to strike with its feet. Still held by the feet, the prey is carried to a perch.

Some territories are occupied by a single bird for years. Individual owls are so attached to their territories that a bird which has lost its mate will remain alone until a new young bird arrives by chance. Once a pair is established, or has survived a winter, nesting begins from February.

Nests are in large, hollow trees, such as poplars or Manchurian ash, high above the forest floor, but also in decayed boles of fallen trees close to the ground. The nest hole may be a large cavity with ample room for the birds to move freely in and out. Usually one or two eggs, and only occasionally three, are laid early in March when the forest may still be under snow. The male hunts for the incubating female and later he provides food for the young. It may be his inability to supply sufficient food for his family that leads to breeding failures every two or three years.

The eggs hatch after about 35 days and the young leave the nest within a further 35 to 40 days. But they still require the care of their parents, and may need to be fed by them for some months. Some may still be fed in this way when a year old and this probably prevents a further breeding attempt the following spring. This could be more evident in the Soviet population than in Japan, where young birds have been found to leave their parents' territory during the winter, leaving the adults free to breed in March.

Blakiston's Fish Owls are certainly among the world's most splendid birds. Though perhaps less handsome than Eagle Owls, they are every bit as strong and domineering and cut equally imposing figures. Yet they live in parts of the world where many people remain indifferent to such great natural treasures. There has been a lack of efficient, practical action in protecting this species. The knowledge and skills to support it do exist; what is needed is concerted action and the will to succeed.

BROWN FISH OWL
Ketupa zeylonensis

LENGTH: *480 to 510 mm*   MAP NUMBER: *72*
DESCRIPTION: *Middle East, south and South-East Asia*
DISTRIBUTION: *Very large, eared owl; bare legs; streaked*
HABITAT: *Riverine woods*
EGGS: *1—2. Nest in abandoned nest in tree or cavity*
STATUS: *Uncertain, perhaps locally frequent, locally endangered*

Brown Fish Owls and Malay Fish Owls (*Ketupa ketupu*) strongly resemble eagle owls, even on close inspection, having brown plumage with dark streaks, pale eyes and flattened, pointed ear tufts. They have somewhat rounder, forward-leaning heads, with less defined edges to the disc of short feathers on the face, and a different expression. This is due partly to the higher position of the bill, which sits squarely between the eyes, instead of a little below them, as in eagle owls. This gives the Brown Fish Owl a more fierce, morose or frowning look, less questioning and less regal. The larger eagle owls may be the most fearsome predators of all but the *Ketupa* fish owls, unlike the African fishing owls (*Scotopelia spp.*), must certainly have evolved from the eagle owl group.

The fish owls have looser feathers than eagle owls and are rather ragged looking and less breathtakingly silent in flight. The chief difference is in the legs and feet. These are longer than those of eagle owls, with bare toes that have rough, spiny scales (rather like those of an Osprey *Pandion haliaetus*) to help them grip slippery fish. Unlike the Osprey, the powerful, curved claws have sharp cutting edges as well as long, sharp points.

Of the four Asian fish owls, this is the commonest and the most widespread. There are, however, few Brown Fish Owls in the Middle East (perhaps still a pair or two in the Golan Heights, for example). The fish owls there have suffered a decline caused by pesticides, poisons and the extraction of water from streams. In Iran they are thought to be extinct and in Turkey it is unlikely that more than a handful of pairs, if any, remain.

The fish owls of Israel and Iraq are pale, rather buff in colour compared with the typically yellow-brown birds of the more humid parts of its range. The main distribution extends from the Persian Gulf eastwards to China, covering in all some 4,400 miles (7,000km) from east to west. Such a southern Asian distribution is most unusual among birds and certainly among owls.

The Brown Fish Owl needs water, of course, and dense tree cover, so is found along well-wooded streams and rivers, beside rice paddies and quiet lakesides. It prefers steep wooded slopes, such as overgrown, eroded ravines and steep, tangled river banks.

In India, it is often a village bird, though not always an obvious one, regularly found in the vicinity of artificial pools, even concrete-sided tanks, and canals. It can be found in the foothills of the Himalayas, up to heights of 5,000 feet (1,500m) in Nepal and Sikkim (even up to 10,000 feet (3,000m) on occasions) and throughout India, Pakistan and Bangladesh.

Pairs often roost together in a large tree or bamboo clump, or in a bushy gorge. They become active well before sunset but do not start to hunt until darkness. They call a lot, and these calls have a curiously human tone with what is often described as a disagreeable, moaning quality. The booming sounds echo around rocky gullies or disturb the stillness of a forest with an unnerving effect. They have given rise to several local names, such as 'hoodoo' and 'bhootoom pecha'.

The Brown Fish Owl does indeed eat fish but much of its food is made up of freshwater crabs and frogs. Fish are caught in a low, skimming flight over the surface of water but crabs may be captured by a bird paddling about on foot or dropping, feet first, into shallow water from a rock or other suitable perch. It does not plunge like an Osprey, nor does it submerge any of the body when fishing, although it is fond of waddling to the water's edge on foot and bathing. Between fishing forays, a fish owl will spend long spells perched on a suitable stump or bare branch overlooking a pool or river. Besides fish, almost any suitable creature that is unfortunate enough to appear before a fish owl is likely to be caught – a small porcupine, jungle-fowl and pheasants have been recorded as food. The habit of scavenging from carcases of animals extends even to eating the remains of a dead crocodile. Carrion-eating is a rare trait among owls.

The nesting behaviour of fish owls is not well-known. Brown Fish Owls breed between November and early spring. This is the dry season in India and China, while in the Middle East it does rain, but only a little. The nest is not far from water, in an old eagle's eyrie, or a ruin, or a large mango or fig tree, and will be used for several years in succession. The birds leave a great many pellets and bits of uneaten food lying around the nest, in which one or two, and perhaps sometimes three, round, white eggs are laid.

TAWNY FISH OWL
Ketupa flavipes

LENGTH: *480 to 510 mm*
MAP NUMBER: 73
DESCRIPTION: *Large, eared owl; bare legs; bright tawny-brown, heavily striped*
DISTRIBUTION: *Central and South-East Asia*
HABITAT: *Mountain riverine forest*
EGGS: *1–2. Nest in tree hole*
STATUS: *Declining and locally threatened*

Large yellow feet, gleaming eyes and a general tawny-orange cast to the plumage, set off beautifully by contrasting black streaks, make this the most attractive of the fish owls. It has particularly long and widely-spread, flamboyant ear tufts, but they can also be depressed and drawn back and downwards alongside the crown. Like other *Ketupa* owls, the head may be sunk into the shoulders or drawn up in a strangely rectangular shape. Birds in Sri Lanka are rather smaller and darker than those on the mainland.

Compared to the Brown Fish Owl (*Ketupa zeylonensis*), this bird has a larger and more powerful bill and the legs are feathered for only about half their length. Like the other fish owls, it lacks the fine fringes to the wing feathers that make the flight of most owls so silent.

The Tawny Fish Owl inhabits streamsides in dense forest, in a narrow belt across southern Asia from the northern edge of the Himalayas to Indo-China. It seems to prefer running water, whereas the Brown Fish Owl lives beside still waters. In the foothills of the Himalayas it may be found up to altitudes of 5,000 feet (1,500m) and in Sri Lanka it frequently lives in the hills to the same height, and sometimes even higher.

Although it is sometimes about by day, the Tawny Fish Owl is basically a nocturnal hunter. It perches high up in trees, swooping down to take fish just like a fish eagle, and often in a more spectacular way than the Brown Fish Owl. Its varied diet includes a large quantity of fish and crabs but also small rodents and birds. The latter may be surprisingly large and include jungle fowl and pheasants. The Tawny

Fish Owl is thought to be the most formidable of the Asian fish owls, except for the remarkable Blakiston's Fish Owl (*Ketupa blakistoni*). Its voice is a deep "*whoo-hoo*" and a mewing, cat-like noise has also been reported. Local names include 'dao hao ho ho' and 'lak kyo-o mung', the latter meaning 'the kyo-o calling devil'. Despite this local reference to its calls, it is little known.

This owl nests in December, January or February, and from January to May in Sri Lanka, where it is the commonest owl. It chooses old nests of fish eagles and other large birds or a hollow in a river bank. Two eggs, though sometimes only one, are laid and the parent birds, especially the female, are bold and aggressive in defence of the nest, attacking most potential predators.

MALAY FISH OWL
Ketupa ketupu

LENGTH: *380 to 440 mm*   MAP NUMBER: 74
DESCRIPTION: *Large, dull brown, eagle owl-like; bare legs*
DISTRIBUTION: *South-East Asia, Sumatra, Java, Borneo*
HABITAT: *Riverine and coastal forest and woodland*
EGGS: *1. Nest in tree or cavity*
STATUS: *Frequent*

The Malay Fish Owl is a bird of forest streams, mangroves and coastal forests, fish ponds and the edges of reservoirs. It looks like a smaller version of the Brown Fish Owl (*Ketupa zeylonensis*) with a simpler plumage pattern. It is found from South-East Asia through Malaysia to Sumatra, Java and Borneo in Indonesia.

This owl is quite at home close to rice paddies and villages so long as there are plentiful trees in which it can hide by day. On Mount Singgalang in Sumatra, it lives at a height of over 5,300 feet (1,600m) above sea level, despite being predominantly a bird of the lowlands and coastal belt. One nest has been found at the base of an epiphytic fern. In Java, it nests in large tree cavities or in old nests of other birds high in the trees. A single white egg with dusky spots is laid. The breeding season in Java extends from September to June. Its voice has been described as more musical and higher-pitched than that of other fish owls.

T. BOYER

FISHING OWLS

THREE SPECIES

PEL'S FISHING OWL
Scotopelia peli

LENGTH: *510 to 610 mm*   MAP NUMBER: 75
DESCRIPTION: *Huge, big-headed, lacks ear tufts; rufous-orange, barred*
DISTRIBUTION: *Africa south of the Sahara*
HABITAT: *Riverine woods and forest*
EGGS: *2. Nest in natural tree hole*
STATUS: *Scarce and isolated*

An ancient riverside tree with its branches sprawling over the water provides an ideal retreat for this tawny-orange owl. It is a resident species, occurring in a range from Nigeria across the Congo Basin and central Africa to the valley of the Zambezi River, with isolated outposts on the Gambia River, in Ethiopia and along the eastern coast almost as far as the Cape. But in few regions is Pel's Fishing Owl at all common.

In Kenya, it is extremely secretive and capable of living in a region undetected for long periods. It is rarely seen and the size of the population is unknown. It is recorded at altitudes as high as 5,600 feet (1,700m), but most of its known sites are below 3,300 feet (1,000m) above sea level. The majority of reports have always been from along the Tana River and in the mangroves at the mouth of the river. In these locations, this owl may be not uncommon. There are recent reports of it from the Mara River, the watercourse providing a barrier to the migrant hordes of wildebeest in the Masai Mara National Park.

Pel's Fishing Owl has a very large, loose-feathered head with no ear tufts, in contrast to the Asian fish owls. This gives its huge, cowled head a look of exaggerated roundness shared by the other two African fishing owls. It does, however, have the same stiff wing feathers as the Asian birds, without the softening fringe of curved barbs on their leading edges so common among owls and which help to achieve their silence in flight. Perhaps there is no need to dive silently onto fish as there is onto small mammals. The Pel's Fishing Owl also has the distinctively bare, long, spiny toes and strong, arched claws of a fish-eater that uses its feet to catch and hold its slippery prey. It is a strong bird that can subdue a muscular fish weighing 4½ pounds (2kg) that is struggling for its life.

How this owl locates its prey is unclear. In southern Africa, its commonest prey are squeakers, fish that can make a sound by moving their fins in their sockets. It is possible this sound helps the owl detect them. Fishing owls are often seen peering into water which seems murky to the human eye, and they may be listening to low frequency sounds generated by the movements of fish below the surface. But it seems more likely that sight is the chief sense used by the fishing owls when they hunt. Fish are particularly vulnerable to the sudden dive of an owl when they rise to the surface to gulp air or snatch a floating insect. On still, moonlit nights in the tropics, they are especially likely to give themselves away to the watching predator as they disturb the surface of the water.

Larger fish, such as the African pike and tigerfish, also wallow in the warm, shallow waters by the edge of rivers, as do bream and catfish when feeding or laying eggs. They, too, figure largely in the diet of Pel's Fishing Owls. Many fish, such as the squeakers, are more active at dusk and after, the hours when the fishing owls hunt, than during daylight when they would be vulnerable to kingfishers, herons and egrets.

A male Pel's Fishing Owl may call soon after dark, but does so mostly just before dawn. He puffs out his throat and upper breast to produce a deep, sonorous hoot that will carry up to two miles (3km). This tremendous performance is often followed by a much, quieter, softer hoot from the female. Some observers believe, however, that it is the female which gives the deeper hoot. The calling is most regular during courtship, especially on moonlit nights among the pans, swamps and surging rivers of the African plains. It is a territorial call and is often answered by booming hoots from adjacent pairs holding territory up and down the river.

The pair roosts together and the trees and ground beneath them become liberally splashed with white droppings, feathers and decomposing pellets of fishbones. It is curious that owls so often have superb camouflage and skill at concealment when they roost, only to betray their presence in such a blatant way.

At dusk, the pair venture out to settle low over water. The gleam of a fish or the merest ripple of water will be enough for Pel's Fishing Owl to launch itself into a dive and snatch a meal in its feet. The bird's body feathers absorb water well and are rarely wetted. The head of the fish is eaten first. Dead fish are ignored.

A pair of Pel's Fishing Owls will spend their whole lives beside one river and in the nearby trees where they roost and nest. In the best fishing areas there may be a pair every 1,000 yards (1km) along a river but densities are often much lower. The birds require a nest site within about 200 yards (200m) of water, deep shade in which to roost, a suitable perch for fishing and deep pools that will not dry out in times of drought.

Nesting usually starts when water levels reach their peak. In certain places, owls move in to nest in areas of seasonal flooding, such as the great swamps of Okavango. The nest is in a natural cavity in a large tree, or in a deep hollow where several branches grow. No lining is added but many dead leaves and flakes of bark fall naturally into the hole and soften the bed for the two white eggs.

The female incubates the eggs, her mate bringing food for her and later for the young. Adult fishing owls defend their nest vigorously, even flying off to chase away a passing African Fish Eagle (*Haliaeetus vocifer*). They have a remarkable distraction display and can lure intruders from the nest by crashing off the branch into deep undergrowth and thrashing through the foliage, calling all the time as though injured.

The second egg may hatch up to five days after the first and the younger chick soon starves. The contact call between parents and young has been described as a weird screech or howl which reaches a crescendo and dies away. The surviving chick may be nine months old before it leaves its parents' territory to become independent and this may be a reason why a successful pair will sometimes let a year pass without attempting to breed.

The decision to breed depends on local conditions. In long periods of drought, many pairs will not breed and the territories break down as several owls congregate, albeit unwillingly, at a deep pool that still holds fish. Starvation accounts for many losses, particularly among inexperienced first-year birds that do not yet hold territories and are unfamiliar with the area.

RUFOUS FISHING OWL
Scotopelia ussheri

LENGTH: *460 to 510 mm*   MAP NUMBER: 76
DESCRIPTION: *Large, round-headed, lacking ear tufts; rufous, streaked; bare legs*
DISTRIBUTION: *West Africa*
HABITAT: *Riverine forest and mangroves*
STATUS: *Declining and endangered*

This large species is the least well-known of the African fishing owls. It is either so rare, or so elusive, that it has been seen by ornithologists only about 20 times. It lives along the rivers of Sierra Leone, Liberia, the Ivory Coast and Ghana in the dense riverside forest and estuarine mangrove swamps. In some of these countries, there is growing interest in wildlife and the management of nature reserves and national parks and this may well improve our knowledge of the status and lifestyle of what surely must be a very dramatic bird. A low, deep, moaning *"whoo"* is the only recorded call. It hunts by night from a waterside perch and feeds on fish, but much else remains to be discovered about its way of life.

Most books state that the eyes of this bird are yellow. In preparing the illustrations for this book, Trevor Boyer examined live birds which clearly had dark brown eyes, as he has shown in his painting.

VERMICULATED FISHING OWL
Scotopelia bouvieri

LENGTH: *460 to 510 mm*   MAP NUMBER: 77
DESCRIPTION: *Brown above, cream below with broad dark stripes; lack ears*
DISTRIBUTION: *West Africa*
HABITAT: *Riverine forest*
EGGS: *1 (2?)*
STATUS: *Probably rare and declining, perhaps endangered*

Knowledge of this species' habits and breeding biology is still far from complete. This, however, appears to be due to its secretive lifestyle, in remote areas, rather than its rarity. Indeed, on the larger rivers and streams of the Congo basin, it seems to be relatively common.

Ornithologists familiar with its vocalizations generally locate this large bird by its low, croaking hoot or the faster, clucking call *"krook krook ook-ook ook-ook"*. These calls are given all the year round but are most frequent in the breeding season from May to October. Like other fishing owls, it is clearly a slow breeder. A pair will usually rear a single chick, which requires much time and intensive parental care to become independent. The Vermiculated Fishing Owl appears to eat rather more crabs and other crustaceans than do most fishing owls, although the Rufous Fishing Owl (*Scotopelia ussheri*) might have a similar diet when living in coastal mangroves.

SPECTACLED OWLS

THREE SPECIES

SPECTACLED OWL
Pulsatrix perspicillata

LENGTH: *430 to 460 mm*   MAP NUMBER: 78
DESCRIPTION: *Striking blackish above, yellow-cream below, white crescents on black face*
DISTRIBUTION: *Mexico, Central and South America*
HABITAT: *Tropical rain-forest, woodland*
EGGS: *2. Nest in hole*
STATUS: *Probably declining, locally endangered*

Forests in Mexico and Central America, and in the northern two-thirds of South America, east of the Andes, support one of the most striking owls in the world. The Spectacled Owl is large and boldly patterned, and acquired its name from the broad, broken circles of white around its yellow eyes. The juvenile — or 'white owl' — has the adult markings in negative with a white head and a black mask.

Although not necessarily uncommon where its rain-forest habitat remains, the Spectacled Owl is little-known, largely because of its elusive behaviour. Dense, unviolated forest gives it a natural seclusion. The Spectacled Owl is found both on the edges and in the dense interiors of tropical rain-forests. In Costa Rica, it is found at altitudes as high as 5,000 feet (1,500m) above sea level and is widely distributed and not uncommon in some areas.

The destruction of the rain-forests may pose a threat to its future but, fortunately, this owl can also be found in drier woods. These include savanna woodlands with quite open, scattered trees and even shelterbelts in coffee plantations and other cultivated areas. Spectacled Owls seem to be more tolerant of deforestation than, for example, Crested Owls (*Lophostrix cristata*), but do need wooded areas of some size for successful nesting. They are adept at hiding in the remains of forest cover when most trees have been felled. Usually nocturnal, these large birds are sometimes active on dull days. They respond to imitations or tape-recordings of their territorial calls.

A territorial pair will call together for long periods, the note of one being a little higher than the call of the other. A typical call is a series of six knocking or tapping sounds, with a popping effect, sometimes described as bubbling or 'thrumming'. This has been rendered as "*PUP-pup-pup-pup-po*" or "*PUM-PUM-pum-pum*", each successive note being lower and weaker, and the rhythm quicker, as the series proceeds. The female is suspected of being the higher-voiced of the pair, and has a hawk-like scream "*ker-WHEEER*" which has been likened to a steam whistle.

The chick — usually only one survives — will be out of the nest, and demanding to be fed, well before it can fly, and its harsh, food-begging call helps pinpoint the whereabouts of a nesting pair. Nests are in tree holes, in which two large, white eggs are laid. In Costa Rica, the egg-laying period is in the dry season or at the start of the wet season. The fledgling may depend on its parents for up to a year, possibly longer, and seems to take several years to attain full adult plumage, unlike other wood owls.

Despite their large size, Spectacled Owls feed chiefly on small prey. They take small mammals, insects, numerous caterpillars and crabs, although at times they will tackle skunks, opposums and birds up to the size of jays. When hunting, the Spectacled Owl perches on a branch as it scans the surroundings, and drops to strike with a swift, agile pounce. Insects are snatched from foliage.

TAWNY-BROWED OWL
Pulsatrix koeniswaldiana

MAP NUMBER: 79
LENGTH: *440 mm*
DISTRIBUTION: *Eastern South America*
HABITAT: *Tropical forest, woodland*
STATUS: *Uncertain, probably rare and declining*

Tawny-browed Owls, also known as White-chinned Owls, have a limited range in South America and are found mostly in the forests of southern Brazil. It bears some resemblance to its close relative, the Spectacled Owl (*Pulsatrix perspicillata*), and the basic aspects of its lifestyle are likely to be similar. The voice has been described as "*brrr brrr brrr brrr*" or "*ut ut ut ut ut*".

BAND-BELLIED OWL
Pulsatrix melanota

MAP NUMBER: 80
LENGTH: *480 mm*
DISTRIBUTION: *Northern Andes*
HABITAT: *Forest*
STATUS: *Uncertain, probably rare and declining*

This beautiful species, erroneously called the Rusty-barred Owl in Burton's *Owls of the World* (the true Rusty-barred Owl *Strix hylophila* occurs further south), is related to the Spectacled Owl (*Pulsatrix perspicillata*) and is probably akin to it in behaviour. It lives in southern Colombia, Ecuador, Peru and Bolivia, in remote highland regions where it has a secretive, nocturnal existence in forests that are seldom penetrated. It has been found mostly at heights of 2,300 to 5,300 feet (700–1,600m).

SNOWY OWL

ONE SPECIES

SNOWY OWL
Nyctea scandiaca

LENGTH: *530 to 660 mm*   MAP NUMBER: 81
DESCRIPTION: *Huge, white or white with grey-brown bars, yellow eyes*
DISTRIBUTION: *Arctic*
HABITAT: *Tundra, bare, rocky ground*
EGGS: *3 – 16. Nest on ground*
STATUS: *Widespread, locally frequent to very scarce*

This is the largest predatory bird in the Arctic. The Snowy Owl inhabits the remote, harsh world of the Arctic tundra between the northern pack ice and the boreal forest to the south. On a map, its distribution forms a narrow ring encircling the Arctic Ocean.

This owl has the whiteness of the winter Ptarmigan and Willow Grouse, the Snow Goose and the Glaucous Gull. It is actually whiter than a polar bear or arctic fox, which can both seem yellow against pristine snow. Adult male Snowy Owls are almost pure white, except for a very few small dark spots and perhaps a bar or two on the wings. Females and the young have variable bars of brown and grey and, apart from white on the face and breast, have a drabber, grey look. In flight, they show strong barring across the uppersides of the wings but the underwings are white.

Whatever its plumage, the Snowy Owl is brilliantly camouflaged in its habitat of broken ground with rocky outcrops and patches of snow. Sitting still, as it does for long periods, this owl looks like another pale rock or lump of snow. From a distance, its eyes appear dark and only at close range are they seen to be black-rimmed lemon yellow or amber.

The general structure of the Snowy Owl resembles that of the Eagle Owl (*Bubo bubo*), and it is one of the few owls to rival the power and size of eagle owls. Strictly speaking, this is not an 'eared' owl, yet it does have minute tufts which it can raise and move from side to side at will. These are usually tucked back out of sight but they suggest some distant relationship with eagle owls. An incubating Snowy Owl may raise its tufts like short, blunt horns.

The plumage of a Snowy Owl is a dense, luxuriant cover of heat-retaining feathers. The thick facial feathers almost hide the strong bill in a forward-pointing tuft which gives this owl its noted feline appearance. No other owl, and probably no other bird, has anything like the enormous, heavily-feathered feet of a Snowy Owl. The individual feathers may be as long as 1.4 inches (3.5cm), three times the length of those of their nearest rival, the Great Horned Owl (*Bubo virginianus*) of the Americas.

In the breeding season, Snowy Owls prefer rolling, low tundra and will not be found in the tundra-like habitats high on mountain ranges further south. The most successful territories have a variety of ridges and rounded hummocks, rocky knolls and the broken, stony ground typical of glacial deposits. These slight eminences are valued by the Snowy Owl, which likes to sit, and to nest, on top of a rise with a sweeping view of any prey and predators that appear on the surrounding terrain.

In the winter, when some owls move south, Snowy Owls will be seen in a greater variety of windswept terrain with meagre cover, including agricultural land, airfields, estuarine flats, marshes and barren, rocky regions near the coast or inland in mountainous regions. Snowy Owls have no need of comfort. They are content to perch on rocky ground or a. wall, even a telegraph pole, eschewing the shelter of woods and isolated trees. A Snowy Owl is a very hardy creature indeed.

These owls bred successfully for a brief period on the Shetland Islands of Scotland, an area well to the south of their normal breeding range. Even in winter they are few and far between in the region. They chose a rocky slope on the moors of Fetlar, where the nest was often shrouded in rain or mist and their neighbours were skuas, otters, sheep and Shetland ponies. Thousands of visitors were drawn to see them from a special hide but many saw little more than the top of the female's head as she sat on the nest, scarcely visible through the fog. On better days, the birds were wonderfully entertaining and extraordinarily impressive.

The male was a splendid white creature, a squat, upright figure sitting still and quiet for long periods on a rock. At one stage, he had two hens on clutches at the same time. The established nesting female was seen to fly along a high ridge to join another female, or an immature bird, and they whirled together in mid-air, feet grappling together, cartwheeling away out of sight over the hill. In time, they reappeared, to be joined by a third, then a fourth Snowy Owl, and finally by the male. Five Snowy Owls together provided an unforgettable sight. Compared to the giant females, the male was neat and compact.

The Fetlar breeding episode ended when the male disappeared, though the females lingered on to lay infertile clutches of unfertilized eggs. Even the release of another male, found exhausted on an oil rig at sea, did not lead to the resumption of normal nesting. This is typical of Snowy Owls on the edge of their range. It is an erratic species whose numbers and presence in a particular area depend on the fluctuations in food supply.

Snowy Owl (*Nyctea scandiaca*)

The cycle of lemmings influences the number of Snowy Owls that remain in the north in winter, their condition in the spring, their own breeding cycle and the number of young that are reared successfully. The lemmings affect the vegetation and soil of the tundra. In simple terms, the owls go where there are plentiful lemmings, particularly brown lemmings, and move on when the supply runs short. Snowy Owls have good breeding seasons every four or five years but the number of lemmings varies from place to place each year, and the cycles of the two species of lemmings also vary. In broad terms, when the population of the brown lemming is at a peak, Snowy Owls breed prolifically, laying remarkably large clutches.

There can be dramatic variations in the number of Snowy Owls in any region. On Banks Island, in northern Canada, some 2,000 may be present in a poor year but, when lemmings are in abundance, between 15,000 and 20,000 Snowy Owls will appear over the 24,600 square miles (63,700 square kilometres) of territory.

In addition to their nomadic way of life, there are regular migratory movements of Snowy Owls. Many will spend winters on the steppes of Siberia and the cold prairies of Canada. When the population reaches a peak after a good breeding season, more owls will move south, especially young birds working hard to survive their first winter. But during the invasions which sometimes occur in North America, and to a lesser degree in Asia, a wholesale southerly movement takes place. Hundreds will migrate across the sea, appearing in such unlikely places as California, central Texas, the Azores, France and even in Pakistan and Korea. Some have landed on ships hundreds of miles out into the Atlantic.

The Snowy Owl, like the Buzzard (*Buteo buteo*), hunts by keeping low and perching immobile for long spells. It also has a rather buzzard-like flight, but with a springy upstroke and slow, deliberate downbeat of the broad, fingered wings. If prey passes its perch, it can accelerate quickly and stoop almost like a falcon in its final attack. It is a more diurnal hunter than an Eagle Owl but shares some of its other hunting qualities. Despite its dependence on lemmings, the Snowy Owl will catch and consume a variety of prey, including many birds. The owls on Fetlar fed largely on rabbits, with some young Oystercatchers (*Haematopus ostralegus*) and medium-sized and large waders and even Arctic Skuas (*Stercorarius parasiticus*). Snowy Owls will take ducks and auks, Ptarmigan (*Lagopus mutus*) and Willow Grouse (*Lagopus lagopus*). Dead animals, such as the remains of skinned seals or foxes, are readily devoured, a rare habit among owls. In winter, wandering Snowy Owls eat rabbits, hares, rats, moles, voles, pikas, ground squirrels, pheasants and partridges, grebes and gulls. In the north, when food is scarce, Snowy Owls can fast for up to 40 days, living off reserves of fat.

Most Snowy Owls are largely silent except around the nest or when claiming their territory in the spring. If disturbed at the nest, they may make loud, grating barks and quacks. The female has a loud, high wail and a hungry young bird makes a high, whistling or humming squeal, which can be ear-splitting. The display call is a rough, hollow-sounding hoot, sometimes recalling the deep call of a Great Black-backed Gull (*Larus marinus*), at other times more drawn out. In the clear, still Arctic air it can be heard from two miles (3km) and even as far as six miles (10km) under certain conditions. It is one of the most far-carrying of all bird calls.

The spring thaw may be early or late in the Arctic and this, like the supply of lemmings, will directly influence nesting success. A late thaw allows too little time for the full breeding process and leaves birds in poor condition in the spring. Good feeding in May is essential to adult Snowy Owls, even if it is the abundance, or lack, of food in July that will determine the survival of the young.

The nest of a pair of Snowy Owls is typically placed on a high ridge or mound. Such spots will be used by generations of owls and even by Rough-legged Buzzards (*Buteo lagopus*) when owls are absent. The years of accumulated droppings, pellets and remains of prey affect the vegetation of the mounds, which can be recognized by their floral richness and will thus attract lemmings. The nest itself is a bare scrape in the ground, without a scrap of lining to cushion the eggs or protect them from the cold ground on which they must sit.

If the thaw is early and the supply of lemmings is adequate, a pair of Snowy Owls will beat the bounds of their territory with a slow, moth-like flight, their deep wingbeats exaggerating the whiteness of their wings and making the birds visible for miles around. At the same time, they make their deep, gruff hooting calls. Territories vary greatly in size, according to the supply of prey. Unlike some of the larger eagle owls – Verreaux's Eagle Owl (*Bubo lacteus*) in Africa, for example – the individual Snowy Owl is attached to neither its mate nor its territory for longer than a single season. Their nomadic lives lack any lifetime bond.

If food is scarce, no eggs are laid; sometimes small clutches are produced but few eggs hatch and almost no young are reared. But when the lemming cycle reaches a peak, the Snowy Owl lays up to 16 eggs, an extraordinary number for an owl. To incubate them, the female has a remarkably large, flabby, brood-patch of bare skin, full of blood vessels. In larger clutches, the difference in age between the first and last hatched can be a month. A tiny chick hatching out beside a brute of a brother or sister faces a tough time unless food is unlimited. In such good years, fledging success can be very high.

The chicks are brooded by their mother for one or two weeks, then move from the nest to find shelter in surrounding hollows, or niches between boulders. They fly after 50 days and soon learn to hunt. Their first autumn and winter are difficult and survival is sometimes poor. It is sobering to imagine a young Snowy Owl setting out alone, facing dreary months of almost no daylight, nearly endless frost, and nothing but trackless wastes to cross until the next brief summer in the north. Should it survive, it will take its place as one of most evocative, memorable birds in the world.

NORTHERN HAWK OWL

——————————— ONE SPECIES ———————————

HAWK OWL
Surnia ulula

LENGTH: *360 to 410 mm*   MAP NUMBER: 82
DESCRIPTION: *Square head with black-edged face; barred breast, long tail*
DISTRIBUTION: *Northern North America, northern Europe and northern Asia*
HABITAT: *Northern forest clearings*
EGGS: *3–13. Nest in old tree nest or tree hole*
STATUS: *Locally frequent*

This unique, magnificent owl is the only member of the *Surnia* genus. The Hawk Owl is found in Alaska, western and central Canada, the northern United States (in winter), in northern Europe, Tien Shan and across most of northern Asia. This wide distribution is similar to that of Tengmalm's/ Boreal Owl (*Aegolius funereus*) but without that species' extensions to the south.

The Hawk Owl is an eye-catching bird with a square, flat-topped head outlined in black on each side and across the throat. Its hawkish qualities are seen in its fierce, gleaming eyes beneath a lowered brow, and the long tail drooped almost vertically beneath its perch or raised between its wingtips. Its underparts are closely barred with grey and, in that respect, even its pattern is hawk-like. The young Hawk Owl, however, is slightly different, having a short tail and broad, black mask.

In flight, the Hawk Owl is long-tailed but relatively short in the wings, which taper abruptly to a point. The soft, loose feather fringes, which assist silent flight in other owls, are weakly developed. This is a dashing bird, often flying swiftly towards a tree, then veering steeply up to perch on the topmost stem. Over long distances, the flight of the Hawk Owl mixes long glides with bursts of quick wingbeats, like a female Sparrowhawk (*Accipiter nisus*). It can accelerate quickly and it then swoops rather like a Little Owl (*Athene noctua*) but, if chasing a small bird or mobbing some large bird of prey, a Hawk Owl can show surprising agility. It can also hover when hunting, like a Kestrel (*Falco tinnunculus*).

These owls live in more or less wooded areas. The northern edge of their range is the southernmost limit of the tundra, so they do not overlap the territory of, for example, Snowy Owls (*Nyctea scandiaca*). Southwards, the species extends to the edge of the steppe and cultivated regions. So it is essentially restricted to the belt of taiga but in areas with access to clear ground, rather than deep within the forests. These clearings may well be marshy areas, such as the muskegs of North America, but open peat hags and burned areas are also frequented.

Hawk Owls like open woods and dry ridges above swampy forest bogs, with clusters of pine, larch, birch and aspen. They especially like tall, old trees with broken tops or bare branches that give them ready lookouts and hunting perches. In North America, though only rarely in Europe, Hawk Owls range over both cultivated prairies, even using haystacks as perches, and open, lowland heaths. In Europe, cultivated landscapes are avoided.

The number of Hawk Owls in any area fluctuates sharply, according to what prey is available. In Sweden it is estimated that there may be 10,000 pairs or more in good years, so this is not necessarily a rare bird, even if never very common. A loss of nesting sites, as hollow trees get cleared away, has caused a decline in many places but, apart from such man-made problems and frequent persecution, it is the food supply that controls the fortunes of this northern bird.

The Hawk Owl eats voles, whose numbers may rise to huge levels in certain areas only to tumble into scarcity. As these variations are not synchronized, the owls generally need make only short journeys to find plentiful prey but when, as sometimes happens, the voles fail over a huge area simultaneously, Hawk Owls make great migratory flights and invade areas from which they have been absent for many years. In Norway, Sweden and Finland, it is rare for Hawk Owls to erupt in this way at the same time. There are usually voles somewhere in Scandinavia to keep most owls 'at home'. But when large movements do occur, they can be dramatic and Hawk Owls outside their normal range always excite attention.

In the spring and summer, small voles form almost the entire diet of Hawk Owls. In winter, small or medium-sized birds such as Willow Grouse (*Lagopus lagopus*) are taken but voles may still be the staple food. In Norway during summer, over 96 percent of prey, by weight, is voles, the remainder being small birds and mammals.

Studies in Finland have shown a higher proportion of birds, some six percent of prey, while in the summer in the Soviet Union, voles formed only 75 percent of prey, with large mammals and small birds both accounting for more than ten percent. In general, the choice of prey reflects the availability of small mammals, but Soviet studies have shown that shrews are avoided, even when quite common. Many predators find them distasteful.

Lemmings are taken but not in great numbers and the fluctuations and movements of Hawk Owls are clearly linked to voles, not lemmings, as was once thought.

Hawk Owl (*Surnia ulula*)

Whereas male Tengmalm's/Boreal Owls are resident in their breeding territories through the winter, when food may be scarce, the male Hawk Owl is sometimes more mobile. Tengmalm's/Boreal Owls need to stay put if they are to secure a nest site in the spring. The nest sites of Hawk Owls are less restricted because they are less selective, and so have less need to defend a territory and nest hole against all comers. Nevertheless, an adult male Hawk Owl might do well to remain on his territory all winter in order to familiarize himself with the localities of prey as well as to find a nest site, so that he is ready to breed early in the spring when a female appears. Males are, indeed, much more likely to remain than females.

Adult female Hawk Owls often move to more lowland areas in winter. For the female, the risks in migrating are outweighed by the prospect of finding more food in areas less likely to be under deep snow. There are often fewer juveniles in the productive lowlands than adult females, which would indicate that older birds claim the best hunting grounds. As with Snowy Owls, it is the social status of these owls that determines their movements and distribution in winter.

Hawk Owls hunt by day, even in bright sunshine, but they also search for prey throughout the lighter nights of the northern summer when they have young to feed. They perch on exposed, high branches, using several in rotation as observation posts. Prey is taken after a smooth, swift stoop. Now and then a Hawk Owl scans the ground while it hovers; it is adept at this style of hunting, which is more readily associated with the Kestrel. In North America, the Hawk Owl has been recorded plunging into snow and emerging with a vole, so it must be able to locate prey by ear. But this is a rare event and it generally relies on its sharp, small eyes.

Outside the breeding season this is a quiet owl, but a long, clear whinnying sound is described as a winter contact call. The typical male song, or territorial advertisement in spring and summer, is a trilling, vibrant "*hu hu hu huuuuuuuuu*" or "*ulyu lyu lyu lyu lyu lyu*", lasting two or three seconds, and sometimes up to 12 seconds. This is a rising, bubbling, rippling sound with about a dozen notes each second. Short bursts are given in a display flight. The female has a shriller note in a shorter sequence and a special sound, given in defence of the nest, described as a sharp, trilling "*kiiiiiiiiirrl*". There are many other calls in its varied and complex repertoire.

The breeding season may begin quite early. Eggs are laid in March in Finland and the Soviet Union, but egg-laying can also extend into June. Territories are sought and defended by the male a few weeks before egg-laying. The male calls a great deal, performs display flights over the forest, and even flies through the trees with noisy wing-clapping.

A hole in a tree is the usual nest site. This may perhaps be where a branch has fallen, or on top of a tall stump that has snapped off, but nest boxes are also used, as are old stick nests of crows and buzzards. The nest is usually close to a clearing where the owls can hunt and often not far from a farmhouse or other dwelling. The hole is unlined, as with most owls. Deep in the dark cavity, the white eggs are dimly visible. There are usually between six and ten in a clutch. If the eggs are lost to a predator early on during incubation, a fresh clutch may be laid, but only a single brood is reared, even if food is plentiful.

The eggs are incubated for 30 days by the female and they hatch out in the sequence in which they were laid over a week or so. After 25 to 35 days, the chicks scramble out to the open air and perch on branches for a few days before they are ready to fly. This is the time when they are most vulnerable but their parents are vigorous and aggressive in their defence, especially the fearless male. If an ornithologist tries to visit the nest, or a forester should stand below it, the adult Hawk Owls will scream loudly and fly at the intruder's head with admirable vehemence. Long after they have flown, the young birds will remain in the nesting territory, often roosting together and relying on their parents for food. Gradually, they disperse and by the following spring they may be ready to find a territory and seek a mate, sending their tremulous bubbling calls far through the forest edge.

Provided that it continues to find suitable clearings in northern forests, where voles are plentiful, there is no reason why the Hawk Owl should not remain a thriving species, its distinctive form on top of an upright pine attracting many a birdwatcher who has travelled north in search of unusual species.

PYGMY-OWLS

FOURTEEN SPECIES

PYGMY-OWL
Glaucidium passerinum

LENGTH: *160 to 170 mm*   MAP NUMBER: 83
DESCRIPTION: *White neck band and eye-rings, long tail, feathered feet*
DISTRIBUTION: *Northern and central Europe, northern Asia*
HABITAT: *Coniferous or mixed forest*
EGGS: *3–10. Nest in tree hole*
STATUS: *Locally frequent*

The pygmy-owl group contains 13 species which range from Alaska and Siberia to Brazil, Argentina and South Africa and to Borneo and India. These *Glaucidium* owls share a general shape, size and character which the Pygmy-Owl typifies. This is a fierce predator, even if it is no larger than a small thrush or starling. The female, in particular, is strong enough to tackle birds of her own size.

This owl will sit almost upright or slanting across its perch. Its relatively long tail is often raised above the drooping tips of its wings, and may be swayed from side to side, giving the owl an air of urgent, nervous activity. The bird is speckled with white all over its forehead and crown, liberally spotted above and neatly barred over its flight feathers and tail. Around the back of the neck is a prominent band of white and around each eye there are broken, concentric rings of white. The cold yellow eyes are small, closely set and almost squint at times, giving this owl a look to match its predatory skills. But, though these eyes are larger than the ears, their night vision is inferior to that of a Tawny Owl (*Strix aluco*), for example, and more comparable to that of a human being.

Eurasian Pygmy-Owls have densely-feathered feet, unlike those of the Northern Pygmy-Owls (*Glaucidium gnoma*) of North America, and the thickest, silkiest, warmest plumage of any *Glaucidium* owl. This is well-suited to a northerly existence. The facial disc is poorly developed, without special feathers at the edge, and the ears are simple in shape and structure.

Flight is quick, undulating, noisy and almost blustering. Pygmy-Owls are often about in the day, chasing small birds or perching conspicuously on treetops, even in gardens during winter. When roosting, though, they keep well out of sight and can adopt an upright, sleeked shape that strengthens their excellent camouflage. Nevertheless, they are sometimes discovered by small birds; Chaffinches, tits, Goldcrests and Treecreepers will mob them mercilessly.

The distribution bears some similarity to that of Tengmalm's/Boreal Owl (*Aegolius funereus*) and the Hawk Owl (*Surnia ulula*) in Europe and Asia, but does not extend to the Americas. It runs from the Nordic countries east to Siberia and turns south somewhat to the east, with a few pockets in central and eastern Europe. This is essentially the area of taiga with southern relics that is also inhabited by Tengmalm's/Boreal Owl.

This species is a resident in central Europe, except for occasional movements downhill during snow. But in the north it is a more nomadic creature that has irregular outbursts when its usual range cannot provide adequate food, though these movements are less frequent and less obvious than those of Tengmalm's/Boreal Owls.

Mountain forests to altitudes of 5,400 feet (1,650m) above sea level are preferred in central Europe but deforested or partially-cleared areas are also occupied. The amount of mature timber in a territory varies greatly. In Sweden, Pygmy-Owls select oak forest mixed with dense spruce but also live in well-wooded parks where they can be encouraged by nest box schemes. In Finland, they live almost everywhere but have a particular liking for mature spruce woods. Like most owls, they nest in tree cavities, especially those chiselled out by Great Spotted, Three-toed or Grey-headed Woodpeckers. These are smaller than the holes occupied by other European owls and allow greater flexibility and more protection from predators. Pygmy-Owls prefer to be far from human habitation but, if nest holes are very scarce, they may occupy a suitably sized garden nest box.

The territorial song is heard throughout the year but peaks in the spring. It is a soft, piping whistle, *"peeu-peeu-peeu"*. The quality of this call, which is repeated, is much like that of a Bullfinch (*Pyrrhula pyrrhula*). It varies in pitch and strength as the bird turns its head from side to side. Another song is a more vibrating sound in which the *"peeu"* notes are interspersed with a hard trill.

Pygmy-Owls react strongly to recordings or imitations of their calls, as do many owls. These should be used with care and restraint for the birds can become frustrated and confused by the apparent presence of an unseen and unremitting competitor. A male may even attack a tape recorder or imitator of its call.

Once Pygmy-Owls have established their territory and found a suitable nest, around five eggs are laid at two-day intervals. Occasionally, in the north, as many as ten eggs may be found in a single clutch but in central Europe there will seldom be more than five or six. Unlike the vast majority of owl species, Pygmy-Owls do not go in for the staggered hatching that ensures that some chicks are strong

Pygmy-Owl (*Glaucidium passerinum*)

at the expense of smaller, later ones in years of food shortages. Instead, the female waits until the clutch is complete before incubating the eggs, which all hatch at about the same time, after 29 days.

The size of the clutch is nevertheless influenced by the availability of food and, specifically, the supply of small mammals. Owls that feed mainly on birds lay smaller clutches, while a diet with mammals enables them to lay larger ones. The owl depends on voles to feed the young; perhaps birds are too difficult to catch in sufficient numbers to feed a hungry brood.

The male hunts while the female incubates. Once the young have hatched the male leads a somewhat harrassed life. The female feeds his prey to the young and refuses the male access to the nest. Her aggression apparently provokes him into catching and supplying more and more food. Young chicks in the deep nest are unable to clamber about the nesting tree, unlike the young of birds such as the Tawny Owl (*Strix aluco*), which are more likely to fall from their shallower nests, and try to struggle back up to the nest hole. The chicks leave the nest when they are about 30 days old, already able to fly. They are looked after for a few more weeks but quite quickly leave the territory and fend for themselves.

Although their breeding is strongly influenced by the supply of voles, Pygmy-Owls are not so specialized in their diet as many species. They eat a broad spectrum of prey and can supplement their diet with small birds and the occasional lizard. Unlike all other European owls, they keep their nest holes clean and free of the remains of prey, but much can be discovered by examining their pellets — the indigestible, regurgitated bits of food. In Finland, prey consists of shrews, voles, mice, bats, lizards, insects, birds and even fish. Bank voles and, to a lesser extent, short-tailed voles are most commonly eaten. The birds include Chaffinch (*Fringilla coelebs*), Willow Warbler (*Phylloscopus trochilus*), Siskin (*Carduelis spinus*) and Pied Flycatcher (*Ficedula hypoleuca*). From time to time, birds up to the size of Great Spotted Woodpecker (*Dendrocopus major*) and Song Thrush (*Turdus philomelos*) will be taken.

Of the many birds caught by Pygmy-Owls, species found on the edge of woodlands are typical prey, though the owls show their opportunism by catching scarcer birds such as Pine Grosbeak (*Pinicola enucleator*), Hawfinch (*Coccothraustes coccothraustes*), Crossbill (*Loxia curvirostra*), House Martin (*Delichon urbica*) and Dipper (*Cinclus cinclus*). In winter, fewer birds were eaten in Finland, which sees an exodus of small birds in winter, and more shrews were found in the diet.

The Pygmy-Owl remains unknown to many ornithologists in western Europe as it rarely strays from its homes in the north and the remote fastnesses of the Alps. It is unfortunate that these areas are often neglected by bird-watchers from other parts of the world. This is a bird of great spirit and deserves a wider audience.

NORTHERN PYGMY-OWL
Glaucidium gnoma

LENGTH: *170 mm*   MAP NUMBER: 84
DESCRIPTION: *Small, round-headed, rather pale, streaked below*
DISTRIBUTION: *Western North and Central America, Mexico*
HABITAT: *Open and mature coniferous or mixed forest*
EGGS: *2–7. Nest in tree hole*
STATUS: *Locally frequent*

The American species of pygmy-owl is much like that of Europe and Asia. There was a time when ornithologists described the Northern Pygmy-Owl as 'bloodthirsty', 'rapacious', 'a fiend' or 'a villain'. Such descriptions showed little objective understanding of an owlish mind, but did give a fair hint of this bird's character.

The Northern Pygmy-Owl lives in mixed woods and open areas in western North America from Alaska to California, and along the western mountain ranges of Mexico and Central America south to Honduras. It is found in woodland at altitudes between 1,300 feet and 10,000 feet (400–3,000m) above sea level, often right up to the tree line, but in northern coastal areas it can be found down to nearly sea level. It overlaps extensively with Flammulated Owls (*Otus flammeolus*) and is often found lower than Northern Saw-whet Owls (*Aegolius acadicus*). It prefers to be high in the canopy but is sometimes found in rather stunted, windblown woods with small trees. In the massive redwoods and sequoias at lower heights, this owl may be very difficult to see on its high perch, concealed in dense evergreen foliage. It also likes mature spruce forest and a variety of mixed woods on both humid and more arid mountain slopes, as well as woodland at the bottom of valleys and the edges of forest adjacent to much more open countryside.

The Northern Pygmy-Owl is a resident. The mountain races move to milder areas only during the harshest weather. In areas where it is little-known, it may prove commoner than expected simply because it is so difficult to see in dense woodland. Even so, it may sit on the topmost twig of a tall pine and call during the day. At other times it will perch on top of smaller trees, appearing to enjoy the sun spilling into a clearing in a deep forest.

Some races, at least, have a false face in the feather

pattern of the back of the head. The effect is to confuse predators, which may be uncertain which direction the owl is looking. The plumage is almost identical to that of the Eurasian Pygmy-Owl (*Glaucidium passerinum*) although the tail, which is a shade longer, appears rather more spotted than fully barred. This owl has bristly toes, whereas those of the European bird are fully feathered.

This is an owl which calls regularly by day. In the northern half of its range (western Canada to Arizona) it gives a slow, regularly-spaced series of toots or short whistles. From southern Arizona south through Mexico, the song is similar except that the pace is irregular and the notes tend to be roughly paired. In excitement, the bird will give a variety of chattering or chuckling notes.

Northern Pygmy-Owls are territorial and their territories appear to be unusually large. The calling males are often one mile or more (2km) apart. A suitable hole in a tree, often an abandoned woodpecker nest, is selected and up to seven white eggs may be laid, though the average is usually three or four. The availability of food probably affects the size of a clutch and breeding success, at least among the populations of the harsher north. The female incubates while the male hunts and feeds her. Fledgling

birds, like young Tawny Owls (*Strix aluco*), often miss a perch in their early flights, or fall from the tree before they are able to fly. They use their sharp claws and strong grip to scramble back up the trunk.

Daytime hunting is frequent, but this owl is most active at sunrise and sunset. It is tiny but fearless, attacking birds and mammals much larger than itself, such as quails and ground squirrels. Its main prey, however, is small fare such as grasshoppers, beetles, lizards and small birds. It differs from the European species in the greater number of insects it consumes. These comprise about 60 percent of all food items, though they make up a much smaller percentage in terms of overall weight of food.

Warblers, finches, wrens, juncos, chickadees and even woodpeckers gather from far and wide to mob an unfortunate owl found by day until it flies off to find a quieter spot. It flies low over the ground, skimming the vegetation in a series of shallow swoops, then rises steeply to its new perch. Curiously, the Northern Pygmy-Owl has noisy wingbeats, possibly because daytime hunting is less dependent on silent flight than is the nocturnal searching by most other owls. The Northern Pygmy-Owl appears far less reliant on sound to locate its prey.

CUBAN PYGMY-OWL
Glaucidium siju

LENGTH: *170 mm*   MAP NUMBER: 85
DESCRIPTION: *Small, pale, barred below*
DISTRIBUTION: *Cuba and Isle of Pines*
HABITAT: *Open woodland*
EGGS: *3–4. Nest in tree hole*
STATUS: *Restricted, perhaps declining*

Cuba and the Isle of Pines are the only places where this day-flying owl is found. Even in this restricted range, the Cuban Pygmy-Owl has two races, one on each island. It can be found in two forms, a redder one and a greyer version. Each has the typical shape of a pygmy-owl and the habit of cocking its tail as it perches on a branch or wire. It nests in a tree hole, laying three or four eggs. A typical call is a series of notes rising in pitch.

LEAST PYGMY-OWL
Glaucidium minutissimum

LENGTH: *120 to 140 mm*   MAP NUMBER: 86
DESCRIPTION: *Tiny, round, long-tailed, streaked*
DISTRIBUTION: *Mexico, Central and South America*
HABITAT: *Dense tropical forest, open woodland and bush*
EGGS: *? In tree hole*
STATUS: *Uncertain; locally common but probably declining*

This is one of the tiniest owls in the world. The Least Pygmy-Owl is the size of a sparrow but stronger and more solidly-built than the similar sized Elf Owl (*Micrathene whitneyi*). It has the classic round head, bright eyes and full-faced look of the pygmy-owls, with false eyespots on the back of the head. It also has the typically raised, rather long and full tail and strong, needle-sharp claws.

This owl is active by day and night in forests from Mexico to Colombia, Venezuela, Guyana, Peru, northern Bolivia and much of Brazil and Paraguay. This range is irregular and patchy, covering humid forest and drier forest edges, and the Least Pygmy-Owl is probably a declining bird. It is found in some parts of the range occupied by the more common Ferruginous Pygmy-Owl (*Glaucidium brasilianum*), but in different habitats. The Least Pygmy-Owl is often a rare bird, though locally common in parts of Mexico.

In Costa Rica, where it is less rare, the Least Pygmy-Owl likes the woodland canopy and the more open edges of wet forests. But it also lives in tall, established secondary growth nearby and in more open places if tall trees are present. Old cacao plantations seem to be suitable. In Mexico, this bird lives in open woods and even arid scrub.

Its call varies from place to place. It has been described as unusually high-pitched, but also as a series of four low whistles. In Venezuela, it produces a short series of low, staccato notes, uttering as many as 12 notes in a burst lasting two seconds. The typical call in Costa Rica is described as between two and five notes, and most frequently four. These are clear, pure toots, evenly spaced and a little like the call of the Stripe-breasted Wren (*Thryothorus thoracicus*) but deeper, more resonant and repeated more quickly. An excited bird may give ten or more hoots in succession, followed by a slurred, rolling note or trill. This owl calls most regularly just before dawn, much less so at dusk and only rarely by day. It is possible that the 'Least Pygmy-Owl' comprises more than one species, which would help to explain the variation in calls.

A hunting Least Pygmy-Owl, for all its tiny size and insignificant weight, is a bird to be reckoned with in the forest. It can apparently catch and subdue many small birds such as tanagers and honeycreepers. It also takes lizards and many large insects, which may form the bulk of its diet although its food has yet to be fully studied. Its flight through vegetation is described as fluttery and moth-like but with a remarkable ability to manoeuvre. This perhaps indicates a facility for catching flying insects.

In the dry season, this diminutive owl nests in a cavity in a tree, perhaps most often an old woodpecker hole, but very little is know about its breeding behaviour. It is an owl about which much remains to be discovered.

ANDEAN PYGMY-OWL
Glaucidium jardinii

LENGTH: *150 mm*   MAP NUMBER: 87
DESCRIPTION: *Dark, strongly patterned with pale spotting*
DISTRIBUTION: *Central and northern South America*
HABITAT: *Montane forest and forest edges*
EGGS: *3. Nest in tree hole*
STATUS: *Uncertain*

This bird, once known as Jardine's Pygmy-Owl, is found in the cloud- and dwarf-forests of the Andes at altitudes between 6,500 and 13,000 feet (2,000–4,000m) and in western Panama and Costa Rica. It is the darkest and most strongly-patterned of the New World pygmy-owls. There is a rufous phase as well as the more common, dark brown type which has heavier pale spotting.

In Costa Rica, the Andean Pygmy-Owl is quite widespread, and sometimes not uncommon, in the hills of the Cordillera Central and the Cordillera de Talamanca, from a height of 3,000 feet (900m) to the upper edges of the forest on high slopes. It prefers wetter, more densely forested areas than the closely related Ferruginous Pygmy-Owl (*Glaucidium brasilianum*). The two differ, also, in their coloration and voices and have a slightly different ecology. In some places, the two live side by side and therefore have strong claims to be regarded as separate species. Some authorities, however, regard the Andean Pygmy-Owl as a race of the Northern Pygmy-Owl (*Glaucidium gnoma*) which is found in the western United States and Central America.

This typical pygmy-owl prefers the high canopy and edges of forest as well as more open spaces, overlooked by the large forest trees. At times it will also occupy pasture land with scattered trees. It is an aggressive, active hunter, dashing into a tree to catch prey unawares. A small bird or lizard needs to be quick to elude it. If the prey does escape, this owl will not set off in prompt pursuit but will perch quietly before its next dash to another tree. In contrast to other pygmy-owls, it tends to take more birds as prey but it will vary its diet with lizards and insects.

If excited or agitated, an Andean Pygmy-Owl jerks its tail from side to side and peers about, perhaps giving a very quick burst of five high-pitched hoots. It calls mostly in the early morning, and again in the late afternoon and during the night. The normal song is a long series of clear hoots, each of them even and pure in tone but delivered in an irregular rhythm. The hoots may be heard in twos, then in threes, and sometimes as a whole series in even time before the owl switches back to pairs or trios.

Like other pygmy-owls, this bird searches holes in trees until it finds a suitable nesting site. This will often be an old cavity chiselled out by a woodpecker. Three eggs are laid.

FERRUGINOUS PYGMY-OWL
Glaucidium brasilianum

LENGTH: *165 mm*   MAP NUMBER: 88
DESCRIPTION: *Small, long-tailed, dark brown with pale spots above, pale with dark streaks below*
DISTRIBUTION: *Central and South America*
HABITAT: *Desert, forest, savanna woods, plantations*
EGGS: *3–5. Nest in tree hole*
STATUS: *Uncertain, probably scarce but locally fairly common*

A bird of lower altitudes than the Andean Pygmy-Owl (*Glaucidium jardinii*), this is mostly a tropical owl, living in forested valleys from the extreme southwestern United States to Argentina. One race is found as far south as Tierra del Fuego; this bird, however, is often considered to be a separate species, the Austral Pygmy-Owl (*Glaucidium nanum*). Ferruginous Pygmy-Owls in south-west Ecuador and north-west Peru may also be of a separate species. Despite its wide range, the Ferruginous Pygmy-Owl is not well-known. In Costa Rica, where perhaps the best studies of it have been made, it is a fairly common resident from sea-level to a height of 5,000 feet (1,500m). In the highest parts of this range it overlaps with the Andean Pygmy-Owl.

This is a typical pygmy-owl in appearance and general behaviour. The plumage varies from brighter, more rufous shades to duller, greyer colouring. Its habits and food vary according to habitat. In the tropics, this is a bird of relatively dry forest but, in the United States, it inhabits the saguaro cactus desert and eats lizards and small birds.

The habitat in Costa Rica varies from deciduous and evergreen forest to more open savanna woodlands, coffee plantations and suburbs with tall trees, which the owl uses for nesting. It is most active at dawn and dusk but can hunt equally well in broad daylight or full darkness. It usually sits quietly on a concealed perch, sizing up prey and waiting for its chance. In a sudden dash, it will snatch a small bird, large insect or lizard in its claws. Its longer flights are rapid and quite direct, with bursts of whirring wingbeats interspersed by short glides.

Its song is a series of up to 30 short hoots, evenly spaced and about two seconds apart. An alarmed or excited bird may give more disyllabic notes and end the sequence with a sharp barking note. Up to five tiny white eggs are laid in a tree hole, usually one made by a woodpecker. Sometimes a cavity in a termite nest is occupied. The nest site is generally quite high above the ground.

PEARL-SPOTTED OWLET
Glaucidium perlatum

LENGTH: *170 to 200 mm* MAP NUMBER: 89
DESCRIPTION: *Small, long-tailed, streaked; false eye patches on neck*
DISTRIBUTION: *Africa south of the Sahara*
HABITAT: *Savanna and open woodland*
EGGS: *2−4. Nest in tree hole*
STATUS: *Locally frequent*

Almost the whole of Africa south of the Sahara, save the dense forests of the Congo basin and the West African coasts, is occupied by the Pearl-spotted Owlet. It is a bird of open acacia woodland and bushy savanna, perching on open twigs and swooping on prey like a small hawk. This owl has particularly strong feet and can kill birds larger than itself, such as the doves that throng the African bush. In denser woods, its place is taken by the Barred Owlet (*Glaucidium capense*).

By day, Pearl-spotted Owlets can occasionally be seen perched on branches of tall trees above the general level of

the surrounding woodland. They seem small, long-tailed and rather rounded and dumpy in form. When alarmed, however, they stretch upright to become taut, and slight bumps appear on the corners of the head, like ear tufts that have not fully developed.

Their patterning is delicate, but difficult to see at long range. On the back of the head is a realistic false face, so the bird appears to face would-be predators creeping up from behind. The eye spots are especially obvious when the owl bends its head to look for prey beneath its perch. This is perhaps when Pearl-spotted Owlets are at their most vulnerable to an attack.

These are the most diurnal of all owls in southern Africa, but Pearl-spotted Owlets hunt mainly by night, catching grasshoppers, beetles and moths, snails, small birds such as queleas and waxbills, and small mice. They also catch bats and large insects in flight and may show unexpected dexterity in turning to snatch a small bird from a noisily mobbing group. Pearl-spotted Owlets also steal food from other species and, at times, will eat carrion.

Females are distinctly larger than the neat, agile males and tend to eat larger items of food with longer intervals between feeds. Daytime hunting offers a wider range of potential prey and carries less risk of interference from larger owls, but it does make Pearl-spotted Owlets vulnerable to predators such as hawks. Despite this danger, Pearl-spotted Owlets may be seen basking in the warmth of the sun after a cold night and they frequently bathe during the day, letting the rain wash through their feathers or flying down to soak in a pool.

A pair requires a territory of about 150 acres (60ha) all year round. This will be proclaimed by the rising, twittering whistle of its song. A woodpecker or barbet nest hole is selected from a short list of several examined; though this may be used in successive years, a new one is usually selected each spring. The female spends up to a month perching at the entrance hole, calling for the male to bring food. This helps to stabilize the pair, to establish a commitment to the nest site and provides the female with the extra food needed to form the eggs.

Three white eggs are laid. Most of the incubation is done by the hen and the eggs hatch after 29 days. If disturbed, the incubating owl lies flat in the nest, hardly looking like a bird at all, but displaying her false face to the intruder. Later, the young birds do the same before leaving the nest, and seem to have even more prominent eye-spots on their hindnecks. Food is brought to the nest both day and night until the young fledge. Each takes 31 days, though there are intervals of two days in their ages. The chicks remain in dense cover close to the nest for a while but later follow their parents and begin to hunt for themselves. It is rare, if not unknown, for the full clutch of eggs to hatch and be reared successfully to this stage.

RED-CHESTED OWLET
Glaucidium tephronotum

LENGTH: *170 to 180 mm*   MAP NUMBER: 90

DESCRIPTION: *Dark head and upperparts; rufous on breast; streaked underparts*

DISTRIBUTION: *West, central and East Africa*

HABITAT: *Equatorial forest*

EGGS: *2–4. Nest in tree hole*

STATUS: *Uncertain, probably rare and declining*

Tiny but ferocious, this owl is found very patchily in central Africa from Liberia eastwards to Kenya. It is always rare and hard to locate in its habitat of primary forest and patchy forest with scrubby clearings, but is sometimes active during the day.

The Red-chested Owlet belongs to the same group as the Pearl-spotted Owlet (*Glaucidium perlatum*) but its ecological niche is quite different. In Kenya, at the edge of its range, it is uncommon and little-known, occupying humid forest to heights of 7,000 feet (2,150m) above sea-level. Pearl-spotted Owlets reach similar altitudes but in drier, open bush.

This owl eats a mixture of insects, such as crickets, cicadas, cockroaches and moths, and some much larger prey, including rats and small birds. Like other pygmy-owls, it seems able to tackle prey larger than itself. The nesting behaviour, and much else about the Red-chested Owlet, remain unknown. In Kenya, where it is presumed to be a resident, only one fully confirmed record of nesting exists. The call is a series of up to 20 high whistles at intervals of one second.

BARRED OWLET
Glaucidium capense

LENGTH: *210 to 220 mm*   MAP NUMBER: 91

DESCRIPTION: *Strongly barred buff and blackish, spotted on belly*

DISTRIBUTION: *Liberia, Kenya, Southern Africa*

HABITAT: *Open savanna woodland and bush*

EGGS: *2–3. Nest in tree cavity*

STATUS: *Uncertain*

From Kenya south to Mozambique, Zimbabwe and Angola, this owl is a bird of the lowlands, inhabiting woods beside rivers, and clumps of large trees in wooded savanna. There is also a small outpost in the denser forests of Liberia. Its varied habitats all include patches of dense bush with little ground cover, though there will be leaf litter abounding in insects, and some tall trees. In Kenya, the Barred Owlet is local, uncommon and easily missed in its densely forested habitats below altitudes of 3,900 feet (1,200m). It is thought to be resident in Kenya, and is assumed to breed, but has not been proved to do so.

The Barred Owlet is larger than the Pearl-spotted Owlet (*Glaucidium perlatum*). It has a larger, more rounded head and lacks the tail-flirting behaviour which characterizes its smaller relative. Its plumage is a splendid, harmonious mixture of grey and white barring over the head, around a white facial disc. It has pale brown and buff barring above with white scapular spots, a barred chest and a distinct zone of thrush-like spotting on the lower underparts. The bright yellow eyes are rather small, close-set and intense. There are at least six separate areas of distribution in Africa, each with races that can be distinguished by size and variations in the plumage pattern.

This owl is active mainly at dawn and dusk and tends to perch less openly than other species, although it can sometimes be seen on a high, open perch by day. But it is neither so visible nor so vocal as the Pearl-spotted Owlet, which often occupies the same area. Like other pygmy-owls, the Barred Owlet flies low and fast, with bursts of whirring wingbeats, before it swoops steeply up to the next perch. Its food consists largely of insects, mice and small birds, though tree scorpions and frogs are also taken. The preference for small food is reflected in its feet, which are smaller and weaker than those of Pearl-spotted Owlets.

Up to ten low whistles are given at half-second intervals with short pauses between series. The notes tend to rise and fall in volume. The calls are used to identify the territory of a pair but are less regular than those of many other owl species. The nest is a natural cavity in a tree, since woodpecker and barbet holes are too small for this rather hefty owl. Two or three oval white eggs are laid but details of the nesting behaviour have been little studied.

ALBERTINE OWLET
Glaucidium albertinum

LENGTH: *200 mm*   MAP NUMBER: *92*
DISTRIBUTION: *Eastern Zaire, Rwanda*
HABITAT: *Forest*
STATUS: *Rare/endangered*

There are five known specimens of this rare and little-known owl. The first was collected at Lundjulu, west of Lake Edward, in eastern Zaire, in 1950, from a forest 3,700 feet (1,120m) above sea level. The next encounter was at the same locality in 1953. Also in 1953, another was collected from the Nyungwe Forest in Rwanda. In 1966 one was taken in Zaire's Itombwe Mountains, north-west of Lake Tanganyika, from forest at 5,550 feet (1,690m). Finally, one more was collected in 1981, at an altitude of 4,750 feet (1,450m), at Munga, another site in the Itombwe Mountains.

It is, of course, possible that these few reports reflect a wider distribution, but there is nothing to suggest that the species is anything other than very rare. The area where it has been found is relatively well-explored. It was once thought to be a race of the Chestnut Owlet, itself now thought to be just a race of the Barred Owlet (*Glaucidium capense*). Museum studies have shown, however, that the Albertine Owlet is indeed a separate species, one of several threatened species of birds restricted to the Itombwe Mountains area in central Africa.

If it is already rare, the outlook is for an even bleaker future. The Nyungwe Forest in Rwanda has been reduced in size by logging and forest clearance, while mining in the Itombwe Mountains threatens its survival there. With increasing human populations in the mountain villages, clearance of the forest for agriculture is almost certain to take place at an increased rate.

It is to be hoped that conservation measures already planned will actually be implemented by the governments of Zaire and Rwanda, but this is by no means certain as yet. Until they are, the Albertine Owlet faces an insecure future in its dwindling forests and is one of many species endangered by man's activities. It is not illustrated.

COLLARED PYGMY-OWL
Glaucidium brodiei

LENGTH: *150 mm*   MAP NUMBER: *93*
DESCRIPTION: *Barred orange-buff, false eye patches on neck*
DISTRIBUTION: *Himalayas, China, South-East Asia, Sumatra, Borneo*
HABITAT: *Mixed forest and forest edge*
EGGS: *3—5. Nest in hole*
STATUS: *Uncertain*

The range of this lovely owl sweeps across South-East Asia, along the length of the Himalayas to China and Indo-China, the Malay Peninsula and over the sea to Sumatra and Borneo. It also takes in a large altitudinal range. The Collared Pygmy-Owl can be found as low as 2,000 feet (600m) above sea level and up to a height of at least 10,500 feet (3,200m) in the mountains.

This is an an evenly-barred owl, crisply marked with white around the eyes and more broadly across the lower face, with another band or rounder patch on the upper chest. It has strange rufous, black and white marks on the back of the neck, like a staring face, which probably protects it while hunting from exposed perches by day. The underparts of the Collared Pygmy-Owl, below the white chest, are heavily barred with dark brown, becoming more spotted and streaked lower down. There are well-marked grey, rufous and chestnut colour types with little intergradation. Like other pygmy-owls, it has a fairly long tail, which is very neatly barred with brown and yellowish-buff markings.

Typical habitat is mixed forest with oak, deodar, rhododendron and fir trees but this bird also occupies the edges of woodland and clumps of tall trees left during the clearance of agricultural land. Its adaptable lifestyle, wide distribution, and its taste for daylight hunting, make it quite an easy owl to see.

This species usually perches close to the trunk of a tree, where it is often mobbed remorselessly by smaller birds which buzz it and chivvy it from perch to perch. This actually assists birdwatchers who know how to imitate the calls of these owls. By doing so, they can attract a remarkably mixed group of birds into view. This technique is frequently employed by bird-trappers.

Although often mobbed, the Collared Pygmy-Owl is fierce and deadly for its size and should not be underestimated. It has a dash and confidence about it, and pounces on birds as large as itself, grasping them firmly and flying off to a suitable perch. The struggling victim is held under one foot and torn to pieces with the bill. Its recorded victims include woodpeckers, barbets, minivets and magpie-robins, but the number of birds eaten regularly may be exaggerated as such prey are easily observed and reported in any given area. The Collared Pygmy-Owl also eats more predictable prey such as mice, lizards, cicadas and grasshoppers. Like some of its close relatives, which also hunt by day, this owl lacks silent flight.

A calling bird bobs from side to side as it utters runs of three or four groups of four bell-like notes – "*toot toot-oot toot*". The motion of the head gives a ventriloquial quality to the sound. It has been claimed that calls are more frequent on hot days than in cooler weather.

In northern India, the Collared Pygmy-Owl breeds in April and May, after finding a natural cavity in a tree, or forcing woodpeckers or barbets out of their nest hole. From three to five eggs, but usually four, are laid in the deep shade of the unlined hole where, like many owls' eggs, they are made visible by their white colour. The period of incubation and other details of the birds' nesting behaviour are still unknown.

JUNGLE OWLET
Glaucidium radiatum

LENGTH: *170 mm*   MAP NUMBER: 94
DESCRIPTION: *Closely barred bright buff and brown, barred blackish and white on belly*
DISTRIBUTION: *Pakistan to Burma*
HABITAT: *Forests*
EGGS: *3–4. Nest in hole*
STATUS: *Locally frequent*

The range of this bird neatly encompasses the whole of India, Pakistan, Bangladesh and Sri Lanka and extends to western Burma. It is small, rather rounded and marked with a pleasant pattern of cross bars. These are mainly black-brown on buff-brown though they turn more

thickly black on white on the lower underparts. Its striking white eyebrows, cheeks and throat patch impart an air of distinction in comparison with other barred brown owls. In flight, a rufous patch under the wing becomes visible.

The Jungle Owlet lives in the hills to altitudes of 6,500 feet (2,000m), in damp, deciduous woodland, thick forest and secondary growth sprouting from cleared areas of jungle. It is found in pairs and is most active from an hour or so before dusk until about sunrise. But it will also hunt in daylight, especially on dull, wet days with little bright sunshine. When roosting during the day, it hides in a suitable cavity or in thick foliage to escape mobbing by small birds. If a human approaches, the Jungle Owlet tends not to sit still, but bursts out of its hiding place with rapid wingbeats and woodpecker-like glides, to settle again on a nearby tree from which it stares back at the intruder.

These owls have a loose association with other birds, such as tree pies and drongos, and are often found alongside them. They eat locusts and cicadas, as well as the occasional lizard, mouse and small forest bird.

The call of the Jungle Owlet is reminiscent of a distant, crowing Red Junglefowl (*Gallus gallus*). The owl gives a loud, slow and attractive "*kao*" two or three times, followed by a series of double notes that quicken, then fade away. While calling, the owl lowers its head, looks hunch-backed and waves its tail from side to side. There is also a song, "*cur-cur-cur-cur-ur*", which fades towards the end. This is heard in moonlight for perhaps 15 minutes at a time in a monotonous series.

Breeding takes place between March and May and the nest is in a tree hole, either a natural one or one excavated by a woodpecker. Three or four eggs are the normal number but other details of the reproduction of this owl are not fully known. In Sri Lanka, the local race, which is suffering a decline as the natural forest cover disappears, has a clutch of only two eggs.

CUCKOO OWL
Glaucidium cuculoides

LENGTH: *230 to 250 mm*   MAP NUMBER: 95
DESCRIPTION: *Small, round-headed, dull brown narrowly barred with buff*
DISTRIBUTION: *Himalayas, China, South-East Asia, Java, Bali*
HABITAT: *Forest and rain-forest*
EGGS: *3–5. Nest in tree hole*
STATUS: *Uncertain, locally frequent*

One of the largest *Glaucidium* owls, this is a bold, fierce bird, with an expression to match and the agility to catch prey in flight. It is broadly barred in dark brown and buff-brown, spotted with white on the scapulars, and has a distinctive white breast patch. The face has poorly-defined disks but the area around each eye is marked by three or four rings of brown on white.

At rest, the Cuckoo Owl perches with a hunched, almost dejected, look and its white breast patch is often nearly hidden. But an alert or alarmed bird stretches upright, wide-eyed and taut, and the breast patch and broad white bands beneath the cheeks become strikingly exposed. Its usual pose is at an angle to the branch but this little bird is highly mobile and alters its stance frequently.

The Cuckoo Owl resembles the little *Athene* owls but has rounder wings, adapted to life in forests rather than open areas. The wing feathers are simple and lack the fine fringes that modify the sound of the wingbeats of most owls. This is a feature of several daytime hunters. The Cuckoo Owl, however, lacks the protective false face on the neck which has been developed by other diurnal owls in the *Glaucidium* group.

The Cuckoo Owl lives in the Himalayas, across much of South-East Asia, far into northern China and also, in an isolated area, on Java and Bali, though not in the Malay Peninsula. The Java/Bali form is sometimes considered a separate species. In the Himalayas, it is found up to 8,800 feet (2,700m) above sea level, in open forests of pine, oak and rhododendron and in the lower tropical and subtropical evergreen jungle. This is also a jungle bird in Burma, often found in bamboo, where it feeds on mice. In winter, the populations at higher altitudes probably descend to the more sheltered valleys. The Cuckoo Owl usually occupies lower woods than those preferred by the Collared Pygmy-Owl (*Glaucidium brodiei*) but, in China, they may overlap in their choice of habitat.

This is a relatively common owl, often active by day. It perches on open branches in the warmth of the sun and hunts by pouncing on large insects, mice, lizards and small birds. Beetles, grasshoppers, crickets and locusts are probably its chief prey but birds such as quails and some large insects are sometimes caught in flight. It also catches and eats the occasional frog, snake and even fish.

Bulbuls, tits and other small birds of the forest keep up a continual noisy mobbing around any Cuckoo Owl but it sits quite still, save for an occasional wave of its tail. Suddenly, it may fly off, in a fast, undulating flight like other pygmy-owls, before its final swoop up to a new perch away from its tormentors.

The calls of a Cuckoo Owl may be heard at any time of day but the noisiest performances are reserved for the hour or two around dawn. It makes a crescendo of harsh sounds which never seem quite to reach their peak and end suddenly. In the breeding season, in April and May, it has a long, bubbling and musical whistle. This vocal repertoire can be seen as intermediate between the typical *Glaucidium* owl and the *Athene* owls.

Normally, four eggs are laid in a tree cavity though, in Burma, three or five are more common. The nest is in a natural hollow rather high in the main trunk of a big tree, but it also nests in woodpecker and barbet holes in large side branches. The birds are evicted and, in many cases, killed and eaten by this belligerent owl.

SJOSTEDT'S BARRED OWLET
Glaucidium sjostedti

LENGTH: *250 mm*   MAP NUMBER: 96
DESCRIPTION: *Boldly patterned, barred on head and neck; back dark rufous; wings barred with white; underparts barred dark brown and buff*
DISTRIBUTION: *West Central Africa*
HABITAT: *Tropical forest*
EGGS: *1. Nest in tree hole*
STATUS: *Uncertain, probably endangered*

This uncommon African owl is more aptly described by its alternative name of Chestnut-backed Owlet. Larger than other African pygmy-owls, it is restricted to a small range in the forests of Cameroon, Gabon and Zaire, and is the only owl in this area without ear tufts.

Sjostedt's Barred Owlet is found only in primary, lowland tropical forest and hunts at night in the understorey. It usually hunts within a yard or two of the ground as it searches for dung beetles, grasshoppers, small mice, snakes, crabs and spiders. Its call is a short burst of up to four notes in about two seconds. It uses tree holes to nest, but much else remains to be learnt of its nesting behaviour and the respective roles of the two adults. Incubation and fledging periods are unknown.

LONG-WHISKERED OWLET

─────── ONE SPECIES ───────

LONG-WHISKERED OWLET
Xenoglaux loweryi

LENGTH: *130 to 140 mm*   MAP NUMBER: 97
DESCRIPTION: *Densely feathered face with bristles, pale eyebrows, unfeathered legs*
DISTRIBUTION: *North Peru*
HABITAT: *Cloud-forest*
STATUS: *Uncertain, probably endangered*

This endearing, tiny owl was discovered in Peru on 23 August 1976; it probably also occurs in southern Ecuador. The generic name *Xenoglaux*, meaning strange or foreign owl, reflects its unusual character. This is most noticeable in the facial feathers, especially those beside the eyes, which splay out like a wispy ruff. The bristles around the bill are also well-developed, including those that grow upward between the eyes like a narrow brown fan, separating the two broad 'eyebrows' of pale creamy-yellow.

The Long-whiskered Owlet seems closest to the *Glaucidium* pygmy-owls, though it also shares some features with the Elf Owl (*Micrathene whitneyi*), which is in a genus of its own. Like the pygmy-owls, it has a rounded head with no real trace of feathered tufts but, unlike both pygmy-owls and the Elf Owl, it has unfeathered legs and bare, pinkish toes. The number of tail feathers also distinguishes it from other species. However, its most obvious distinctive features are its feathery face, so unlike the traditional owl face, and its staring eyes of mottled orange-brown. Limited evidence suggests that this owl probably flies only rarely, preferring to move by hopping through dense lower growth.

The cloud-forests of the Andes where the Long-whiskered Owlet was discovered are 6,200 feet (1,890m) above sea-level. The region is moistened regularly by the cycle of clouds which condense on the high, forested mountain slopes. This was an area seldom visited by ornithologists. Since 1963, however, ornithological expeditions to Peru have discovered more than 20 species of bird new to science, and others may still await discovery. The owlet was given its specific name, *loweryi*, in honour of the late George Lowery, of Louisiana State University, who played a major role in establishing the intensified studies of Peruvian birds. The lifestyle, numbers and requirements of this beautiful and probably rare little owl still need to be documented so that it can be protected for future generations.

ELF OWL

— ONE SPECIES —

ELF OWL
Micrathene whitneyi

LENGTH: *130 to 140 mm*   MAP NUMBER: 98
DESCRIPTION: *Tiny; dull grey-brown, spotted white on scapulars; barred wings*
DISTRIBUTION: *South-west USA and Mexico*
HABITAT: *Dry woodland, cactus, wet savanna*
EGGS: *2–5. Nest in hole*
STATUS: *Locally threatened*

This dumpy bird has the reputation of being the world's smallest owl, although it actually vies for that title with two other species, the Least Pygmy-Owl (*Glaucidium minutissimum*) and the Long-whiskered Owlet (*Xenoglaux loweryi*). To see the Elf Owl, it is necessary to travel to the extreme south of Texas, the eastern and western parts of Mexico, southern Arizona, New Mexico or lower California. It is resident in much of this restricted range, where it is often associated with the giant saguaro cactus. But in Arizona, Texas and California, the Elf Owl is a summer migrant.

In appearance, this is a typical small owl. Like the Little Owl (*Athene noctua*), it has a rounded body held clear of its perch on strong, neat legs. These are free of the body feathers that often obscure the legs of the larger owls and many small scops owls. The Elf Owl has rather pale, greyish-brown plumage with a row of white scapular spots, and white and buff barring on the flight feathers.

Its facial pattern is poorly marked except for thin, pale eyebrow lines. It has paler underparts with a faint peppering and barring of darker brown. Its eyes are pale yellow but its face has a less intense expression than those of the Little Owl or Burrowing Owl (*Athene cunicularia*). The Elf Owl is round-headed and has a much shorter tail than pygmy-owls or screech-owls.

Away from the cactus desert, the Elf Owl lives in woodland up to 6,500 feet (2,000m) above sea level and on a variety of lowland terrain. Its narrow range is surprising in view of this adaptability. This is often the commonest owl in southern Arizona, where it lives in the low, hot, arid plains of the broad valleys. The ground is hard and stony, covered liberally with the candelabra-shaped saguaros and with mesquite and creosote bushes and a variety of small cacti. In Texas, its numbers are declining, while its range in California has contracted.

The early belief that the Elf Owl lived only in the desert may have delayed its discovery in quite different habitats. In expansive grasslands, it lives in the trees and scattered brushwood that grow in the larger canyons and ravines, and in the oak, walnut and sycamore that survive on slopes sheltered by cliffs. It is also found in cottonwood far from the nearest groves of giant cacti.

Elf Owls spend most of the day hidden inside a hole in a tree, or among dense foliage, and are much more nocturnal than most pygmy-owls. They become active at dusk when they chase large insects. This is by far the best time to observe them. Crickets, grasshoppers, caterpillars, beetles and centipedes are typical prey. Small birds are rarely, if ever, attacked. Elf Owls sometimes fly close to campfires, probably drawn by the insects swirling around the light.

This bird calls very loudly, giving a series of about six yelping notes in rapid succession, the high pitch descending at the end. If discovered while calling, the Elf Owl will usually sit still and upright, looking like a broken stump and relying on its natural camouflage to protect it.

A typical nest site is a hole made by a Gila Woodpecker (*Melanerpes uropygialis*) or Gilded Flicker (*Colaptes auratus*), especially in any of the saguaros riddled with such holes, although cavities in trees are also occupied. Occasionally, one or even two species of woodpecker, and the Elf Owl, may nest in the same saguaro, while flycatchers and screech-owls may nest in others nearby. The saguaros are central to the survival of the varied bird population in these regions. Their melon-like pulp is easily penetrated by a woodpecker and dries to a hard, dry skin inside the newly-bored cavity.

Two to five eggs, but most commonly three, are laid in April or May in the base of such a cavity, where there is no real lining apart from the accumulated chips, food and feathers. The eggs, which are tiny for an owl, hatch after two weeks of incubation by both sexes. The chicks are fed on insects and remain dependent on their parents for some time after leaving the nest. At that time of year, the saguaros grow white blossoms while the lower shrubs, prickly pears and other cacti have glorious yellow and vermilion-red flowers. It is a strange, wild and haunting region, the home of one of the most energetic and charming owls in the world.

Elf Owl (*Micrathene whitneyi*)

PAPUAN HAWK OWL

— ONE SPECIES —

PAPUAN HAWK OWL
Uroglaux dimorpha

LENGTH: *300 to 330 mm*   MAP NUMBER: 99
DESCRIPTION: *Large, long-tailed; rich brown, barred reddish-buff above; streaked below; yellow eyes*
DISTRIBUTION: *New Guinea, Yapen Island*
HABITAT: *Dense forest*
STATUS: *Rare, perhaps endangered*

This is a rare bird of the hot tropical forest, living a secretive life on Yapen Island and possibly throughout neighbouring Papua New Guinea and Irian Jaya. The Papuan Hawk Owl has slightly glossy, warm brown upperparts, all closely barred with darker brown or black. The underside is cream, streaked with black. The face has a plain, open expression and the poorly-defined facial discs are blackish at the edges. The forehead and eyebrows are dull cream-buff with sparse black bristles. This open, V-shaped area separates huge, round eyes of the clearest yellow, so large that they dominate the face. The owl's other main feature is its very long tail, which forms almost half the total length of the bird.

In flight, this tail and the relatively small, round head give this owl the appearance of an *Accipiter* hawk, though the Papuan Hawk Owl is only occasionally a bird-eater. It also lives on small mice and large insects, but little has been discovered of its way of life, numbers and detailed distribution. Since its habitat is steadily disappearing, it must be presumed that the numbers of the Papuan Hawk Owl are, sadly, also in decline.

SOUTHERN HAWK OWLS

—— SIXTEEN SPECIES ——

RUFOUS OWL
Ninox rufa

LENGTH: *400 to 500 mm*   MAP NUMBER: 100
DESCRIPTION: *Large, long-tailed; dark head, closely barred dark brown above, pale with rusty bars below*
DISTRIBUTION: *Northern Australia, New Guinea*
HABITAT: *Rain-forest, thick woodland*
EGGS: *2–3. Nest in hole*
STATUS: *Uncertain, probably scarce, declining*

The owls of several genera in the southern hemisphere are known as hawk owls. Yet, in the far northern hemisphere, this name is given to a quite different species, the Hawk Owl *Surnia ulula*, which is not related to the southern group. The southern hawk owls are only loosely linked but all have generally longer wings and tails than most owls,

and less developed facial discs.

The Rufous Owl is the second largest of this group. Its face is rather pointed with a slightly hawk-like expression. It is closely and neatly barred all over, except for its blacker mask and pale throat. The yellow eyes and yellowish bill give the bird an intense, staring look. It is found in northern Australia and in the lowlands of New Guinea and a few nearby islands.

In New Guinea, it is not well-known, even though its sparse distribution stretches across a large area along both the northern and southern sides of the island, as well as to Waigeo Island and the Aru Islands in the west. The Rufous Owl lives in forest and secondary growth after forest clearances, mainly in lowland regions but also up to 6,500 feet (2,000m) or more above sea level. In Australia, it prefers dense rain-forest and thick woodland on the drier savannas, especially beside rivers and along temporary watercourses. It occupies several rather isolated areas on the northern capes and the north-east coast of Australia but is considered uncommon.

The Rufous Owl is found to the north of the range of the Powerful Owl (*Ninox strenua*), the largest of the southern hawk owls. Although smaller, the Rufous Owl is more aggressive, and the two seem to be mutually exclusive. By day, the Rufous Owl conceals itself in a tree or dense foliage, roosting either singly or in pairs. It calls at night, giving a low, slow "*woo-hoo!*", which is described as similar to the call of the Powerful Owl, though less strong or far-carrying. The Rufous Owl probably eats a variety of small mammals but seems to concentrate on tree-living marsupials, the small opossums.

The nest is in a tree cavity, in which fallen pieces of decayed bark, dead leaves and accumulated scraps form a soft lining for the two or three white eggs. Little is known of its breeding behaviour.

POWERFUL OWL
Ninox strenua

LENGTH: *630 to 650 mm*   MAP NUMBER: 101
DESCRIPTION: *Very large, long-tailed; dark with copious cream bars*
DISTRIBUTION: *South-east Australia*
HABITAT: *Forest*
EGGS: *2–3. Nest in hole*
STATUS: *Rare*

This long-tailed bird, found only in south-eastern Australia, has a round face reminiscent of a buzzard or hawk. Its protruding bill and the distinct brow ridges over the eyes enhance this impression. The plumage is beautifully patterned with neat, complex barring of dark brown, black and cream. Eyes of the clearest yellow complete its severe, rather fierce appearance.

The Powerful Owl is confined mainly to the coastal side of the Great Dividing Range, but is sometimes recorded on the inland slopes of the mountains. Young birds occasionally stray well inland when dispersing in search of new territories. Otherwise, this is a sedentary owl, living

singly or in pairs in a fixed territory throughout the year. This area will contain a number of favoured roosting sites where the owls can hide in dense foliage. Although often difficult to find, roosting owls may be spotted in more exposed locations. They are then fairly approachable. At night, they are shy and hard to observe.

Recent mapping work in Australia has found that streams between ridges covered with eucalyptus forest are a particularly favoured habitat. Powerful Owls hunt at night and take much of their prey within the tree canopy. As a result, they need fairly open forest in which to search freely for small animals. The owls use their long legs and large, muscular feet to snatch such prey.

Arboreal animals make up at least three-quarters of the bird's diet but the particular species vary from place to place, depending on their abundance. Ring-tailed possums may be the preferred prey in one region; sugar gliders or greater gliders may predominate in another. Birds account for most of the remainder of the diet, though a few small ground-living mammals and insects may also be taken from the forest floor.

This dependence on tree-living marsupials has had a marked effect. The range of the Powerful Owl has altered, and its numbers have declined, whenever forest has been burned, cleared or replaced by more uniform tree plantations, whether native or exotic. Monocultures, even of Australian species of tree, are never so productive as the naturally varied forests.

Where prey is abundant in untouched habitat, a pair of owls may still need at least 2,000 to 2,500 acres (800–1,000 ha) in which to live. In areas where species of prey are at lower densities, the territories are correspondingly larger. Even where prey is readily available, the territories tend to be separated by unoccupied buffer zones. Nests may be anything from three to 12 miles (5-20km) apart.

The call is a loud "*who-hoo!*", deep and far-carrying from the male, but higher-pitched from the smaller female. Young birds have a shrill whistle which helps the ornithologist to track down families just after fledging. The nest is in a hole in a tree, in which the female may roost all year round. If disturbed on the nest, she may make a spirited attack but the larger male is less aggressive than the smaller Barking Owl (*Ninox connivens*).

Only two eggs are laid, with an unusually long interval of four days. The female alone incubates the eggs, which take 35 or 36 days to hatch, while the male provides the nightly rations until the young are several days old. The chicks leave the nest after five weeks but are not fully mature for another seven to nine months. During this period, families of three or four may roost together during the day.

BARKING OWL
Ninox connivens

LENGTH: *380 to 440 mm*   MAP NUMBER: 102
DESCRIPTION: *Hawk-like, long-tailed; grey-brown, streaked below*
DISTRIBUTION: *Australia, New Guinea, Moluccas*
HABITAT: *Savanna forest*
EGGS: *2–3. Nest in hole*
STATUS: *Frequent to scarce*

As dusk falls in the forests of Australia and New Guinea, the visitor may be fooled by an abrupt, double bark. It sounds somewhat like a dog but a native would recognize the call of the Barking Owl, whose popular name is derived from this sharp sound. It is higher pitched when given by the female and, at close range, a low growl can be heard preceding the call.

This long-tailed owl with yellow eyes, also known as the Winking Owl, has a repertoire of memorable calls. Another, given in the breeding season, is described as resembling a drawn-out or strangled scream. Such sounds are the very stuff of the superstitions and legends which are woven more around owls than any other birds.

In New Guinea, the Barking Owl lives in open country while the Papuan Hawk Owl (*Uroglaux dimorpha*) occupies the forests. It has a wide distribution and several different races have been recognized in the north Moluccas, eastern New Guinea, Vulcan Island, Dampier Island and in five separate areas of Australia. Some of the Australian populations are quite isolated while others

appear to intergrade in certain areas.

Australian Barking Owls live in pairs in eucalyptus woods. Their calls, at dawn and dusk, are much more familiar than the actual bird, though the confusion of this sound with the bark of the fox has led to difficulties in mapping the range of this owl. Defended territories are usually around 500 acres (200ha) in size, though some are much smaller, and are occupied all year round for roosting and nesting.

When hunting, however, the owls often range well outside the defended territory. Mammals, birds, insects and occasional fish provide a varied diet for this opportunistic bird. Rabbits, rats, mice, opossums and gliders are all captured, and creatures ranging from small insects to birds as large as crows may be snatched up. Like the Powerful Owl (*Ninox strenua*), roosting birds can be seen by day, often clutching the remains of prey caught the night before. However, it is by scientific study of the pellets and through studies at the nest that accurate details of prey species have been obtained.

The nest is in a tree hole, and two or three dull eggs are laid on a bed of random debris that has collected in the cavity. The male rotates within the hollow and scrapes the material with his feet to prepare a smooth pad for the eggs. These are laid at intervals of three days. The female incubates them and is fed and guarded by the male, an aggressive bird that may well attack intruders. Incubation lasts 37 days and the chicks fly after five weeks.

BOOBOOK OWL
Ninox novaeseelandiae

LENGTH: *350 mm*   MAP NUMBER: 103
DESCRIPTION: *Long-tailed, tawny-brown, brown eyes*
DISTRIBUTION: *Indonesia, New Zealand, Australian islands*
HABITAT: *Thick forest, open rocky areas, scrub*
EGGS: *3–4. Nest in hole*
STATUS: *Widespread, frequent to scarce*

The Boobook Owl is widely dispersed across Tasmania, New Zealand and on small, remote islands around Australia. This range, from which the Barking Owl (*Ninox connivens*) is largely absent, almost certainly indicates a

long history of dispersal and the establishment of new populations. At least 15 races can be separated. These are found on islands with such evocative names as Sumba, Alor, Timor, Babar and Kai in the Lesser Sunda Islands of the south Indonesian archipelago, the homes of sandalwood, nutmeg and spices.

This is a beautiful region where mountainous islands rise from a blue sea broken by leaping dolphins. These islands are little known to ornithologists. With the growth of tourism, opportunities to study their owls have seldom been better, but the threat to the habitat and well-being of these birds has increased correspondingly.

The Boobook Owl also occupies islands of a quite different character, such as Lord Howe and Norfolk Islands far to the east of Australia and north of New Zealand. Like

the other islands, these have their own races of the owl, which have local names derived from the bird's call — 'boobook' or, alternatively, 'morepork'.

Hand in hand with this wide range goes an acceptance of a large variety of habitats. The Boobook Owl lives in thick forest and also in open places where it roosts in caves and tumbled rocks, in urban areas where trees grow in parks, in mallee and mulga scrub and in arid places with little cover.

Like other *Ninox* owls, this bird has a reduced facial disc which may suggest that its hearing is less keenly developed than that of other owls. It does, in fact, search for food by day, when it probably relies mainly on its excellent vision. But, like the Barking Owl and the Powerful Owl (*Ninox strenua*), it is essentially a nocturnal hunter. The Boobook Owl is actually smaller than those birds, with shorter wings and tail, and its range and lifestyle suggest a less specialized species.

Its disyllabic call of "*boobook*" used to be attributed to a quite different bird, the Tawny Frogmouth (*Podargus strigoides*). The sound is not, though, a deep, booming sound as might be imagined, but a sharp, high-pitched call, repeated regularly; often, however, it has a hoarse or gruff quality. Occasionally, it makes other noises, including a cat-like squawl and a quick "*yo-yo-yo-yo*".

This owl may spend the day hidden singly, in pairs or in family groups, in a tree or a rocky crevice. If disturbed, they slip silently away but small birds sometimes reveal their position, noisily mobbing them as they depart. Honeyeaters often discover and mob roosting Boobook Owls during the day.

At dusk they emerge to hunt, often perching on exposed branches or telegraph poles as they stare at the ground or look watchfully around. Sometimes a Boobook Owl will catch insects that are drawn to street lights. Unlike other members of its genus, this owl is mainly insectivorous. But it will take small birds and mammals and join in the free-for-all when a variety of birds of prey are attracted by plagues of mice.

The nest is a hole in a tree, much like those of the other *Ninox* species. Three white eggs are laid. The male prepares the hollow but the female does all the incubating. The young leave the nest when about six weeks old and have grown adult-like plumage by the age of three months. These immature birds then disperse and appear outside the range of the breeding adults, which are much more sedentary. In Tasmania, numbers have declined, partly as a result of competition for nest sites from kookaburras, introduced starlings and other hole-nesters.

BROWN HAWK OWL
Ninox scutuluta

LENGTH: *280 to 320 mm*   MAP NUMBER: 104
DESCRIPTION: *Rounded, dark brown with streaked, whiter underparts, yellow eyes*
DISTRIBUTION: *Southern and Eastern Asia, Japan, Borneo, Philippines*
HABITAT: *Forest, wooded cultivation, scrub, mangroves*
EGGS: *2−5. Nest in hole*
STATUS: *Widespread, frequent to scarce*

This thickset bird, also known as the Oriental Hawk Owl, has a wide range stretching from the Indian subcontinent across the South-East Asian mainland to northern China, Korea and the Sikhote Alin Range in the eastern Soviet Union. It also occupies a variety of islands from the Andamans in the Bay of Bengal to Sumatra, Java, Borneo, the Philippines, Taiwan and Japan. This is a remarkable diversity of environments and climatic conditions for a single species to tolerate. Groups on islands have been isolated long enough for at least ten races to evolve. Some northern races are migrants and overlap in winter with resident races to the south. Birds from north-east Asia, for

example, have been found in Sumatra during the winter, and migrants of at least two forms are common from October to March in Sulawesi and the Philippines.

The Brown Hawk Owl has simple needs, as its wide distribution suggests. It thrives in all kinds of forest and bush with taller trees, including cultivated land with remnant stands of mature trees or shelterbelts. This owl also survives happily in mangroves, which provide it with ample cover. In Sumatra, it occupies primary and secondary forest at up to 3,900 feet (1,200m), though usually lower, and is also found in plantations and gardens.

The Andaman Islands have their own species of hawk owl as well as a race of the Brown Hawk Owl, both of which are shared with the Nicobar Islands farther south. Both are much darker overall than the mainland Brown Hawk Owls. It seems likely that an ancient invasion of hawk owls from the mainland established the stock that evolved into the new, darker species, the Andaman Brown Hawk Owl (*Ninox affinis*). A later invasion from the mainland found that the original birds had already evolved into a different species. The later arrivals have also evolved into darker birds, along similar lines to the first. They have not yet been isolated for long enough to be more than a race of the Brown Hawk Owl but, eventually, they too may cross the boundary and form a new species. At that stage, there will be three species of Brown Hawk Owl, all evolved from the original stock.

Brown Hawk Owls living in mangroves eat crabs snatched from the mud at low tide. Even those in dense forest show a preference for the proximity of rivers and eat a variety of amphibians as well as small birds, mammals, reptiles and insects. They are very much adaptable generalists, rather than specialist hunters, and are typical round, brown owls in appearance.

Scientific studies have shown that the ears of the hawk owls of the genus *Ninox* are not especially acute. In this, they resemble eagle owls, scops owls, screech-owls, pygmy-owls and the little owl group. The structure of the ears of hawk owls is unexceptional and their size is similar to that of other birds of comparable size. This contrasts with the huge, complex ears of the barn owls, wood owls and certain other groups. The generalist nature of the southern hawk owls has assisted, not hindered, the present species in its geographical and ecological spread.

In India, the Brown Hawk Owl is active at dusk and through the night, spending the days singly or in pairs tucked away in the shade of thick creepers lying tangled over a big branch. If disturbed, it flies off quickly and steadily, with an upward swoop onto a new perch. At dusk, it ventures out to perch on a favourite stump or pole, often the same one night after night. It can catch flying insects with agile leaps from this perch, or in sudden, short flights like a flycatcher, and is said to hawk insects in the air rather like a nightjar.

The Brown Hawk Owl has a distinctive voice and gives a series of disyllabic calls of "*oo .. uk*" or "*pop-pow*", a second or so apart. There are usually nine to 13 of these calls, but the range can extend from six to 20. Moonlit nights in the breeding season may be filled with this call for literally hours on end. Pairs will call in a duet and be answered by others in the distance. Calls will often intensify just before dawn.

The owls nest in tree holes, laying two to four eggs. The cavity is generally littered with pellets but has no proper lining. Relatively little has been discovered about the breeding behaviour of this widespread owl.

ANDAMAN BROWN HAWK OWL
Ninox affinis

LENGTH: *250 to 280 mm*   MAP NUMBER: 105
DESCRIPTION: *Dark brown overall*
DISTRIBUTION: *Andaman and Nicobar Islands*
HABITAT: *Open forest*
STATUS: *Uncertain, restricted, probably rare*

Found on the Andaman Islands and Nicobar Islands in the Bay of Bengal west of Burma and Thailand, this owl is presumed to have evolved from the larger Brown Hawk Owl (*Ninox scutulata*) as an isolated island offshoot. Like the local race of the Brown Hawk Owl, it is a darker bird than the mainland owl, with much darker underparts. The Andaman Brown Hawk Owl has itself evolved into two races, one on each chain of islands. The call is a single, loud "*craw*", quite unlike the double call so distinctive of the Brown Hawk Owl. This little-known species has received only scant attention from ornithologists.

WHITE-BROWED OWL
Ninox superciliaris

LENGTH: *230 to 280 mm*   MAP NUMBER: 106
DESCRIPTION: *Dark brown spotted with white above; white barred with brown below*
DISTRIBUTION: *Madagascar*
HABITAT: *Forest, wooded savanna and ravines*
EGGS: *3–5. Nest on the ground*
STATUS: *Uncertain, perhaps rare and threatened*

This owl's common and scientific names refer to the bird's broad, white eyebrows which create its distinctive expression. The word superciliary means 'above the eye'. Also known as the Madagascar Hawk Owl, this species is largely restricted to the western half of that island. There is an occasional record from the north-east, but it is certainly most frequent in the west. It is principally a bird of forests, and at risk because much of its natural habitat on Madagascar has been denuded. However, it also roosts in

small caves. It has been reported from forest and wooded savanna, wooded ravines through low hills and in forest clearings near villages. It may be commoner than has been feared, although reports have been contradictory. In the west of the central plateau and in the Bara region numbers appear to be moderately high.

The White-browed Owl is closely related to the Brown Hawk Owl (*Ninox scutulata*) but is barred below, rather than streaked. It eats a variety of prey, from small insects to birds and reptiles, but is principally an insect-eater. Active only at night, it is very vocal, giving two muffled hoots followed by 15 to 20 intense discordant notes. It nests on the ground, laying three to five eggs. The breeding season runs from October to December.

The birds of Madagascar, some of which are endangered, have yet to receive the intensive study that their rich variety deserves, and are poorly served in popular literature. The White-browed Owl could prove to be a fascinating species, a link with the owls of the South Pacific, Australasia and the Indian subcontinent.

PHILIPPINE HAWK OWL
Ninox philippensis

LENGTH: *200 mm*　　MAP NUMBER: 107
DESCRIPTION: *Small, dark, rich brown, spotted white along scapulars; streaked rusty below*
DISTRIBUTION: *Philippines*
HABITAT: *Forest*
STATUS: *Uncertain*

The small Philippine Hawk Owl, which varies in appearance from island to island, is separated into at least three races. One is restricted to the islands of Luzon, Marinduque and Leyte, another to Ticao and Masbate, and the third is found on Panay, Guimaras, Negros and Siquijor. These islands are all part of the complex archipelago between the South China Sea and the Pacific Ocean, where land and sea are closely entwined.

The classification, or taxonomy, of these owls is complex. Some authorities recognize other species, such as the Spotted Hawk Owl *Ninox spilonata* or Tweeddale's Hawk Owl *Ninox spilocephala*. The former is found on Mindoro, Tablas and Sibuyan, the latter on Mindoro, Mindanao, Basilan, Jolo, Bongao and Siasi.

Some experienced ornithologists believe these are simply more races of the Phillipine Hawk Owl, which is a polymorphic species over the whole group of islands. Whether these forms, isolated by fairly narrow stretches of sea, could interbreed or not is an almost unanswerable question. The exact listing of species or races remains a matter of debate. In any case, the island groups will eventually diverge. Classifying the owls of the Philippines is made more complex by visits in winter from several races of the Brown Hawk Owl (*Ninox scutulata*) of mainland Asia. A study of how these various owls are separated ecologically is yet one more task awaiting the attention of ornithologists.

OCHRE-BELLIED HAWK OWL
Ninox perversa

LENGTH: *250 to 260 mm*　　MAP NUMBER: 108
DESCRIPTION: *Pale yellow-brown, spotted above, plain below*
DISTRIBUTION: *Sulawesi*
HABITAT: *Dense, untouched rain-forest*
STATUS: *Uncertain, probably endangered*

This fairly small bird is found in rain-forests across much of Sulawesi (Celebes) in Indonesia. It is more uniformly-coloured than many hawk owls, in a soft, ruddy ochre, with white spots on the scapulars and wing coverts. Like most of its genus, it has piercing yellow eyes and a prominent bill, but ill-defined facial discs.

It is found up to 2,600 feet (800m) above sea level in forests over all but the south of the main island, in contrast to the Speckled Hawk Owl (*Ninox punctulata*) which prefers more open habitats. Ochre-bellied Hawk Owls can be seen also on a few islets to the south-east, including Kabaena, Muna and Butung. They are apparently scarce throughout, even in the deep virgin forest. As forest is cleared, their survival may be threatened. Little is known about the size of the population or about the bird's breeding biology.

The original scientific name of this owl was *Ninox ochracea* which derived, like its English name, from its appearance. The use of *Ninox perversa* since 1938 seems an unnecessary change but both names can be found in recent literature and lists of species.

INDONESIAN HAWK OWL
Ninox squamipila

LENGTH: *300 to 350 mm*   MAP NUMBER: 109
DESCRIPTION: *Very dark; banded reddish-buff and dark brown on wings, closely barred dark brown and cream on belly*
DISTRIBUTION: *Scattered South-East Asian islands*
HABITAT: *Forest*
STATUS: *Uncertain, perhaps threatened or endangered*

Known also as the Moluccan Hawk Owl, this bird is found on the north Moluccas, Buru, Seram, Tanimbar in the Lesser Sundas and on Christmas Island to the south of Java. Each of these far-flung islands has a distinct race, and the species may be a title of convenience for several diverse forms. Some birds are a deeper, redder brown, while others are paler and more yellow. Their barred underparts are also variably marked. This is a typical hawk owl in shape, being quite long, and tapering down from its broad shoulders and large, round head. It is not, however, markedly long-tailed.

The Indonesian Hawk Owl is found in thickets and forests to an altitude of 5,700 feet (1,750m) but, in common with most hawk owls, has attracted little attention or study. It has the usual large and sensitive eyes, but relatively uncomplicated ears. This suggests a greater reliance on vision than is found in, for example, a Tawny Owl (*Strix aluco*) of the European woods. Even so, its ability to move comfortably through the island forests, to see and hear its prey in near darkness, and to swoop down to the ground to catch it neatly in its feet, is still impressive. The hawk owls may be ordinary in the world of owls but their faculties are still remarkable.

BROWN OWL
Ninox theomacha

LENGTH: *200 to 250 mm*   MAP NUMBER: 110
DESCRIPTION: *Very dark; black-brown above and on face,*
dark reddish below
DISTRIBUTION: *New Guinea archipelago*
HABITAT: *Lowland forest*
STATUS: *Uncertain, perhaps threatened*

Several owls around the world are known colloquially as
'brown owl', and this one has therefore also been called
the Papuan Boobook Owl, Jungle Boobook Owl and
Brown Boobook Owl, all of which have a certain logic. A
more clumsy name is the Sooty-backed Hawk Owl. The
simple 'Brown Owl' has, however, become its accepted
common name.

   This small, dark owl has deep, umber-brown upperparts
and rich, rust-coloured underparts. Its yellow eyes form a
vivid contrast with the dark, peppered-grey plumage of the
head. The Brown Owl can be found on several islands of
New Guinea. It lives in lowland forest but, in some places,
its range extends to an altitude of 8,200 feet (2,500m)
above sea level. It has been reported to be less common in
lowland areas than in some of the hills.

There are four recognized races. Besides the typical form
of New Guinea, a duller race with a browner head is found
on Misool Island and Waigeo Island off Irian Jaya, a larger
bird with white marks beneath lives on the
D'Entrecasteaux Islands and one with even more white is
found on Rossel Island in the Louisiade Archipelago. These
last two chains are at the eastern edge of Papua New
Guinea in the Solomon Sea.

   The Brown Owl is an insect-eater, but its diet is poorly
documented. The bird is not uncommon and can
sometimes be seen at night catching large insects that are
attracted to street lights. Forests, gardens, tall trees at the
edge of clearings and a variety of similar terrain may be
home to this adaptable creature. In the forests of New
Guinea, it replaces the Boobook Owl (*Ninox*
novaeseelandiae), which prefers more open country.

   This bird lives either a solitary life, or roosts in pairs. The
call most often heard is a simple, double note of "*kyo kyo*"
or "*yow-yow*" which has a notably eerie effect. Each part
of the call has a marked downward inflection. The calls are
repeated every three to four seconds and continue with
rare persistence throughout much of the night.

SPECKLED HAWK OWL
Ninox punctulata

LENGTH: *200 to 260 mm*   MAP NUMBER: 111
DESCRIPTION: *Pale brown, spotted white above; white*
throat; pale below
DISTRIBUTION: *Sulawesi*
HABITAT: *Open forest and cultivation*
STATUS: *Uncertain but appears fairly common*

This is the commoner of the two hawk owls of the
Sulawesi Islands (Celebes). It occupies more open, less
densely wooded habitats than the forests preferred by the
Ochre-bellied Hawk Owl (*Ninox perversa*). The Speckled
Hawk Owl has creamy-white spots all over its head, back
and wings on a subtle buff-brown background. The facial
pattern is a striking one with white eyebrows, a blackish

mask and a large, white throat patch.

   The owl gives a trisyllabic call of two short notes,
followed by a longer and more high-pitched sound. This
owl is widespread, often living close to villages and human
habitations, so its calls are heard far more often than those
of the Ochre-bellied Hawk Owl. The Speckled Hawk Owl
is more at home in disturbed habitats, in cultivated regions
with a few remaining trees and in open, or secondary
woodland. The fortunes of the two hawk owls have
differed markedly in recent decades. The forest species has
declined with the loss of forest, while the cleared areas
have helped the Speckled Hawk Owl to thrive. But the
species remains one of many in the region whose
behaviour in the field has yet to be fully studied.

ADMIRALTY ISLANDS HAWK OWL
Ninox meeki

LENGTH: *200 to 250 mm*   MAP NUMBER: 112
DESCRIPTION: *Dark on head and back, white spots on wings; belly white with spear-shaped streaks*
DISTRIBUTION: *Admiralty Islands off New Guinea*
STATUS: *Uncertain; restricted, rare*

Of all the hawk owls on the smaller islands and archipelagos of South-East Asia, this is the most handsome. With gleaming yellow eyes in a dusky face, a forehead of rusty-brown, and a yellow bill above a pale chin patch, the Admiralty Islands Hawk Owl ranks with the most beautiful owls in the world. The body plumage is a mixture of barred rufous-brown, blackish with crisp spots of white, and broad spear-head marks of red-brown standing out against the clear white underparts.

The Admiralty Islands, just north of Papua New Guinea, are one of several island groups in the region which have their own species of hawk owl. These species are closely related and almost certainly evolved from the same ancestral stock. Classification (taxonomy) is difficult because such hawk owls never meet and any question of interbreeding is hypothetical. Although little-known, the Admiralty Islands Hawk Owl is very different from the other species and presumably must have evolved into a separate species long ago.

NEW IRELAND HAWK OWL
Ninox solomonis

LENGTH: *250 to 300 mm*   MAP NUMBER: 113
DESCRIPTION: *Dark; barred on back and underside, rufous breast*
DISTRIBUTION: *Bismarck Archipelago off New Guinea*
STATUS: *Uncertain, restricted and probably rare*

New Ireland, a thin island north of Papua New Guinea, shares this owl with New Britain, its neighbour in the Bismarck Archipelago, which also has its own separate species. The New Ireland Hawk Owl is larger, darker and more heavily-barred than the New Britain Hawk Owl (*Ninox odiosa*) but otherwise remains little-known. Despite its scientific name, this owl is not the species found on the Solomon Islands. A separate race of the New Ireland Hawk Owl is found on New Hanover Island, to the north-west of New Ireland.

NEW BRITAIN HAWK OWL
Ninox odiosa

LENGTH: *200 to 230 mm*   MAP NUMBER: 114
DESCRIPTION: *Reddish brown, spotted white*
DISTRIBUTION: *New Britain Island off New Guinea*
HABITAT: *Forest*
STATUS: *Uncertain, restricted*

The crescent-shaped island of New Britain has its own hawk owl as well as sharing a species with nearby New Ireland. New Britain is the largest island in the Bismarck Archipelago, north-east of Papua New Guinea. The New Britain Hawk Owl has small, whitish spots and is a redder species than the New Ireland Hawk Owl (*Ninox solomonis*). It is also a smaller bird, which is probably why the two can survive together on the same island. In the same way that the scops owl genus *Otus* of the Asian islands has formed many species, the hawk owls have developed into a complex variety of species and races during long periods of isolation on islands between the Indian and Pacific Oceans that are in close proximity.

SOLOMON ISLANDS HAWK OWL
Ninox jacquinoti

LENGTH: *250 to 310 mm*   MAP NUMBER: 115
DESCRIPTION: *Dark brown, closely barred buff above; very dark breast; unmarked cream belly*
DISTRIBUTION: *Solomon Islands, near New Guinea*
STATUS: *Uncertain, probably rare*

This species is slightly larger than the Brown Hawk Owl (*Ninox scutulata*) and has more barred underparts, but the colouring of the underside differs from island to island. During its period of isolation on the Solomon Islands, which are due east of New Guinea, several different races have emerged on the major islands in the group. This bird is clearly closely related to the Brown Hawk Owl and to the hawk owls of New Ireland, New Britain and the Admiralty Islands and probably has a similar lifestyle, eating mostly insects and nesting in hollows in trees.

BARE-LEGGED OWL

ONE SPECIES

BARE-LEGGED OWL
Gymnoglaux lawrencii

LENGTH: *200 to 230 mm*   MAP NUMBER: 116
DESCRIPTION: *Small, upright, long-legged; white eyebrows; streaked below; yellow eyes*
DISTRIBUTION: *Cuba and Isle of Pines*
HABITAT: *Forest in limestone areas*
EGGS: *? Nest in rock or tree hole*
STATUS: *Uncertain, restricted*

This small, upright owl is found only on Cuba and the Isle of Pines in the Caribbean. Its long, bare legs recall those of the Burrowing Owl (*Athene cunicularia*), but it is often known as the Cuban Screech-Owl. There has been debate over whether it should be classified with the scops owls or screech-owls of the *Otus* genus, but most authorities favour its separation into a genus of its own.

Unlike the screech-owls and scops owls, the Bare-legged Owl has no feathery tufts or 'ears' on its head. It lives in limestone areas with eroded gullies and cavities which provide it with both roosting and nesting places, but it also nests in holes in trees. By day, the owl hides away in a dense bush or tree, or deep inside a rocky cave.

The call is a soft, accelerating "*coooo-cooo-coo-cu-cu-cu*" and one of its local names is 'cucu'. This run of notes becomes gradually higher in pitch, and may be answered by the other member of a pair with a more clearly enunciated "*hui-hui-hui*".

LITTLE OWLS

FOUR SPECIES

LITTLE OWL
Athene noctua

LENGTH: *190 to 230 mm*   MAP NUMBER: 117
DESCRIPTION: *Small, flat-headed; dark grey-brown to buff-brown with streaks and spots; yellow eyes*
DISTRIBUTION: *Europe, Central and Eastern Asia, North Africa, Middle East*
HABITAT: *Woodland, cultivation, parks, semi-desert*
EGGS: *2–8. Nest in tree hole or in wall*
STATUS: *Widespread and locally frequent to common*

Athene, the goddess who came forth from the supreme deity Zeus, embodied his divine wisdom. She symbolized victory in battle, fertility, and the lunar and menstrual cycles. In ancient Greece, Athene was seen as a goddess from across the sea, already linked to birds, and soon associated with the Acropolis in Athens. The Little Owl must have dwelt among the rocks and high buildings of the city for it became both a symbol of Athene, and her constant companion in legend.

Little Owls were released in battle to raise morale and were also linked to matriarchal societies which held

Athene in awe. The goddess was the opposing symbol of Dionysos, who represented mystical frenzy, drunkenness and debauchery. As a result, the Little Owl was also seen as an opponent of these states. It was thought that eating the egg of a Little Owl could ward off the spell of such influences and this belief spread through Europe. In time, it widened into the legend that the eating of owls and their eggs could cure gout and other ailments associated with persistent drunkenness.

The ancient linking of owls with wisdom also became widespread; the phrase 'wise old owl' remains common. Even in Africa, where owls are often associated with death and madness, witchcraft and doom, owl symbols are used in initiation ceremonies to indicate a transition from ignorance to wisdom.

In some societies, owls are said to ward off evil spirits and, in Britain, an owl nailed to a barn door was, until quite recently, accepted as a way to avoid troubles. In Germany, owls were once thought capable of calming lightning and preventing hailstorms. Elsewhere, rituals involving owls were thought to protect people from being bitten by a mad dog or dying of snake bite. Legends, some doom-laden, some more sanguine, have also evolved about the presence or calls of owls during pregnancy or childbirth.

Little Owls choose habitats which encourage these legends of the supernatural. They are often seen in places steeped in religious significance. They may be observed slipping quietly out of ancient ruins in Israel or, in Egypt, roosting in cavities high in the great Temple of Horus in Edfu, or at floodlit displays at the temples at Karnak or the Great Pyramids at Giza. The ancient Egyptians, a practical people who must have been familiar with owls in everyday life, nevertheless took them to be creatures of great power.

It is a far cry from the goddess Athene to the myths of an English village, where the species of owl became less significant than the general characteristics of an upright stance, round head, flat face and large, forward-facing eyes. The ability to blink with the upper eyelids adds one more human feature to the most anthropomorphized birds on earth. Yet it was not until the late 19th century that the Little Owl itself was introduced by man into England.

Its range already spread across mainland Europe, from Iberia north as far as Denmark, and east towards Asia. It was also found in Arabia, down the western side of the Red Sea, across the whole of North Africa and in isolated parts of the Sahara, and eastwards through the Himalayas and China, but not India. The introduced British population now thrives over much of England and Wales but only in the south-east corner of Scotland. The Little Owl was also introduced into New Zealand, several shipments being released between 1906 and 1910. It is now well established on South Island.

Little Owls live in regions of scattered trees, preferring old ones with cavities and holes where branches have snapped off. English parkland is ideal for them, as are rows of pollarded willows alongside lazy lowland rivers. In Central Europe, these owls love to perch in ancient oaks or sit on a grassy tussock in a rich green meadow. Farther south, they are birds of hotter, drier places where olives, cork oaks and palms grow from stony ground, and where ruins or clusters of fallen rocks create pockets of shade and concealment during the heat of the day.

The desert owls are paler, with more clearly defined patches on the neck that form false eyes, as if the bird is facing both ways at once. Western birds are a rather dark, liver brown with paler spots and white freckling on the forehead. The underparts are dull white, densely marked with smears, streaks and spots of brown. The face is pale, with severe dark and light eyebrows low over the glistening yellow eyes, giving the bird a typically fierce, quizzical or frowning expression.

Though seen often by day, perched on some prominent rock or branch, Little Owls hunt mostly at dusk or by night. If disturbed, they fly off quickly with deep, swooping undulations and quick bursts of their broad, rounded wings, before swooping steeply up to a new perch. Once in the open, they attract noisy flocks of small birds, which alternately buzz the head of the dreaded owl and then withdraw in fear to a safe distance from which to call loudly in alarm.

Little Owls nest in holes in trees and walls, especially in the mouldering carbuncles of pollarded willows and poplars. They lay three to five white eggs, but occasionally as few as two or as many as seven. There is no real nest but the male may scrape the litter in the hollow to smooth and soften a pad of decaying material on which the eggs are laid. The young hatch after a period of up to 29 days, to be fed initially by the male and later by both parents.

For much of the year, Little Owls eat invertebrates such as cockchafers, earwigs and moths, with a good many earthworms and a few small mammals. When they have young to feed, Little Owls take more small birds, particularly sparrows and thrushes. Most hunting is done from a perch from which the owl surveys its territory. A hunting Little Owl has an intent, determined air as it bobs about, peering at the ground.

Much of what seems to be the bulk of an owl is its thick layer of soft feathers, and a hot Little Owl in Spain, or a busy one in Britain, can look sleek and slim. However, an owl resting in daytime may look as round as a ball with just two tiny legs raising its rotund form above the perch.

Little Owls frequently perch out of sight in the foliage of a tree and call loudly with beautifully musical and far-carrying calls. A single, liquid "*kiew*" or "*quilp*", or a yelping, rising and repeated sound described as "*wherrow*" are the most familiar. In Britain, at least, the calls of Little Owls are seldom so readily identified as the hoots and contact calls of Tawny Owls (*Strix aluco*), or the shrieks of Barn Owls (*Tyto alba*). They are also less easily put into words or imitated than those of the more traditional owls of the English countryside.

The chicks make loud, hissing sounds and, if angry, Little Owls snap their bills with a loud, hollow click. The song is used by the male in early spring to define his territory and several competing males may be heard calling in all directions when seeking a mate in March. The female shrieks a reply and pairs often call in a synchronized duet.

Territories in England may be a mere 90 acres (35ha) and pairs may nest only a few hundreds yards apart. Pairs of Little Owls may sometimes share a barn with Barn Owls and even Kestrels (*Falco tinnunculus*), but they tend to avoid territories of the larger Tawny Owl, which anyway prefers more wooded districts. Little Owls across most of their range will, once mature and well-established, spend their lives within the confines of a small territory.

Little Owl (*Athene noctua*)

SPOTTED LITTLE OWL
Athene brama

LENGTH: *190 to 210 mm*   MAP NUMBER: 118
DESCRIPTION: *Small, flat-headed; barred below*
DISTRIBUTION: *Southern Asia*
HABITAT: *Open woodland, cultivation, villages*
EGGS: *3—5. Nest in hole in tree or wall*
STATUS: *Locally common*

This bird virtually replaces the more northerly Little Owl (*Athene noctua*) in a range which runs from Iran across the whole of India (except Sri Lanka) to Burma and Indochina. Visitors to the great Indian national parks, such as Bharatpur, will find Spotted Little Owls peering at them from overhanging branches, or looking out comically from beneath a shaky roof or through a hole in a ruined wall.

The Spotted Little Owl is similar to the Little Owl but has clearer white areas on the face and underparts, and less complex patterns on the underparts in the form of short, neat, crescent-shaped barring. This bird is common, particularly in India, and is found in gardens and parks, cultivated areas with scattered trees and open, bushy places, as well as the extremes of semi-desert and moist forest. They usually prefer mango groves and orchards, overgrown ruins and the outskirts of villages. The species can be found to altitudes of about 5,000 feet (1,500m) above sea level in the Himalayan foothills.

These birds are most active at dusk and dawn, preferring to spend the hours of daylight hidden away in a hole in a banyan, mango or tamarind tree. A tap on the trunk of almost any old tree will bring the round, surprised face of a Spotted Little Owl to the entrance of a hole, or put one or two to flight from a hidden cavity. They often dash out and perch in the open on a nearby tree, concerned not with concealment but with assessing the intrusion by twisting and turning their heads and bobbing up and down in the typical, charming way of *Athene* owls, trying to see the problem from every angle. If a Spotted Little Owl is abroad by day, it will be mobbed ceaselessly by small birds.

Family groups of Spotted Little Owls remain together for long periods and can be found in parties of three or four more often than Little Owls. They breed from February to April, laying up to five eggs in a hole in a tree or old stone wall. Both members of a pair incubate the eggs and feed the growing brood of hungry chicks.

Spotted Little Owls behave very like Little Owls; they are active and alert, they perch upright and fly from place to place with a quick, but deeply undulating action. They watch carefully for prey and drop to the ground to take it in their strong feet, which are equipped with needle-sharp claws. The victim may be an earthworm, a beetle or a lizard. For variety, a small mouse might be caught or even a small bird while it sleeps. Insects are often hawked in the air around street lights or fires, and flying termites are caught in the feet. The owls will take larger items back to a favourite perch, where they feel safe, and dismember them at leisure, holding the prey with one foot and tearing it with their bill, in a parrot-like fashion.

The breeding season is the best time to listen for the calls of Spotted Little Owls, but they are quite vocal all the year round. They produce a variety of notes, all more or less discordant, and a rapid, harsh, screechy chatter or churr is among the most common.

FOREST SPOTTED OWL
Athene blewitti

LENGTH: *230 mm*   MAP NUMBER: 119
DESCRIPTION: *Dark, short-winged little owl*
DISTRIBUTION: *Central India*
HABITAT: *Moist forest*
STATUS: *Endangered, if not extinct*

The story of the Forest Spotted Owl is a sad one. Always rare, it was once thinly distributed over a substantial area of India. Today, however, there is doubt whether it still exists; if not already extinct, it may soon be so. Slightly larger but shorter winged than the Spotted Little Owl (*Athene brama*), it is known to be more diurnal but much shyer. It keeps itself to itself in dense, moist deciduous forest and native mango, seeming to favour the neighbourhood of streams. Little more is known about other details of its behaviour.

It was once recorded as 'not uncommon' in the dense jungle of West Khandesh but recent searches have failed to locate it there. The bird was known from the Tapti River, 125 miles (200km) north of Bombay, and in the area eastwards to Sambalpur. There have also been reports from Madhya Pradesh. After special expeditions failed to track down the Forest Spotted Owl, it was thought that it no longer existed. However, hopes for its survival were raised in 1968 when a bird identified as this species was photographed. This was the first report since a Forest Spotted Owl was collected near Bombay in 1914. Even that was only the sixth specimen ever taken.

BURROWING OWL
Athene cunicularia

LENGTH: *200 to 260 mm*   MAP NUMBER: 120
DESCRIPTION: *Small, flat-headed; mottled and barred; long, spindly legs; yellow eyes*
DISTRIBUTION: *North, Central and South America*
HABITAT: *Open grassland*
EGGS: *2–11. Nest in burrow in ground*
STATUS: *Locally threatened, declining*

Few owls are so characterful as the Burrowing Owl. Its long legs, upright stance yet rounded, dumpy shape form a caricature of the Little Owl (*Athene noctua*). This bird wears an intense frown and a look of impatience, even distrust. The white eyebrows are flattened down over large yellow eyes which, like those of so many owls, appear dark at a distance under the shadow of the brows, unless the light is low and full on the face. The Burrowing Owl will be rounded and squat one moment and, the next, become upright, taut and alert, bobbing and twisting its head. It may stand looking back over a shoulder, or rest comfortably on one leg with its head drawn in, trying not to doze off in the sunshine. Once placed in a separate genus, *Speotyto*, the Burrowing Owl is now recognized as one of the *Athene* species.

Burrowing Owls have a surprisingly large range. In the north, where they are summer visitors, their distribution stretches as far as southern Alberta and Saskatchewan in Canada. A broad band over the western United States covers the Great Plains and the Great Basin and there is also an isolated population, with a special race, in Florida and on the Bahamas. Some of the Caribbean islands are also occupied. The whole of Central America is home to these owls, as well as the greater part of South America, though not Tierra del Fuego and the Amazon forests. At least 18 races are recognized in this vast area of distribution.

Within this range, the owl is restricted to its particular habitat of open, treeless grassland. Its natural range includes short-grass prairies, sagebrush heath, deserts and semi-deserts, llanos and tropical savanna grasslands, the great pampas in the south and alpine grasslands high in the Andes. The Burrowing Owl is now also often found on farming and ranching land, in forest clearings, on the grassy surrounds of airports, in the rough of golf courses and even in suburbia where there is undisturbed grass or an area of quiet, open parkland.

This is a bird of the ground, unusually so for an owl. The Burrowing Owl both roosts and nests in holes in the ground. Other owls may do so occasionally, but no other species is so strictly tied to such a habitat. As its name suggests, this owl is able to dig burrows but it mainly takes over holes made by small mammals. The same burrow may be used for nesting for several years in succession. But, despite folk tales to the contrary, the burrows are not shared with prairie dogs or rattlesnakes, with which the Burrowing Owl does not get on well.

It also differs from most other species in being colonial. Up to ten or a dozen pairs nest in loose association. The nest chamber itself may be a yard or so below ground and the clutch of eggs seems to be extremely variable, between two and 11 in number. With an average of over six eggs, the clutch is the biggest of any raptorial bird in North America. The eggs are incubated by both adult birds in turn for four weeks.

Burrowing Owls resemble Little Owls in general behaviour and, like them, they explore visual images and sounds from various angles. The owls bob and turn and twist their heads to judge the exact distance to any intruder or prey. They fly briefly, low and fast, with bursts of wingbeats and swooping glides.

Their prey includes a variety of insects, especially large, crunchy beetles and Jerusalem crickets, small rodents such as kangaroo rats and voles, and small birds. They tend to hunt most actively at dusk, and at sunrise and sunset, but occasionally search by day and through the night. Moths and lizards may be caught in the hour or two before midday. Burrowing Owls are most active by day in the cool of spring and autumn and are at their least diurnal during the heat of midsummer. They hunt either from a perch, or by aerial chasing or by hovering above the ground until a suitable creature appears, to be snatched up in their sharp claws.

The song of the male Burrowing Owl is heard in courtship and in defence of a territory. It gives two notes, "*coo cooo*", of almost even pitch. In parts of the West Indies, the owl is known as '*el cucu*'. Intruders are greeted with a six-note alarm call but the most disconcerting of the calls is given by the young in the nest. This is a rasping rattle very like the sound of a threatening rattlesnake. However, this is more likely to be coincidence than adaptive mimicry as chicks of other species, such as the Northern Saw-whet Owl (*Aegolius acadicus*), produce similar sounds from trees, far from rattlesnakes.

Nesting attempts by Burrowing Owls frequently end in failure and up to half the nests may be deserted. Studies in the United States have shown that they use the burrows of prairie dogs, ground squirrels and badgers. Burrows with short grass and good visibility are preferred. The prairie dogs and squirrels crop the vegetation by constant nibbling and so provide the owls with a better view of both prey and predators. Short grass may also mean a greater number of small rodents for the owls to feed on. Badgers leave a longer growth, to the disadvantage of the owls. At the same time, the badgers from nearby burrows may raid the nests of the owls, causing a large number of failures.

Other pairs may desert their nests because there are too many Burrowing Owls competing in too small an area. This may be precipitated by adverse weather and a slump in the numbers of the small mammals that form their chief prey in the spring. Later in the summer, the owls switch to insects. Studies have concluded that nests lined with livestock dung are less prone to predation than others, the odour obscuring the tell-tale smell of the owls. If dung was removed, the owls replaced it. Burrowing Owls and Short-eared Owls (*Asio flammeus*) are the only owl species which are known to actually carry material of any kind to line the nest. There is, interestingly, a recent record of a Burrowing Owl nesting above ground.

In the Great Basin, west of the Rocky Mountains, where the Burrowing Owl is a widespread visitor in summer, it may be more common in the sagebrush areas than was supposed, as well as in the typical grasslands. Studies made just after dawn in the early summer revealed far more owls than were believed to be present. At that hour, the owls perched on small bushes, basking in the early sunlight. At other times, a bird so fond of perching quietly on the ground is easy to miss.

Although the area of distribution is so large, the best habitat in the north is now more restricted than ever. The cultivation of the plains has deprived the Burrowing Owl of much of its range. Campaigns in the United States early this century to eradicate prairie dogs wiped out Burrowing Owls in many areas, reducing the overall population. In much of South America, a decline in numbers was noted as long ago as the early 19th century and that decline continues. Sheep introduced onto Tierra del Fuego have trampled burrows there and caused the owls to move out. Clearances of forest have helped Burrowing Owls in some places but rodent control has often set them back again almost immediately.

To see a bird so full of life, so amusing and fascinating to watch, it is worth seeking out those places that still offer small colonies a good living in the unique prairie communities of small mammals and birds that have evolved such close relationships.

Burrowing Owl (*Athene cunicularia*)

WOOD OWLS

—— EIGHTEEN SPECIES IN TWO GENERA ——

MOTTLED OWL
Ciccaba virgata

LENGTH: *350 mm*   MAP NUMBER: 121
DESCRIPTION: *Dark grey-brown head and upperparts,
speckled white; underparts white, streaked; dark eyes*
DISTRIBUTION: *Mexico, Central and South America*
HABITAT: *Tropical forest, plantations, open woods*
EGGS: *2. Nest in tree hole or bird of prey nest*
STATUS: *Uncertain, locally common*

The *Ciccaba* genus is generally believed to include only five species. Four are found in a range from Mexico deep into South America while the African Wood Owl (*Ciccaba woodfordii*) is widespread across its own continent. Like the *Spizaetus* hawk eagles, the *Ciccaba* wood owl species have been seen as proof of past links between South America and Africa, and the subsequent continental drift. Other authorities have suggested that such links would have produced more closely-related birds than only these two small groups. In any case, the Mottled Owl could arguably be included in the genus *Strix*.

The genus *Ciccaba* could be described as an artifical grouping of separate species. The African member is perhaps not more closely related to the South American ones than to many northern Eurasian birds. In one important respect, the structure of its ears, the Mottled Owl is clearly a *Ciccaba* type, lacking the complex aural system of the *Strix* species. But it does have the asymmetry of ears so typical of the latter.

In its behaviour and place in the ecology of the tropical forests, the Mottled Owl is the equivalent of the more northerly Barred Owl (*Strix varia*) and Fulvous Owl (*Strix fulvescens*). Birds of the *Ciccaba* group resemble the Tawny Owl (*Strix aluco*) in general shape, having round heads without ear tufts and large, open faces, well-defined facial discs, quite upright but broad bodies and short legs. Their wings and tail are moderately long but not striking. They are, indeed, quite 'average' owls. The South American birds, however, are not well-known.

The Mottled Owl is a neat, attractive bird, dark liver-brown above and white beneath, with dark streaks. The mottled chest contrasts with the clearer streaks on a whiter ground lower down on the underparts. The tail is usually clearly barred. The owl has huge, dark eyes, set rather centrally in a domed head. The irises are dark brown with a purple sheen but, in dim light, the pupils are so wide open that the eyes look all black. The eyebrows, the back-to-back C-shapes beside the bill and the lower rims of the

facial disc are white, producing a quizzical look.

This owl is widespread with eight recognized races and a number of colour variations around the basic theme. Some owls are more tawny-buff below, some more or less white in the markings on the upperparts, while others are marked buff and even orange on a redder background. The presence of light and dark types in the same area is akin to the variation often seen in Eurasian *Strix* owls.

Mottled Owls are fairly common across their wide range. They occur on both sides of the Sierra Madre in northern Mexico, throughout Central America and are found west of the Andes in Colombia and Ecuador and east of the Andes from the Colombian lowlands to the mouth of the Amazon River and southwards over the Mato Grosso to the coast of Santa Catarina in Brazil. They occupy forest habitats in humid lowlands as well as more open places with scattered woods or plantations and cultivated regions with remnants of woodlands and shelterbelts. In Colombia they live in forests, usually occupying the area from the middle of the tree canopy to the topmost branches.

In Venezuela, they occupy a wide range of habitats, from rain-forest or the humid cloud-forest in the mountains to the lower deciduous woods, thickets, mangroves and even open fields. Although essentially a lowland species, the Mottled Owl is found in Guatemala at heights of 7,200 feet (2,200m) above sea level.

These owls live solitary lives, except when breeding. Strictly nocturnal, they are among the 40 or so owls in the world that can claim to be birds of the deep night. So, despite their frequent occurrence, they are little-known. Their prey is made up largely of small rodents but is probably varied with small birds, insects and reptiles. What little is recorded suggests that the bird is a versatile, opportunistic feeder rather than a specialist.

The nest site is selected from holes in trees or old nests of birds of prey. It is often around 25 feet (7—8m) above the ground. Territories are established with frequent calls, variously described as a rather deep hoot or a rising, whistling screech. In Colombia, the call is a resonant "*whooou*". This is usually repeated two or three times and sometimes in sequences of five or six notes. More rarely, a cat-like scream is heard. In Panama, the call of the Mottled Owl is a more screeching "*keeooweeyo*", with an occasional gruff growl. In Mexico, the typical call is a series of four low, short, widely-spaced hoots, the last one being softer and lower.

This is one of the most vocal of the larger South American owls and may respond to imitations of its calls by calling back and flying towards the mimicking observer. Two dull white eggs are laid in April or May but few details have been documented about the breeding cycle. One nest has been found, on the abandoned old nest of another bird, deep in a hole in a tree.

Black And White Owl
Ciccaba nigrolineata

LENGTH: *350 to 380 mm*   MAP NUMBER: 122
DESCRIPTION: *Very dark black-brown, barred white on upper back and breast; dark eyes; yellow bill and feet*
DISTRIBUTION: *Mexico to Ecuador*
HABITAT: *Forest edge and clearings, damp woods*
EGGS: *1—2. Nest in tree hole or old stick nest*
STATUS: *Uncertain*

A round-faced, dark owl with light brown eyes, the Black and White Owl lives in forests from southern Mexico south to western Ecuador. It is sooty black-brown above and on the face, with a slight, mottled, pale line above each eye. It has a noticeable black bib and underparts closely barred with black. This owl is less brown than the Mottled Owl (*Ciccaba virgata*) and is barred crosswise below, rather than streaked. Its feet and bill are a rather bright orange-yellow.

A single race of this owl occupies its entire range. In Panama, the owl lives in forests and the edges of forest clearings and has been recorded at 6,500 feet (2,000m), but it is largely nocturnal and seldom seen. In Colombia, the Black and White Owl is found locally in similar habitats to heights at least 5,000 feet (1,500m) above sea level. In Venezuela, the bird is rare, living in rain-forests and clearings from sea level to altitudes of 3,000 feet (900m).

The Black and White Owl is a bird of the middle and higher branches of forest trees. It lives a solitary life, or roosts with its mate close by. This bird seems to prefer wet places, as do other *Ciccaba* owls, with a particular liking for riversides and woodland with a swampy or flooded floor. Perhaps such damp conditions help provide the rotten stumps of old trees that have suitable holes for nesting, or possibly these conditions produce a larger supply of prey. Its food is a variety of small rodents, insects such as cicadas and beetles, and even some bats.

The call is variously described and appears to vary across its range. It has been noted as loud and high-pitched, like a long "*who-ab*". In Panama, the call is described as a long, nasal "*oo-web*" with a marked upward inflection, rather quieter than the similar call of the Mottled Owl. Another call is a more explosive, sharper sound which is often repeated; in Panama, this is a deep, resonant and deliberate "*whoof, whoof, whoof*". Birds tape-recorded in Colombia have a rising and falling scream which becomes strained and cat-like, as well as a deeply resonant "*hu, hu, hu hoo-ah*" and a series of perhaps nine to 14 "*hoo-ah*" notes, with an occasional single, deep "*boo*".

Little is known of the breeding behaviour of the Black and White Owl, but it lays one or two white eggs in a tree hole or in the old stick nest of another bird high in a tree. The young of all the *Ciccaba* owls grow a sequence of plumages before they eventually become adult.

BLACK-BANDED OWL
Ciccaba huhula

LENGTH: *350 mm*   MAP NUMBER: 123
DESCRIPTION: *Wholly barred dark brown and white; yellow bill; orange eyes*
DISTRIBUTION: *Northern and central South America*
HABITAT: *Rain-forest and plantations*
STATUS: *Uncertain, probably generally scarce*

The South American *Ciccaba* owls are all closely related and some ornithologists prefer to group Black-banded Owls and Black and White Owls (*Ciccaba nigrolineata*) as a single species. The Black-banded Owl is a splendid creature. Although it has none of the vivid contrasts of colour and striking patterns of some owls, it has a complex, delicate colouring and a perfection of detail which must be seen at close range to be appreciated fully.

Its eyes are orange and the bill and feet are yellow. The plumage has close barring of white on black; the white barring is a little wider on the underparts than on the upperparts and the tail has several narrow white bars with a broader white tip.

The survival of this species offers a grain of hope for other South American owls, since it is a bird of the rain-forest that in some areas has managed to adapt to man-made habitats. Although it can be found in coffee and banana plantations, it remains essentially a forest owl. The destruction of the rain-forest and its replacement by monocultures and ranch land almost certainly pose a threat to this species.

The Black-banded Owl lives in the Amazon basin and is quite widely distributed from Guiana to southern Brazil. In Colombia, the owl is known only from a handful of specimens and infrequent encounters in the wild, but it is assumed, probably correctly, to be widely distributed in the forest. In Venezuela, it is found in clearings within the rain-forest to a height of 660 feet (200m) above sea level. Very little is recorded about its diet or breeding biology.

Its voice is well-described, being a rising cat-like scream followed by a loud hoot, "*whoeeruh, booo*"; there is also a deep, resonant "*hu hu hu HOOOO*". At times its voice is identical to that of the Black and White Owl, and they routinely respond to each other's calls.

RUFOUS-BANDED OWL
Ciccaba albitarsus

LENGTH: *300 mm*   MAP NUMBER: 124
DESCRIPTION: *Barred rufous-brown and orange-buff; dark brown eyes*
DISTRIBUTION: *Northern Andes*
HABITAT: *Humid temperate mountain forest*
STATUS: *Uncertain, probably threatened*

This is the high-level, Andean mountain equivalent of the lowland Black-banded Owl (*Ciccaba huhula*). The Rufous-banded Owl is found in humid forest at heights of up to 12,000 feet (3,700m) above sea level in Venezuela, Colombia, Ecuador, Peru and Bolivia. The altitude keeps the forest cool, and it is therefore much more temperate than tropical. The mountains are kept moist by the daily condensation of cloud around the high hills, producing an eerie, yet magnificent, landscape in remote and difficult regions. Small wonder that this bird is so little known and little understood.

In Venezuela, the Rufous-banded Owl occurs in open spaces, between the forests, where there are scattered trees. Everywhere it appears to be rare, and a prize for any visiting ornithologist. It has a clear white throat and buff-white eyebrows and feathering beside the bill. The chest is dark brown, barred and spotted with a rusty or tawny colour and white, creating a distinct band across the chest. The rest of the underparts are marked with silvery-white in squared spots, unlike the streaky pattern of the similar

Mottled Owl (*Ciccaba virgata*).

Birds whose calls have been recorded in Colombia gave deep, resonant notes with a deliberate pattern repeated at eight- to 11-second intervals. The sound is "*hu, hu-hu-hu, HOOOa*". This differs in rhythm from the basically similar call of the Black-banded Owl. In Venezuela, local names such as Borococo and Surrucuco are thought to be imitations of the call.

The species is nocturnal, and presumably eats a variety of insects and small mammals. Practically nothing is recorded about its breeding behaviour. It is to be hoped that this owl survives the depredations of its forest habitat and receives full scientific study.

AFRICAN WOOD OWL
Ciccaba (Strix) woodfordii

LENGTH: *350 mm*   MAP NUMBER: 125
DESCRIPTION: *Large, brown head; spotted brown upperparts, barred lower underparts; dark brown eyes*
DISTRIBUTION: *Africa south of the Sahara*
HABITAT: *Forest and open woodland*
EGGS: *1–3. Nest in hole or old bird of prey nest in tree*
STATUS: *Widespread, common*

This is the only member of the small *Ciccaba* genus which is found outside the New World and so might offer evidence of past links between South America and Africa. Some recent authorities, however, have placed the African Wood Owl in the genus *Strix*.

The African Wood Owl, very similar to its South American counterparts, is of medium-large size with a rounded, cowled head and big, dark, pink-rimmed eyes surrounded by a smudge of dusky brown. The dark neck and upper chest contrast with the rest of the underparts, which are barred. The owl has a fairly long, barred tail, white scapular spots and a white area around the bill and between the eyes. This broadens out into a blunt, short V at the top and widens to a broad triangle at the bottom, an hour-glass pattern shared with many owls.

This is the common African forest owl south of the Sahara. Five races are recognized and there is some variation in colour, with blackish and more rufous types. The rain-forest birds are redder than those of drier woods. African Wood Owls replace the common *Strix* species, such as the Tawny Owl (*Strix aluco*), which live in the woods of Europe and much of temperate Asia.

This species is common in a range from Senegal and Gambia east through the coastal forests of West Africa and in a broad swathe to Ethiopia, Kenya and south to the Cape. However, it is absent from sizeable parts of Tanzania, Zimbabwe, Botswana, Namibia and South Africa. African Wood Owls prefer forest but only the edges of the denser tracts of rain-forest, and also survive well in plantations and strips of woodland along watercourses. They can be found at sea level and up to altitudes of at least 12,000 feet (3,700m), in habitats ranging from wild, undamaged forest to the suburbs of towns. It is clearly a successful and adaptable bird.

The African Wood Owl is rarely seen at dusk, being one of the most nocturnal of owls, and is best located by listening for its calls as full darkness sets in. After roosting in tangled creepers, or among thick leaves high in a tree, an African Wood Owl leans forward, blinks and stretches one wing at a time with evident enjoyment. After fanning its tail and loosening up for the night's activities, it moves to a more open perch and begins to call.

Tape-recordings of these calls, used judiciously, may help to attract a bird into visual range. On some occasions, several may be drawn. The quick, aggressive response shows the importance of regular calling in keeping each pair within their boundaries. The owls can even be drawn out of their forest habitat into dry bush which they would not normally enter, so determined are they to see off their rivals. In the bush, they are extremely clumsy, crashing noisily through the scrub, probably unable to see the detail of these unfamiliar surroundings. In the forests, which they know intimately, African Wood Owls move about silently and easily.

Curiously, for a nocturnal bird, the calls are sometimes heard in the late afternoon in full daylight. They are usually given from the top of the forest canopy. Both sexes have a series of rapid hoots, those of the female being the more high-pitched. The calls begin loudly and evenly but fade away into an uneven rhythm – "*whu-whu-whu whu-uh uh-uh-uh*". The female also utters a high "*wheeow*", which is often answered by a low hoot from the nearby male. Like several other species, the pair will call together but the performance may vary from a co-ordinated duet to a much less organized series of overlapping hoots.

The African Wood Owl watches for prey from a perch and swoops down to gather it with broad feet and sharp claws. It may chase the prey after an initial near-miss. In the depths of a gloomy forest, dark even by day, it is unlikely that this owl sees much prey but it can pinpoint the sounds of insects and rodents with its sharp hearing. The broad dish of its face helps to focus the slightest sound into its large, sensitive ears. This owl shows a degree of adaptability by catching flying insects in the air and snatching insect prey from leaves as it flies past. Typically, it moves just 200 to 300 yards (200–300m) in the course of a night's hunting.

The bulk of the food is made up of insects, ranging from katydids, crickets, grasshoppers and mantises to cockroaches, moths, wasps and beetles. Being fairly large, the African Wood Owl is capable of taking a variety of small mammals, frogs and snakes and various small birds, or the young of larger birds such as doves. Now and then, it captures an adult bird as large as a Speckled Pigeon (*Columba guinea*).

African Wood Owls roost alone or in pairs, using regular sites over long periods. Each member of a pair has a number of roosts which are used in turn. After the young have fledged, the whole family may sometimes be found roosting together in a close huddle. The roost site is often betrayed by accumulated droppings but the pellets contain few bones and quickly break up. They rarely form noticeable piles, even beneath regular perches. It takes a

lot to disturb an African Wood Owl from its roost and, if it does fly off, it soon attracts a flock of small birds making loud scolding calls.

A pair will occupy a territory all year, needing about 125 acres (50ha) of forest for their needs. They call each night to announce their presence and to reinforce their claims to the territory. As the breeding season approaches, the calls become more frequent and continue throughout the night. The owls choose a nest hole in a tree, often where a large branch has fallen and left a rotten cavity in the bole. It is frequently only six to 13 feet (2–4m) above the ground.

More rarely, the nest may be at the base of a tree, in a hollow in the fallen leaves and twigs on the forest floor, or higher up in the deserted nest of a large bird of prey. In a tree cavity, a few leaves and flakes of bark are used to line the rough hollow and provide a softer bed for the eggs. Both nest sites and roosts have been found next to bees' nests, which may provide a degree of protection against genets and baboons.

Usually two eggs are laid, but occasionally one or three. Often, and always in dense forest, only one chick is raised.

The female incubates the eggs, each taking 31 days to hatch. Although the male feeds her at the nest, she may leave it for lengthy spells to hunt for herself. The chick is inactive by day but climbs about the cavity at night. The young are tended by the female, although the male brings food and both adults guard the nest. If a predator, such as a genet, approaches, an adult owl will perform a distraction display, feigning injury by calling weakly and fluttering down to the ground in an effort to lead the predator away. This is equally valuable when the young have left the nest but are unable to fly. They leave the nest after 23 to 37 days and fly well when 46 days old.

The young owl will remain as long as possible with its parents, which may eventually have to chase it off when they next begin to breed. It is essential for the youngster to establish a territory with plenty of food and to master its terrain. Without this security, it will face hardship; many young African Wood Owls die during their first year. As most territories are already occupied by dominant adults, which remain there all the year round, the opportunities for the newcomer are slim indeed.

HUME'S TAWNY OWL
Strix butleri

LENGTH: *330 mm*   MAP NUMBER: 126
DESCRIPTION: *Rounded, barred and streaked owl; pale orange eyes*
DISTRIBUTION: *Middle East*
HABITAT: *Desert wadis, oases*
EGGS: *5. Nest in rock cavity*
STATUS: *Uncertain, rare and localized*

Until quite recently this was claimed to be one of the world's least-known owls, but a number of regular sites, if not actual nests, have at last been located in Israel. One nest has been discovered and watched and the birds have been photographed. Some have even been kept in captivity. Studies have dismantled the theory that Hume's Tawny Owl may be a desert race of the Tawny Owl (*Strix aluco*). It is clearly a desert species of the genus *Strix*, which is certainly remarkable, given that the *Strix* species are essentially woodland owls.

It is thought to be fairly widespread in the Middle East, from Israel south-east to Saudi Arabia. In February 1982, it was recorded in Egypt, 33 miles (54km) west of the Red Sea. This first record of the bird from the continent of Africa raised the possibility that it may be resident in the Egyptian desert. By 1981 it was known from 27 sites in Israel and from four sites in Sinai.

At Ein Gedi beside the Dead Sea in Israel, the owl feeds around palm groves and near floodlights which attract moths. It perches on tall posts and has been watched hawking insects like a round-winged nightjar. In other areas it prefers desert gorges close to water, which is apparently present at all known sites.

This is a pale, sandy brown owl with a golden-brown nape, very pale underparts, a buff facial disc and orange eyes outlined with black. Some birds have a more golden tone than others. Its toes, in contrast to those of a Tawny Owl, are unfeathered apart from a few wisps of hair-like plumes and a silky feathering on the underside.

The call is variously described. It has been reported to resemble that of a Tawny Owl in quality, in the form of a single, long, even note, although without the typical quavering of a Tawny Owl. It is also described as a hoot followed by two shorter, double notes – "*hoooo huhu huhu*". An agitated call, given in response to a tape recording or when another owl is nearby, has been written as "*hu-hu-hu-hu-hu-hu-hu*"; it lasts for two or three seconds. Two birds have been heard calling in duet. One report from the southern tip of Israel, a hot wilderness of dry wadis and scattered acacias, described a series of 12 notes, sometimes 13, given at dusk. The notes increased slightly in speed and, more noticeably, in volume. The final note was lower and suddenly cut short. The sound had a deep, slightly booming but rather muffled quality – "*hu hu hu hu hu hu hu BU BU BU BU b*" – and was unlike any Tawny Owl call in pattern or sound.

The flight of Hume's Tawny Owl when hunting is said to be silent, agile and even butterfly-like. At times it certainly flies with markedly arched wings. It seems to eat mainly small rodents, and several have been killed by cars at night, so it probably feeds regularly by roadsides. The rock gerbil is likely to be the mainstay of its diet, with insects adding variety but less bulk.

The nest must normally be in a small cave or rock crevice but the full details of its breeding biology remain to be discovered. The first nest to be studied was found in 1974, in a well at Nahal Sekher, in the western Negev. Five eggs were laid, early in May. The chicks were in the nest for 28 days, and greater Egyptian gerbils formed two-thirds of their diet; they were also fed on Tristram's jirds and lesser jerboas. The adult male was later killed by an Eagle Owl (*Bubo bubo*).

This owl is said to be the bird mentioned in Leviticus and the Book of Isaiah, the Lilith Midbar or desert Lilith, a female demon that haunted wild wadis and gorges before Adam and Eve were created. The species was first described scientifically from Baluchistan in 1878 but, for many decades, little else was learned.

The first specimen, which remains the most easterly record, was obtained by a Mr Nash, who passed it to Captain E.A. Butler, a naturalist and expert taxidermist, who handed it to the ornithologist and game hunter, Allan Hume, founder of the Indian National Congress. Hume named the bird after Butler, who had made a sizeable contribution to ornithology in India, but, in popular literature, it has remained Hume's Tawny Owl. Poor Nash was virtually forgotten.

Hume is remembered for several other birds as well but suffered the tragedy of having 25 years' notes and correspondence for a definitive volume on Indian birds accidentally sold as waste paper in his absence. His interest in ornithology died with the project.

Hume's Tawny Owl (*Strix butleri*)

SPOTTED WOOD OWL
Strix seloputo

LENGTH: *400 to 450 mm*   MAP NUMBER: 127
DESCRIPTION: *Dark red-brown, spotted white, barred below; dark eyes*
DISTRIBUTION: *South-East Asia*
HABITAT: *Lowland forest and woodland*
EGGS: *1–2. Nest in tree hole*
STATUS: *Uncertain but appears common*

To see this bird of the lowlands, the ornithologist must travel to the South-East Asian mainland (Indo-China, south Burma and Malaysia) or to the islands of Java, Bawean in the Java Sea and Palawan, west of the Philippines. This is an unusual distribution, as Borneo (between Bawean and Palawan) and Sumatra (between Java and Malaysia) are large and noticeable gaps in its range.

The Spotted Wood Owl lives in fairly open country with scattered woods, copses and belts of trees in farmland. It is striking in appearance, with big, brown eyes in a round, buff face and attractively patterned plumage of grey-brown, white, black and buff. It is largely nocturnal but sometimes hunts before sunset.

Because of its ability to cope with unnatural and semi-natural habitats, this is not a rare bird. It may even be found in town parks and gardens; indeed, it is one of many owls that have learned to live close to human communities, perhaps simply by ignoring the noise and activities of people around them.

Its calls include a series of low, musical notes that end with a longer, deeper hoot. It eats insects, notably large and nutritious beetles. Little is known in detail of its nesting behaviour but it lays a small clutch of one or two eggs. The nest is usually in a hole in a tree; rarely in a crude stick nest of some other bird in the fork of a tree.

MOTTLED WOOD OWL
Strix ocellata

LENGTH: *380 to 460 mm*   MAP NUMBER: 128
DESCRIPTION: *Closely barred; broad white throat band; dark eyes*
DISTRIBUTION: *India, western Burma*
HABITAT: *Open woods, cultivated areas, plantations*
EGGS: *1–3. Nest in hole*
STATUS: *Uncertain, locally common*

The name of this owl hardly conveys the complexity of pattern and exquisite detail of its plumage. Like the Great Grey Owl (*Strix nebulosa*), it has a facial disc lined with fine, concentric rings around the eyes, which are large and dark. A broad white throat patch is strikingly clear and the underparts are marked with orange-buff on white, all overlain with fine dark bars. The upperside is a mixture of brown and white in a finely barred and streaked pattern, with larger spots of white and orange-buff. In flight, large areas of yellowish-buff are distinctive.

Mottled Wood Owls can be found in western Burma and across most of India, from a height of 2,600 feet (800m) in the north to sea level on the plains, in all kinds of open woodland and plantations. There are three races. The Mottled Wood Owl of Saurashtra is the largest, the northern race being rather small and paler, while the southern race is small and darker. Northern Mottled Wood Owls live in mangos and groves of ancient, densely foliaged banyans and tamarinds, often beside cultivated land and close to villages. In the south, similar habitats are occupied over the Indian plains, where the bird is a common and widespread resident.

Pairs roost together by day, well hidden in thick foliage. If disturbed, they fly well and far, if need be, swooping up into the canopy of another thick tree, unlike eagle owls (*Bubo spp*) which tend to settle on a side branch. At dusk and dawn, Mottled Wood Owls give loud, eerie calls. These are described as *"chuhua-aa"* during the breeding season. At other times, their calls are a simpler, mellow hoot or a sharp screech.

Being quite large owls, they are capable of killing birds up to the size of a pigeon. Their main food, however, is rats and mice, with a variety of insects, crabs and lizards. The nest is an unlined hole in a tree, where two, and occasionally three, creamy-white eggs are laid between November and April.

BROWN WOOD OWL
Strix leptogrammica

LENGTH: *460 to 530 mm*   MAP NUMBER: 129
DESCRIPTION: *Large, dark brown, spotted white; orange face; dark eyes*
DISTRIBUTION: *India, south China, South-East Asia*
HABITAT: *Highland and lowland forest*
EGGS: *2. Nest in tree or on ground*
STATUS: *Uncertain, locally common*

This is the most widely distributed *Strix* owl in South-East Asia. It occupies a vast range from the Himalayas and India to the edge of the East China Sea, south to the Malaysian peninsula, Sumatra, Java, Borneo, Hainan, Taiwan and many other islands.

There are no fewer than 15 recognized races. Some have extensive ranges of their own, while others are restricted to single, small islands. It is possible that further study would show some of these races to be closely related species. A process of isolation and speciation may well be occurring, in the same way that scops owls have evolved in different ways in the same region.

The birds of Indonesia are smaller than other races, but all are essentially dark brown owls marked with bright orange-buff. The head is very dark with tiny white speckles, and the face is a warm orange-buff edged with dark brown. The chest has thick dark barring and is spotted with buff, while the lower underparts are whiter with finer blackish barring. Brown Wood Owls lack the complex outer ears so characteristic of *Strix* owls and perhaps should be grouped with the ill-defined tropical genus *Ciccaba*.

Brown Wood Owls manage to take advantage of the variety of woodland habitats within their range. These include the remaining rain-forests of Borneo, the lowland forests and woodlands of India and the evergreen forests found in the Himalayas up to at least 9,200 feet (2,800m) above sea level. On occasion, Brown Wood Owls have been recorded as high as 13,000 feet (4,000m).

Nocturnal in their habits, Brown Wood Owls roost in pairs, well-hidden in dense foliage. They are difficult to see because, disturbed by the slightest sound, they fly swiftly and easily away through the forest and are silent and elusive. Attempts to follow them usually result in little more than a fleeting glimpse, as the owls disappear deeper and deeper into the trees. When roosting, this bird may compress its plumage and half-close its eyes, taking on the appearance of a piece of wood.

In India, the calls have been described as a low, double hoot, or a repeated, hollow *"hooo hoo-hoo hooo"*, a cooing sound like a pigeon or a squawk in alarm. In the south, a hollow, musical *"tu-hoo"* is repeated every few seconds, preceded by a low, faint *"tok"* which is audible only at very close range.

Prey varies from insects to large birds and rodents, and apparently even fish at times, especially in Sri Lanka where the birds are partly diurnal. In the Himalayas and South-East Asia, they are regarded as bold, powerful birds, capable of catching small pheasants and jungle-fowl as well as a variety of smaller birds and mammals. The nest is in a hollow trunk, with a few twigs and feathers added, or is set in a cavity in a cliff or at the base of a tree or rock in a shady ravine. Two eggs are usually laid, in January to March.

TAWNY OWL
Strix aluco

LENGTH: *360 to 460 mm*   MAP NUMBER: *130*
DESCRIPTION: *Large, big-headed; dark red-brown to grey, spotted and streaked; dark eyes*
DISTRIBUTION: *Europe, Asia, North Africa, Middle East*
HABITAT: *Mixed, coniferous or deciduous woodland, woodland edge*
EGGS: *1–8. Nest in tree hole or old tree nest*
STATUS: *Locally common*

The Tawny Owl is widespread in most of Europe and parts of Asia. It occurs in Britain and ranges across Europe, north to Norway, Sweden and Finland and southwards to the Mediterranean and Morocco. It is also found in the Middle East, from Turkey and The Lebanon to Iraq, and in a separate area stretching from west of the Himalayas to the Korean peninsula. Across this wide range, the Tawny Owl lives in many different habitats and climatic zones, and overlaps with numerous other species of owl. It is, almost everywhere, a common and adaptable bird.

It is most frequently seen at dusk, perhaps silhouetted on a chimney pot or a television aerial. Large suburban gardens with hollies and evergreen oaks make perfect hideaways by day and good hunting grounds at night. The Tawny Owl is among the most strictly nocturnal of owls. By day, it roosts out of sight, perching upright in thick ivy or dense foliage – a holm oak is ideal – or in a dark cavity in a hollow tree.

A roosting owl can sometimes be located by the splashes of white droppings which accumulate beneath its perch. This method, however, is less reliable than when employed to search for the Long-eared Owl (*Asio otus*). Tawny Owls change roosting sites quite regularly and leave less evidence of their presence. But their roosting site can often be revealed by the noisy mobbing of small birds, especially Blackbirds, Chaffinches, tits and Mistle Thrushes. Squirrels and birds to the size of a Jay will all mob a Tawny Owl if they chance upon one in daylight.

Although the Tawny Owl will regularly kill all these species when hunting at night, it rarely attacks its persecutors during the day, even when driven off to find a more secluded perch. When roosting on a branch or in foliage, it relies on its rigid, upright stance and splendid camouflage to hide it from view. In this posture, it simply looks like a piece of wood.

Most Tawny Owls are a rich, reddish brown in colour, streaked and barred in brown and white below, and spotted with white along the line of the scapulars, the feathers on the 'shoulders' of the bird. A few are much more grey. There is a lot of variation in colour across this bird's range but there are no differences related to age or sex. The head is large, round, smooth and without ear tufts, and the face itself is rather plain with big, almost black eyes. A Tawny Owl stretched up against the trunk of a tree, head up and plumage tight, appears to have faint 'ears', or angular corners, each side of the crown.

In flight, a Tawny Owl is big and broad, large-headed and round-winged. It moves quite heavily, yet is surprisingly manoeuvrable within woodland and flies with breathtaking silence. At the nest, adult Tawny Owls are sometimes aggressive to intruders (but not usually) and may attack. Because of the bird's silent flight the attack is usually totally unexpected. The first an intruder may know of the owl's presence is through feeling, rather than hearing, the merest swish as the bird swoops past his head. Exceptionally, a Tawny Owl will actually draw blood, raking its needle-sharp claws across the intruder's scalp.

The Tawny Owl has excellent night vision. It cannot, of course, see without some light, but a pitch black night is rare. In real darkness it can see little better than humans. At dusk, the owl sees very well, for its eyes are extremely large, with a rather tubular shape that exposes a greater area of retina. The retina itself is crammed full of light-sensitive organs. Most of these are rods, which increase perception of detail, but there are also cones, which suggests that some colour is seen in better light. Although bright sunlight will dazzle an owl, especially one recently disturbed, the size of the pupil has an exceptional range. The pupils contract for daytime vision and open up remarkably wide at night. A thickened cornea gives, in effect, an additional lens. Despite these adaptations, the eyes of the Tawny Owl are not what make it such a wonderfully efficient predator in the dark. Its real strength is its exceptional hearing.

Tawny Owls and Long-eared Owls can each hear a range of four octaves. The Tawny Owl's range is 0.4 to 0.7 kHz, which is inferior to that of the Barn Owl (*Tyto alba*), but far better than most scops owls, eagle owls and other species. The ears are large, with moveable flaps over an outer tube-like opening. The inner ear is very large and the auditory region of the brain is equipped with more nerve endings than in most other birds, so its hearing is clearly acute.

Moreover, the ears are asymmetrical. One is higher and further from the bill than the other. This is why owls look so intently, and bob their heads, when hunting. They are literally getting a fix on the tiny sounds that they have picked up. The sounds are focused into the ears by the concave facial disc, and the different positions of the ears allow the bird to pinpoint prey with exactness. A Tawny Owl can hear the rustle of a mouse, the squelch of a worm, or the buzz of an insect's wing at a considerable distance. Even in the dark it can work out the exact position of the creature, and will launch itself in a deadly swoop. Legs outstretched, toes extended, it hits the victim with a powerful blow and the feet envelop it in a killing grip.

Significantly, the owl does not dive towards a rustle, but listens to the rustle and dives to the point at which it stops. Its reliance on hearing is underlined by its almost complete inability to hunt when rain and winds are producing a crashing din in a wood.

Because Tawny Owls are sedentary, some ornithologists believe that it is their intimate knowledge of their surroundings, rather than their acute hearing and good vision, that allows them to move easily in woodland by night without crashing into branches. Some bird species which bury food and recover it months later, sometimes from hundreds, perhaps thousands, of sites, prove they have remarkable memories for the landmarks within their area. Knowledge of its home range is clearly of immense value and helps the Tawny Owl survive periods when the weather is harsh and the supply of voles is low.

Tawny Owls are extremely vocal. The song of the male serves as a territorial call, a courtship call and a message to the female that her mate is returning with food. Whatever the function, it is always hauntingly evocative. First there is a long, pure, or faintly wheezy, hoot, followed by a short

Tawny Owl (*Strix aluco*)

pause, then a brief, abrupt "*hu*" and a long, resonant, wavering "*huhuhuhoooo*". The typical pattern is "*Hooo. Hu huhuhuhoooo*". Females hoot as well, especially in autumn, but with a less clear and pure delivery.

The other common call is a contact note, more or less sharp, sounding like "*kewick*". This note, followed by a hoot, is no doubt the origin of the somewhat inaccurate "*tu-wit tu-woo*", but such a combination is rarely heard. The "*kewick*" call is the most frequent call of the female. Fledged young have a similar call but it is more wheezing, or strained, and is a lower and less explosive "*tsi-weep*". This call is less high-pitched and squeaky than the similar food-begging call of the young Long-eared Owl. As night falls in a wood, the outburst of "*kewick*" calls from Tawny Owls on all sides can be loud, energetic and more than a little unnerving.

Hooting songs are most frequent during territorial defence and courtship, with one peak in late winter and spring and another in late summer and autumn. They are heard least often in June and July. Cold, wet and windy weather all reduce the frequency of the calls, and a bright moon may also decrease the vocal output of the owls.

A Tawny Owl, once established, will remain in a territory all its life. The pair-bond is also a lifelong one, so young birds struggle to find a suitable place to live unless an adult has recently died. Males fight to defend a territory, while the female selects the nest site. The territory has to supply food for the whole family. In winter, Tawny Owls survive well even in severe weather, if sufficient prey is available. If voles are scarce, and the weather harsh, many Tawny Owls die. Studies in England revealed territories of 30 acres (12ha) in thick woodland and 50 acres (20ha) in more mixed woods and open ground. Although territories can be smaller still where prey is abundant, those in northern Europe are often as large as 250 acres (100ha), reflecting a much lower density of prey.

Tawny Owls eat a wide variety of prey, being generalists rather than specialists. They frequently eat worms, which they can hear beneath the surface and snatch up from wet ground and leaf litter. They also relish cockchafers, moths, beetles, mice, voles, fish and frogs. Roosting birds are often killed and eaten. Studies of pellets, the undigested material coughed up by an owl after a meal, show that many items, including the larger voles and mice, which are known to have been eaten are not detected in the pellet analysis. Nevertheless, it is clear that small rodents, birds and frogs are most important in the owls' diet.

Most nests are in natural holes, but the old nests of Magpies (*Pica pica*) or other birds, upturned tree roots and hollows in the ground are also used quite regularly. Tawny Owls appear able to drive Barn Owls from their traditional sites and take over their tree cavities, but there are also records of Tawny Owls being moved on by Jackdaws (*Corvus monedula*). Some Tawny Owls have been reported as so persistent in their efforts to incubate their eggs that they have eventually suffocated or starved as Jackdaws have built their nests on top of them.

In the north, two to six eggs are laid. In Russia, seven or even eight eggs are sometimes found. In Britain, the average clutch size is smaller and the Tawny Owl has much less erratic and opportunistic breeding behaviour than, for example, the Barn Owl. The eggs are incubated by the female from about the time when the second one is laid, though this varies. They hatch after some 29 or 30 days and the young often leave the nest a little before they can fly, at between 28 and 37 days old. Once they have learnt to hunt and must leave their parents, the young face their toughest test and many fail to meet the challenge.

Tawny Owls are beautiful, common and widespread. They have been closely studied and are easily heard. Compared with other nocturnal birds, they are also quite easily seen. Most people have a pair or two close to their homes. Yet these owls retain an air of mystery and can, on a dark night, send a chill down the spine of anyone who suddenly hears a "*keewick*" or that incomparably beautiful, quavering, drawn-out hoot.

SPOTTED OWL
Strix occidentalis

LENGTH: *405 to 480 mm* MAP NUMBER: 131
DESCRIPTION: *Large; red-brown, spotted whitish*
DISTRIBUTION: *Western North America, Mexico*
HABITAT: *Ancient mixed and coniferous forest*
EGGS: *2–4. Nest in hole or old raptor nest*
STATUS: *Threatened, locally endangered*

The northern race of the Spotted Owl is a rare and threatened bird, but the species is found in a broad band of western North America, from southern British Columbia to central Mexico. Its preferred habitat is ancient woodland, where the trees grow large and have deep holes in their venerable trunks. These cavities make ideal nests, though this species will also adopt old nests left by other large birds and will nest in holes in cliffs. Wooded ravines and the mountainous forests of the Rocky Mountains are favourite haunts of the southern race.

Spotted Owls are medium-sized, upright owls, without ear tufts on the rounded head. The facial disc is well-defined, and fairly pale buff against the darker red-brown of the sides and top of the head. The eyes are large and dark, the bill pale and yellowish. Their upperparts are a dark, rich red-brown. The top of the head and back of the neck are spotted with white and the rest is mottled with buff. The underside is a complex pattern of rusty-brown with faint dusky crossbars and spots and dashes of white.

Strictly nocturnal, this owl can be difficult to observe. Once tracked down at the daytime roost or at the nest, however, it can allow remarkably good, close views. It has been described as one of the tamest, or stupidest, of owls. It will fly close to an intruder at the nest but not, apparently, with any aggressive intent. It was once thought to possess neither the courage to defend its nest nor the intelligence to fly away and protect itself. Spotted Owls simply sit at the nest and watch people looking at them from only a few inches away.

One preening owl was said to be so indolent of manner that it appeared to fall asleep half-way through. Another was reported by two ornithologists on a collecting expedition to be perching, unconcerned, in a conifer while they approached. While one distracted it, the other crept up behind and killed it with a blow to the head.

If discovered by day, a Spotted Owl will be mobbed by a mixed flock of smaller birds. Quite why they do it is uncertain. Adult birds may be teaching their young to

recognize a predator, or they may be trying to drive the owl away, though usually with little effect. It is possible that they are trying to catch the attention of a larger creature that will succeed in banishing the owl, or perhaps they are simply venting their anger.

At night, the Spotted Owl leaves its hideaway in a dense tree or cavity to hunt for flying squirrels, deer mice, woodrats, shrews, moles and bats, with a wide variety of small birds, insects and frogs to add spice to the diet. As a predator, it is powerful and opportunistic. Roosting birds as large as small owls are not safe from its attentions. Recent studies in California compared breeding pairs with non-breeding pairs. The birds that nested successfully ate more large mammals, and fewer small ones, compared with those that had no nest.

In the Pacific north-west, Spotted Owls eat mainly woodrats and flying squirrels. In the Californian studies, the same prey species were identified as the most important, with pocket gophers and Steller's Jays (*Cyanocitta stelleri*) also frequently taken. Moles, grey squirrels and several other species were taken less often.

Spotted Owls probably hunt largely by perching quietly, watching intently for suitable prey. When potential prey is detected, by sight or sound, the owl bursts into action, taking the victim with a muscular grip of its feet. When it creeps along a branch, with less deadly intentions, it is said to have a decidedly parrot-like appearance.

The call is a high-pitched, explosive hoot of "*oh oo ou ow*". This is usually three to five notes which are described as similar to a baying hound. The last note is more emphatic than the first. There may often be two quick notes, then a pause before a third, to produce a call of "*hoo hoo – hooo*". Birds disturbed at the nest make a low, rising whistle, and there are also dove-like hoots.

The Spotted Owl was discovered in March 1858 by a pioneering naturalist of the Pacific Coast by the name of Xantus, after a specimen was collected in the southern Sierra Nevadas. The Spotted Owl was next discovered in Arizona in 1872, and a decade or so later was found to be not uncommon in the most dense conifer forests of Calaveras County. Little more was learned for years.

Four races were described, but only three were generally accepted, as they are still. A dark bird, the endangered race, is found from British Columbia to California and a second race occurs in southern California. A third, also dark but with clearer white spotting, is found in the southwest United States and central Mexico, where it lives in dense spruce and fir trees in shady canyons, or thickets of aspen and maple, at up to 9,800 feet (3,000m).

Early studies of this species involved all-too-frequent shooting of the adults and collecting of their eggs. Two eggs are laid, and less often three and only rarely four. At one nest, eggs were collected in one spring, the eggs and both parent birds next spring and two eggs on the next visit 15 years later. The following year, eggs were taken again from the very same hole. The nest was in a deep canyon, in a cavity 16 feet (5m) up in a granite cliff at the foot of a rock face 200 feet (60m) high.

Other early nests were found in an old raven's nest, on the floor of a small cave, on bare ground at the base of a large rock and in a variety of hollow trees. Museums and private collections benefited from the old naturalists but little was learned about the biology of the bird. Most eggs were taken before they could hatch and much remains to be discovered about the development of the young.

The Spotted Owl requires dense, ancient, natural coniferous woods. It is unable to settle in new plantations and disturbed woods. Logging in the remnant forests of the northwestern United States brought conservationists to the defence of the northern race of the Spotted Owl and the case became a complex legal issue between ecologists and timber merchants. Ornithologists are now taking the lead in efforts to protect the remaining untouched forests from the timber companies. Large parts of the forest have already been put aside as reserves, but it is unlikely that these alone will be sufficient to save the northern race.

BARRED OWL
Strix varia

LENGTH: *405 to 600 mm*   MAP NUMBER: 132
DESCRIPTION: *Large, brown with whitish spots above; barred on chest, streaked below*
DISTRIBUTION: *North America, Mexico*
HABITAT: *Coniferous and mixed northern woods, swampy forest*
EGGS: *2–5. Nest in tree hole*
STATUS: *Locally frequent*

This large-headed owl of North America and Mexico is a bird of temperate forest and one of the commonest owls of North America. The Barred Owl is neatly patterned in subdued colours, largely a drab olive-brown with clear spots and bars of off-white above. It is paler below with brown, crescent-shaped bars across the chest. It has lengthways streaks lower down on the abdomen and its face is pale, with a series of concentric semi-circles near the outer edge of its facial disc. The eyes, though quite large, are set close together and look intensely black.

It is distinguished from the Great Horned Owl (*Bubo virginianus*) by its lack of ear tufts and from the Spotted Owl (*Strix occidentalis*), which it resembles, by the contrast between its barred chest and striped lower

Barred Owl (*Strix varia*)

underparts. In appearance and behaviour, it is much like the European Ural Owl (*Strix uralensis*). In the north and east of its range it prefers conifers, hemlock or mixed woods and, farther south, it lives in deep, dark forests along streams and beside swamps.

There are three races of the Barred Owl: in a broad belt across Canada from the Rocky Mountains of British Columbia east to Nova Scotia; in the southern and south-eastern United States, west to the Great Plains but not beyond; and in parts of Texas, north and central Mexico. Another group, in southern Mexico, Guatemala and Honduras, is best treated as a separate species, the Fulvous Owl (*Strix fulvescens*). In the north-west, the Barred Owl is increasing and expanding, and already overlaps with the range of the declining Spotted Owl.

Open terrain is used for hunting in the same way that the Long-eared Owl (*Asio otus*) often flies from its roost at the edge of a forest to hunt over open ground. But the Barred Owl hunts by pouncing from a perch so it is not dependant on such large open spaces. In dull weather this owl may be seen hunting by day. Nevertheless, it is essentially a nocturnal bird, well equipped for survival in the dark. It has excellent vision at dusk and, once the light has faded, it can detect its prey by sound. Focusing on rustles and squeals with its large, asymmetrical ears, the owl is able to pinpoint their source to perfection, and a feet-first dive soon dispatches any creature incautious enough to make a noise. It does not, however, have very large feet and this limits the size of the prey it can grip.

The prey is quite varied and is chiefly small mammals, but includes hares and squirrels, as well as mice and shrews and even some fish, frogs and birds. In southern swamps, the Barred Owl will catch large numbers of crayfish and frogs and apparently catches fish by wading into the shallows, an unusual habit except among Asian fish owls.

Barred Owls are residents, keeping within a territory all year round unless forced out of the frozen north by deep snow. By day, they hide in dense foliage but seldom rely on their good camouflage to keep them from harm. Instead, they fly at the least disturbance, not tolerating any close approach, and so are hard to see and observe. Yet the Barred Owl can at times be quite tame, and distinctly curious. Its personality has been said to be as mild and engaging as any predator can have.

The call of a Barred Owl is easily put into words. It sings "*who cooks for you, who cooks for you all*". The song is heard most often early in the spring, when breeding begins, and can sometimes be heard by day. A pair will often call in duet, when the male's version will be distinctly the deeper of the two.

The nest is usually in the hollow trunk of a large tree but if none is available a large old nest of another bird will be used. If old trees remain undamaged, a suitable hole may be used by a succession of owls over two or three decades. A big beech with a rotten heart, encompassing a large cavity reached through a deep crevice, is ideal. The main threat to the future of the Barred Owl is a lack of old trees with cavities in forests which have been over-tidied.

Two, three or even as many as five eggs are laid on the bare floor of the cavity at intervals of two or three days. While the smaller male hunts, the female incubates the eggs alone, beginning with the first so that the early eggs are not left to freeze in the spring. This means that the first egg hatches two or three days before the next, and so on.

Each egg hatches after 28 days' incubation. The early chicks will be stronger and bigger than later ones, which may not survive if food is scarce. The larger young may fight their smaller siblings for supplies. The female stays with the chicks for three weeks, then helps with the hunting until, some six weeks after hatching, they are able to fly. The young may remain reliant on their parents until the autumn but eventually move away to face an exacting winter alone in unfamiliar territory. It is a period of great mortality among young owls, but if young Barred Owls can survive, they can expect many more years of life in the deep, damp forests.

FULVOUS OWL
Strix fulvescens

LENGTH: *405 to 450 mm*   MAP NUMBER: 133
DESCRIPTION: *Rusty-brown; barred breast; black eyes*
DISTRIBUTION: *Southern Mexico, northern Central America*
HABITAT: *High-altitude tropical and temperate forest*
EGGS: *2–5. Nest in tree hole*
STATUS: *Rare*

Until quite recently this was considered by most people to be a race of the Barred Owl (*Strix varia*). Now, however, it is generally treated as a separate species, following the lead of the American Ornithologists' Union, among other authorities. Dr K H Voous concurs with this view, treating the Fulvous Owl as a different species, but closely related to its northern counterpart.

Known also as the Guatemala Barred Owl, it lives in humid upper-tropical and temperate pine-oak forest in southern Mexico and northern Central America. It is a fifth smaller than the nearest races of the Barred Owl, which come to within just 30 miles or so (50km) in Oaxaca, southern Mexico. Its hooting calls resemble those of the Spotted Owl (*Strix occidentalis*) more than those of the Barred Owl, one reason why its separation has been justified. The Rufous-banded Owl (*Ciccaba albitarsus*) is closely similar in appearance to the Fulvous Owl.

RUSTY-BARRED OWL
Strix hylophila

LENGTH: *355 mm*   MAP NUMBER: 134
DESCRIPTION: *Densely barred rusty-red, dark brown and orange-buff; dark eyes*
DISTRIBUTION: *Brazil, Uruguay, north-east Argentina*
HABITAT: *Woodland*
STATUS: *Probably scarce*

There are two species of *Strix* owls found only in South America. This one occurs largely in Brazil and is sometimes known as the Brazilian Owl. A fairly small *Strix* species, it is pleasantly barred with brown, white and orange-buff, and has a fairly strong orange suffusion over much of its body and head. Its face has broad, concentric rings of brown around the large, brown eyes, making the bill stand out. Calls include a rolling "*rrrrro*", a rhythmic, descending "*gu gu gu gu gu, u, u, u, u*" and a long-drawn "*i-u-a*".

The Rusty-barred Owl is not very widespread, being found largely in the south of Brazil around Sao Paulo and down to the Uruguayan border, as well as inland towards Paraguay and the north-eastern tip of Argentina.

RUFOUS-LEGGED OWL
Strix rufipes

LENGTH: *330 to 380 mm*   MAP NUMBER: 135
DESCRIPTION: *Dark face with cream crescents; dark brown back; yellowish underparts barred dark and white*
DISTRIBUTION: *Southern South America*
STATUS: *Uncertain*

A South American species, this neat and attractive owl is found in Paraguay, Argentina, south to Tierra del Fuego, and southern Chile. It also occurs on Chiloe Island, which has one of three recognized races. It may possibly be a rare breeding bird on the Falklands Islands as well, and has reached the more remote island of South Georgia.

Strong contrasts, even of fairly unremarkable colours, make many birds look handsome, and so it is with the Rufous-legged Owl. It is basically a brown bird, but the deep brown upperside has fine whitish barring, and the underparts are clear yellow-orange or orange-buff, crossed with very sharp, regular barring of very dark brown and cream. The face is a dark rusty-brown, barred in some races, with a pale throat running upwards to a broad triangle of white around the bill, topped by a wide, whitish V between the eyes.

The details of the Rufous-legged Owl's life are obscure. Much research has yet to be conducted into its behaviour and habits. When these are elucidated, this owl and the Rusty-barred Owl (*Strix hylophila*) may eventually be removed from the *Strix* genus and placed in a separate new genus of their own.

URAL OWL
Strix uralensis

LENGTH: *580 mm*   MAP NUMBER: 136
DESCRIPTION: *Big; pale grey-brown; small dark eyes in plain face*
DISTRIBUTION: *Central and northern Europe, central Asia, Japan*
HABITAT: *Old woodland and forest*
EGGS: *2—6. Nest in hole or old raptor nest, broken stump or nest box*
STATUS: *Generally scarce and threatened, locally frequent and increasing*

Despite having one of the widest of ranges across Europe and Asia, this bird is not well known to most birdwatchers, although it has been well studied by dedicated owl specialists. It is often elusive and difficult to find and, for the many ornithologists in western Europe who rarely travel north, the Ural Owl remains a picture in a field guide.

It is actually quite widespread in Scandinavia, where local birdwatchers have such a different perspective, and is found in central Norway, Sweden, and around the top of the Baltic Sea into Finland. Ural Owls also occur in the Baltic states south to Lithuania and in a few isolated outposts in eastern Europe. The mountain beechwoods of the Carpathians in northern Romania, a forest or two in Czechoslovakian Bohemia and the high beechwoods and conifers of the Dinaric Alps of Yugoslavia all have small populations at a low density.

From Europe, the distribution of the Ural Owl is essentially a broad band across central Asia, extending through Siberia to the Sea of Okhotsk, south as far as Korea and on several island groups from Sakhalin southwards throughout Japan. This broad range includes at least nine recognizable races of Ural Owl. A tenth, a dark, isolated race occurring in China, is sometimes treated as a separate species, David's Wood Owl (*Strix davidi*).

The Ural Owl remains an unfamiliar bird because it lives, for the most part, in remote, undisturbed forests far from human communities. It is by nature drawn to old conifer forest or mixed woodland with clearings. But in Finland it has begun to move into forest bogs where wet ground underfoot is overgrown by a mixture of spruce and birch, and it is most frequent in areas of damp heathland with scattered trees. This has also brought the Ural Owl closer to home, as it were, and it will now nest in buildings and specially provided nest boxes.

The Ural Owl is a large bird, tall and heavily-built, with a rather long tail and elongated shape for a *Strix* owl. It is basically pale grey-brown but is attractively marked with dark brown streaks along the centres of the upperpart feathers and rows of white spots on the scapulars. These rows run as diagonal bands on either side of the back, in the style of a Tawny Owl (*Strix aluco*). It has broad pale bars on all the flight feathers and tail, and strong streaks of dark brown on the underparts.

In flight, the Ural Owl has a large, pale, barred area on the outer wing. The underwing is largely buffish-white, marked with heavy dark bars around the trailing edge and tip. The long, white-tipped tail often hangs down a little as the bird flies. Despite the bars and streaks, a Ural Owl in flight looks remarkably pale and might briefly be mistaken for a well-marked Snowy Owl (*Nyctea scandiaca*). The flight is buzzard-like, but with deeper, more relaxed wingbeats, enhancing the very large, powerful impression that this owl gives in the wild.

Its head is large but the eyes are quite small and closely set and lack the fierce, intense expression that is so characteristic of the Great Grey Owl (*Strix nebulosa*). The eyes are dark, not yellow, and the facial disc is unusually plain, pale grey-buff, without any concentric rings. The face is actually almost round, except for a tiny V-shaped indentation at the top, and the disc is neatly edged with a chequered pattern like the wing of a blue butterfly.

The small eyes may give a clue to the behaviour of this species, which is less nocturnal than most other owls of its genus. Summer nights, of course, are long and light in its northern range and the owl must hunt in partial or full daylight. But winters are equally long and dark and it then needs good night vision.

Like other owls, it relies heavily on magnificent hearing. Ears discriminate so much more than eyes. A small vole in a large patch of dead leaves is not easy to see, but a squeak penetrating the rustle of wind-blown leaves is instantly recognized, even by human ears. Sounds travel around corners and from dark shadows, so the ears pick up things the eyes cannot see.

A hunting Ural Owl is adaptable and can switch from one kind of prey to another with more ease than the Great Grey Owl. This allows it to stay in its territory all year, like a Tawny Owl. It can survive the years when voles are scarce, or hard to trap in deep snow, by switching to birds or squirrels. In addition to voles and squirrels, it takes small mammals such as rats, rabbits and hares, as well as frogs, insects and birds up to the size of thrushes. Sometimes the Ural Owl excels itself and manages to subdue larger prey such as Black Grouse (*Tetrao tetrix*).

Ural Owl roosts are widely scattered and the task of collecting enough pellets to achieve a meaningful analysis of its food is usually difficult. Studies showed that mammals formed 86 percent of the diet in Sweden, and 75 percent in Finland. Birds varied from species as small as the Goldcrest (*Regulus regulus*) to grouse, and included several Tengmalm's Owls (*Aegolius funereus*), a Long-eared Owl (*Asio otus*) and even Ural Owl chicks. In Japan, voles formed 68 percent of 419 prey items examined, with various small mammals accounting for most of the remainder and birds forming 12 percent.

Ural Owls have a double, barking hoot, and pairs may call together from early March onwards as they reinforce old partnerships and defend their territorial boundaries. The pair remains together for life. The song is a simple repetition of hoots, "*huow-huow-huow*", the female's version being lower, weaker and harsher in quality. The male also calls "*wohu*" and, after a pause of four seconds or so, gives a call of "*wohu-huwohu*" as a territorial defence or to keep contact with his mate. A loud, sharp "*korrwick*" is longer and harsher than the "*kewick*" note of the Tawny Owl. Despite these calls, and the food-begging note of the young, the species is generally very quiet and it is quite possible to spend half a day and night in an occupied Ural Owl's territory and hear nothing at all.

The territory is large, and successful nests in Finland are rarely less than 1¼ miles (2km) apart, and usually more than 2½ miles (4km). But in the Soviet Union and elsewhere, in really good habitat, the territory may be about 1,100 acres (450ha) and the density of owls fairly

Ural Owl (*Strix uralensis*)

high. Territories are defended against other owls and birds of prey, and Ural Owls frequently kill Tawny Owls and Tengmalm's Owls in such disputes. But they are vulnerable to Goshawks (*Accipiter gentilis*), which may take over their nests even after eggs have been laid.

The nest site is normally a broken stump, with the heartwood rotted out to leave a neat, rounded cavity, or a hole in a tree trunk. Such a hole may be used year after year; in Finland, a hole in a birch tree was used for 18 successive years. But, if alternatives are available, the pair may switch from site to site over a period of years. Recesses in cliffs, an old Goshawk nest (which may have to be vacated if the Goshawk pair choose to reoccupy it), the nest of a Buzzard (*Buteo buteo*) or Honey Buzzard (*Pernis apivorus*), ruined buildings and, increasingly nowadays, nest boxes are also used.

Even in years of plentiful voles, some pairs of Ural Owls seem unable to breed for want of suitable nest sites. Small boxes intended for Tawny Owls are often taken over by Ural Owls when natural holes are impossible to find. The loss of undisturbed forest with old, rotting trees is really the biggest threat to Ural Owls in the future, except perhaps for the threat of global warming. An increase in parts of the Soviet Union and northern Europe in recent decades has been attributed to cooler weather after a warmer period early in the century. A return to warm weather would presumably have the opposite effect.

In Sweden, this species is known as the Attacking Owl because Ural Owls are very aggressive at the nest and swoop noiselessly and with great determination at anyone who climbs up to the hole. Up to six eggs are laid. The number laid by northern owls tends to be larger than by species in the tropics, and this species illustrates that general rule quite well. Nevertheless, the average is around three. They are incubated for 27 or 28 days and the young remain in the nest for about five weeks.

If nest boxes continue to be provided, and if old trees are left alone in managed forests, Ural Owls should continue to thrive. All the same, because they are so strictly resident, and so sparse in the south of their range, birdwatchers must continue to travel north if they wish to see these large, impressive owls.

DAVID'S WOOD OWL
Strix davidi

LENGTH: *580 mm*   MAP NUMBER: 137
DESCRIPTION: *Dark, heavily streaked; small dark eyes*
DISTRIBUTION: *China*
HABITAT: *Mountain forests*
STATUS: *Rare and probably endangered*

This is an isolated owl of China, its range centred on western Szechwan. This area lies at the eastern end of the southern region of the Tibetan plateau, bisected by the Yangtze river in the great mountains west of Chengtu. David's Wood Owls are resident in the mountain woods of Heilungkiang, south to Shenyang in Liaoning, in Szechwan and in south-east Tsinghai.

This little-known species may be simply a strongly-marked race of the Ural Owl (*Strix uralensis*). If so, it would be the most striking and well-defined of the races. It is darker than any Ural Owl, with blackish-brown markings, particularly the streaks beneath, and a more clearly marked edge to the facial disc. It has a similar lifestyle to the Ural Owl, living in coniferous and mixed woods between 13,000 and 16,500 feet (4,000–5,000m) above sea level. David's Wood Owl has never been studied comprehensively, but its calls are described as a long, quavering hoot and barking "*khau khau*".

This species is not illustrated as no adequate reference was available to the artist.

GREAT GREY OWL
Strix nebulosa

LENGTH: *610 to 840 mm*   MAP NUMBER: 138
DESCRIPTION: *Huge; upright; grey-brown, with ringed facial disc, small yellow eyes*
DISTRIBUTION: *Northern Europe, northern Asia, northern North America and western mountains*
HABITAT: *Old mature forest*
EGGS: *1–9. Nest in old tree nest, broken stump*
STATUS: *Locally declining, rare*

The Great Grey Owl is one of the 'superstars' among owls and stands out as a unique, extraordinary bird. It may be a less formidable hunter than the Eagle Owl (*Bubo bubo*), Great Horned Owl (*Bubo virginianus*) or Snowy Owl (*Nyctea scandiaca*) but it carves its niche by the sheer aggression it shows towards human intruders at the nest.

Although huge, it is largely a bundle of loose feathers covering quite a small, lightweight body. Yet a Great Grey Owl will swoop and deliver a frightening strike at the head with powerful feet equipped with needle-sharp claws. It can rip open a deep wound, tear out an eye and even fracture a cheekbone. The naturalist David Attenborough, in his television series *The Living Planet*, wore a protective helmet when climbing to the nest of a Great Grey Owl.

It is said that there are more significant differences between the Great Grey Owls of North America and those of Europe, than between the European Eagle Owl and the American Great Horned Owl. But the various Great Grey Owls remain members of a single species found over a broad northern belt right around the Arctic. Great Grey Owls do not live on the tundra, but occupy the huge boreal forests of the taiga to the south of the Arctic circle. This area extends from northern Scandinavia across the north of Siberia to Mongolia and Sakhalin Island, and through western Alaska south into the Rocky Mountains and east to the Great Lakes. This vast range holds just three commonly recognized subspecies.

These splendid coniferous forests are enchanting places, yet present great challenges to an owl, especially when the ground and trees are deeply swathed in winter snow. The very scale and remoteness of the largely untouched woods make them difficult places in which to search for owls. The Great Grey Owl, despite its size, is adept at melting away among the pines, and its upright, long-tailed shape and cryptic colours are outstanding examples of camouflage.

In Europe and Asia, it occupies lichen-covered spruce,

Great Grey Owl (*Strix nebulosa*)

fir and pine, often mixed with larch and poplar, and sometimes birch woodlands. In North America, black ash and basswood forest and woods of big aspens are also frequented. The owls extend to subalpine conditions at altitudes of 10,500 feet (3,200m) above sea level in Utah and 8,000 feet (2,400m) in the Sierra Nevada of California. In winter, swamps at the edges of forests, rough grasslands and even farmland and golf courses are visited for food.

The facial disc, seen from the front, is the largest, roundest and perhaps most perfect of any owl. With a circumference of about 20 inches (50cm), it is an excellent receiving dish that focuses sound into the ears and helps the bird locate its prey by hearing, rather than seeing, its movements. The ear openings are large, mobile and complex, the most highly developed of any *Strix* owl.

The skull is slightly asymmetrical, so that the right ear opening points a little below the left. This assists the owl to trace the source of sound with remarkable precision. As films have often shown, it is well able to catch a vole beneath deep snow, diving head-first into the white blanket to strike its prey just as accurately as if the vole were sitting in the open in broad daylight. The headlong plunge ends in a punch with the feet, striking the prey as deep as 18 inches (45cm) below the surface of the snow.

By contrast, the eyes of the Great Grey Owl are small and set close together. The diameter of the eye, at 0.47–0.55 inches (12–14mm), is tiny compared to 0.67 inches (17mm) in the Tawny Owl (*Strix aluco*) and 0.94 inches (24mm) in the Eagle Owl. The eyes are clear yellow, each set deeply in a comma-shape of jet black, with very pale, back-to-back crescents almost meeting above the bill between them. The bill looks small and yellow. The face is a beautiful, clear, soft grey, closely marked with slightly wavy, concentric rings of darker grey pencilling. This serves to emphasize an intensity and alertness of expression that few birds can rival.

From the side, the head has a strange, flat-fronted shape. It is actually quite narrow at the top and more or less triangular. Although most of the plumage is grey and grey-brown, marked with dull white, the wings have broad bands of orange-buff just beyond the wrists — these show well in flight. In North America, Great Grey Owls are fractionally larger, darker and are barred beneath, rather than streaked.

The great thickness of its plumage is an essential adaptation to the extreme cold. Whereas Eagle Owls may weigh up to 8lbs 13ozs (4kg), a big male Great Grey Owl weighs only around 2lbs 3ozs (1kg) and some weigh as little as 1lb 3ozs (535gm); even females weigh less than 4lbs (2kg). The small body requires much less energy than that of the Eagle Owl and allows the Great Grey Owl a better chance of survival in low temperatures.

Clearly, this owl is less strong and musclebound than its size would suggest. This is reflected in its prey. Whereas Eagle Owls can tackle prey up to the size of a small roe deer, or a Capercaillie (*Tetrao urogallus*), Great Grey Owls are chiefly dependent on voles and shrews. They are also much more specialized in their diet and less opportunistic in their hunting; in years of low vole populations, they have to search for food far from their home territories.

Sometimes they move out in great numbers and invade regions far to the south. The fact that they are interested in catching voles and that most have never seen a human or, if they have, are indifferent to people, has prompted ringers to use unusual methods in order to catch them and ring them. In North America, these owls have been caught by baiting fishing lines with artificial mice to tempt the owls within range of giant nets.

When hunting, Great Grey Owls are attracted to open country, such as clearings in the forest, the edges of forest bogs and muskegs, and felled areas. They usually perch on a tree and wait, watching and listening intently for any sign of a vole. Given the slightest hint, they are able to glide down, sometimes as much as 330 feet (100m), to the exact spot and snatch their tiny prey. Compared with either the Tawny Owl or the Eagle Owl, this bird has much less weight per unit area of wing and has a relaxed, easy, heron-like flight. It is able to thread its way through small gaps in the intricate texture of the forest and has a lightness of touch that is remarkable for a bird of its size.

By mid-February, the males may already be calling regularly to advertise their return to the breeding territories. The song is deep and booming, in a regular series of "*hoo-hoo-hoo*" notes which can rise gradually in pitch. However, the sound does not carry far through the dense stands of tree trunks.

Pairs nest in a variety of sites, including the frequently-photographed option of a large, broken tree snapped off well above ground level, with a deep hollow rotted down into the heartwood. But most birds use old nests of Goshawks, Buzzards, Ospreys, Ravens and Magpies in Europe, and those of Red-tailed and Broad-winged Hawks, Ravens and American Crows in North America.

The birds may scrape and prod at the nest material, but add no new material and usually seem content to sit openly on a flat nest, whereas Ural Owls (*Strix uralensis*) sit deeper in a hollow nest and are scarcely visible from the ground. Unlike other *Strix* owls, Great Grey Owls have never been reported nesting inside a hole.

The number of eggs may vary from one to nine, with an average in northern Europe of just over four. The determining factor is the amount of food, particularly voles, and this also affects the survival rate of the chicks. The eggs hatch after being incubated for 30 days by the female. During this period, the male brings food to the nest. Incubating females must be among the least mobile birds in the world. One female moved for only 0.63 percent of the total incubation period.

The male continues to provide food for the young, who leave the nest after three weeks but cannot fly well for six or eight weeks. If food is scarce, the smaller, weaker chicks die. Since the female starts to incubate before laying the full clutch, the chicks vary in age by several days.

Most hunting seems to take place when the light is low, not during the sunniest time of day nor during the darkest part of the night. In the summer, the birds have little choice but to hunt in some light, as they live in the land of the midnight sun and cannot wait for darkness. But, even then, they prefer to hunt during the slightly darker night. In winter, the position is reversed and the owls may hunt during the twilight which passes for day in the north.

Although Canadian trappers have killed huge numbers of Great Grey Owls, and still do when opportunity arises, the species seems to be in no danger and should have a secure future as long as the cold, northern forests are left empty and undamaged. But, in northern Europe, death is often due to shooting, trapping and collisions with traffic and overhead wires. The owl is often persecuted.

EARED OWLS

SEVEN SPECIES

Striped Owl (*Asio clamator*)

T.BOYER

STRIPED OWL
Asio clamator

LENGTH: *305 to 380 mm*   MAP NUMBER: 139
DESCRIPTION: *Eared owl, with dark eyes in white face; striped underparts*
DISTRIBUTION: *Mexico, Central and South America*
HABITAT: *Deciduous lowland forest and woods*
EGGS: *3−4. Nest on ground or low branch*
STATUS: *Uncertain, probably threatened*

A single species of owl, given a genus of its own, may always be the subject of debate about its classification. The Striped Owl was once listed close to the genus *Asio*, the eared owls, and yet placed in a single-species genus *Rhinoptynx*. It has even been credited with some links to the genus *Tyto*, the barn owls.

A cross-pairing of Barn Owl (*Tyto alba*) and Striped Owl has produced eggs in captivity, but the embryos died before hatching and cannot be considered to have been fertile. Structural features show little resemblance and, superficially, the Striped Owl is much more like the eared owls. Indeed, it is a slightly odd species of *Asio* after all.

Certainly it looks like an eared owl. It has marked ear tufts that are longer even than those of the Long-eared Owl (*Asio otus*), and a strongly-defined white facial disc which gives it a similar appearance to the Long-eared Owl, except for its much darker eyes and larger, almost blackish, bill.

The eyes may be orange or deep hazel but appear dark in the field. Like the Long-eared Owl, the Striped Owl is basically yellowish-brown, mixed with greys and matt black, its warm buff underside strongly striped with dark brown. Its back is also striped but with broader, dark stripes. Its primary feathers are, like those of a Long-eared Owl, barred grey-brown and bright buff.

Compared with the Long-eared Owl, this species has a rather long tail and short wings. This might suggest a lifestyle less dependent on open ground and more adapted to hunting in a woodland environment. But it is, in fact, a bird of open spaces. Although only fractionally longer than a Long-eared Owl, it is substantially heavier, over three-quarters as heavy again in the case of the larger females. Its ears are very like those of the Long-eared Owl in their complex and asymmetrical structure. They are large and extraordinarily sensitive.

In many ways, the Striped Owl seems to combine the characteristics and lifestyles of Short-eared Owls (*Asio flammeus*) and Long-eared Owls but its precise relationship to them is unclear, particularly in view of its restricted tropical distribution.

The Striped Owl is found across a large area of South America, from northern Argentina and southern Brazil north to the southern edge of the Amazon basin. The range narrows northwards, to swing around to the west of the great forests through Bolivia and along the northern coast of South America, completing a broad belt around the rain-forest. There is apparently a larger race on Tobago, although it is virtually unknown and may be extinct.

Another separate area of distribution, occupied by the smallest of four races, stretches through Central America into south-east Mexico. There is a a very large geographical separation between this race and the nearest Long-eared or Short-eared Owls but it is found in much closer proximity to the Stygian Owl (*Asio stygius*).

Although so clearly absent from the bulk of evergreen rain-forest, this is nevertheless a forest-edge owl at times, living in deciduous woods, wooded savanna and in marshland with stands of trees. In Venezuela, it lives in clearings within, and at the edge of, the rain-forest, as well as in deciduous forest close to the Orinoco River. In Panama, however, it is a bird of more open habitats.

It prefers open country with scattered thickets and copses and so it is at home in agricultural land where forest has been cleared, leaving relict patches between fields and pastures. In Venezuela at least, it is sometimes found on the edge of towns and villages. It shares the habit of Long-eared Owls and Short-eared Owls in gathering in communal roosts outside the breeding season. A dozen or so birds may sometimes be flushed from some favoured spot in rank grass or a dense thicket.

The Striped Owl eats small mammals, large insects and a few reptiles and small birds, but its greater weight and power and longer claws indicate larger average prey than is the case with the Long-eared Owl. Mammals such as spiny pocket mice, rice rats and Cayenne spiny rats and rat-tailed opossums are caught at night. Hunting often begins around sunset.

A typical technique, despite its short-winged form, is a low, quartering flight over open countryside, with sudden swoops after prey. But it will also wait and watch from a perch, ready to drop onto some small creature.

The Striped Owl gives a series of short, dog-like barks and low, muffled hoots, often seven in number. There is also a longer, shriller call note, lasting about a second with the emphasis in the middle − a whistled "*hooOOOoh*". The calls of the female are higher pitched. Nests are found on the ground in long grass or any clump of material that has gathered by chance around the base of a low branch or oil palm frond. Three or four eggs are laid in a rudimentary scrape made by the male, and incubation lasts 33 days. Probably it is usual for just a single chick to be raised successfully to the fledging stage.

LONG-EARED OWL
Asio otus

LENGTH: *350 to 400 mm*   MAP NUMBER: 140
DESCRIPTION: *Upright, streaked brown and warm buff to grey; long ear tufts; orange eyes*
DISTRIBUTION: *North America, Europe, Middle East, Asia, parts of Africa*
HABITAT: *Forest, isolated thickets, woodland/marsh edge*
EGGS: *3−10. Nest in old nest of other bird in tree, rarely on ground*
STATUS: *Locally frequent*

The Long-eared Owl can, with justice, be thought of as one of the world's most beautifully adapted owls, and one of the most finely-tuned of all birds. It is certainly a supreme master of nocturnal hunting for small mammals.

Its four recognized races occupy a wide range. One is found in North America, from southern Canada to a belt from coast to coast across the centre of the United States. Another occurs farther north in Canada, virtually into Alaska and to the northern tree limit. A third is much more restricted, and thus rare, and is found only on the Canary Islands. The fourth ranges far more widely, from western Europe − even occurring in Ireland, a land of few owls −

Long-eared Owl (*Asio otus*)

eastwards to Japan, south to the Middle East and even spreading into North Africa.

Long-eared Owls like both broad-leaved and evergreen forest. But, though they will roost in the depths of the darkest stands of trees, they prefer being close to the forest edge and to hunt over more open ground. They can be seen in Scotland's pine woodlands, or in a sycamore in a sheltered garden on the bleak Shetland Islands. On the island of Texel in the Netherlands, they collect in surprising numbers on the tops of pines between coastal sand dunes and pastureland. In complete contrast, they can also be found high in tall date palms in the arid Israeli desert. In southwestern USA, this species will nest in mesquite groves in the desert, and is rarely found in coniferous forests in the mountains. In the east of Europe and Asia, winter roosts may hold up to 150 owls.

The size and colour intensity of this owl varies throughout its range. Island forms tend to be dark, but there may be variation from pale, yellowish-brown to deeper, more chestnut-brown colours, even within quite small areas. In North America, Long-eared Owls have distinctly red-brown faces, quite unlike European birds.

The basic colour is usually a tawny- or yellowish-brown, rather pale, with very fine spotting, mottling and peppering of darker brown and grey. There are whitish spots and dark bars above, and broad streaks, usually with fine cross-bars, on the rich buff underside. The whole breast and belly are darker and more striped than on the Short-eared Owl (*Asio flammeus*).

The wings have dark carpal patches and broad panels of buff or almost orange across the bases of the primaries, a more rich, emphasized version of a pattern found on many species of owl, including the Short-eared Owl and the Great Grey Owl (*Strix nebulosa*).

The face is extremely mobile and expressive. A sleeping owl has its eyes sunk beneath the feathers of the facial disc, closed up into narrow, vertical slits beside the strong V of the deep forehead and bill. Wide awake, the owl has a rounded face, with a relaxed, open, near-perfect disc. The long, feathery ear tufts can be flattened back over the head, almost to the point of being undetectable, or raised dramatically like the ears of a curious cat.

In daylight, the pupils of the eyes are small and the irises look pale and vivid, varying from deep orange to orange-yellow. In duller light, when the pupils are wide open, the colour is hard to see at all and the bird can look dark-eyed.

The shape and posture of the Long-eared Owl are very elastic. If it wants to hide against the branch of a conifer, it stretches upright and smooths its feathers into a tight, cylindrical shape, often with one wing pulled around in front of the body like a cloak. When this owl feels safe and undetected, it can sink into a relaxed, dumpy ball of loose feathers every bit as round as a Tawny Owl (*Strix aluco*). Hunting birds have a sloping posture when perched, unlike the tense, upright shapes of birds that know they have been discovered at their roosts.

It is unclear what purpose the ear tufts serve. One explanation is that they have a cryptic effect, looking like two projections from a snapped-off stump. Another function seems to be communication with other owls. It is certainly true that the tufts are raised in what seem to be expressions of feeling when owls are close together, but they would be hard to see in a dark wood when the birds are active at night. It could also be that they impart ferocity

to an owl that needs to challenge a predator, or to drive another bird from the area of its nest.

It is interesting that tame Long-eared Owls enjoy being gently stroked on the head and neck, but react strongly if their ear tufts are touched. Perhaps the skin at the base of these feathery horns is especially sensitive and has a more direct sensory function. The reasons for these ear tufts may combine a number of these possibilities.

The ear tufts do not, however, have any function related to hearing. But the real ears of this refined owl are still exceptionally acute. The openings are long, vertical slits, running almost the whole height of the skull, but the structure and size differ from left to right. There is a large, movable flap of skin in front of each ear which, with the broad facial disc, serves to concentrate sound into the ears.

Although the range of hearing is little different from that of a human ear, the ability to hear low and medium-pitched sounds could be as much as ten times better. The greatest sensitivity is at a higher pitch than in man or in diurnal birds. The major facility offered by these remarkable ears, however, is due to the differing size and position of the left and right ears, which enable the owl to pinpoint a sound with impressive accuracy. This is ideal for locating and swooping on prey in complete darkness. This owl also has excellent vision in poor light, for it is one of the most nocturnal of owls. It has been likened to a night harrier, hunting over open ground with a light, wavering, elegant flight as it quarters an area.

The Long-eared Owl is also remarkable for its extended vocabulary. Its basic song is a dull, low, almost moaning hoot, audible for half a mile (1km) or more. The notes given by the female are rather higher and softer than those of the male, and both can be imitated quite accurately by blowing across the neck of a bottle.

Deep hoots and higher, questioning responses are frequently given by male and female in turn. Other calls include a cat-like hiss, a barking "*woof-woof*", a high "*yip-yip*" like the flight call of a Barn Owl (*Tyto alba*), and a variety of bill-snapping and tongue-clicking noises. In addition to its vocal dexterity and the clicking sounds, the Long-eared Owl makes loud claps with its wings during display flights. It gives a single clap each time, but may perform up to 20 such claps during a single flight.

Hunting Long-eared Owls concentrate on the edges of woodland and open spaces with rough grassland, and over young trees and waste ground of all kinds. They fly low and slowly, pouncing on small mammals such as mice, voles and rats and also on roosting birds. The importance of the voles in their diet is reflected by the cyclical nature of the owls' breeding success, which is firmly linked to the fluctuating numbers of voles. Years with large numbers mean that many pairs of owls breed and, on average, they lay and hatch more eggs, and rear more young. Poor vole years result in pairs often missing a breeding season, or laying fewer eggs and feeding fewer young. The Long-eared Owl, like many species, starts incubation from the very first egg and only if there is plenty of food will the smaller, weaker chicks be fed.

The old nest of another bird, or a flattened squirrel drey, is usually chosen as a nest site by the Long-eared Owl. Typical nests may be on the flat platforms of Sparrowhawks (*Accipiter nisus*) or in the bigger, deeper bowls of old crows' nests. Others will be on the flimsy, see-through lattice of sticks made by Woodpigeons (*Columba palumbus*). The owls will nest in wicker baskets specially placed for them in trees. The nest may be in a conifer, or a dense willow beside a marsh, or perhaps in a hawthorn thicket on the edge of a heathery moor.

Territories are reported to vary between 125 and 250 acres (50–100ha) in Finland in years when voles are plentiful. In other areas, between 10 and 50 pairs may nest in 40 square miles (100 square kilometres), including hunting areas. The actual territory defended by each pair is unusually small and is restricted to the area around the nest. Hunting ranges can be shared. Nests may sometimes be rather close together, with several pairs using the same small patch of wood in an area of extensive open ground used for hunting. Pairs of Long-eared Owls usually occupy their territory all year round but they prefer to use a different nest each year, even if the alternatives are close together. Past sites may be re-used after a year's gap.

The eggs, which number anything up to seven and even as many as ten in a vole plague year, are incubated for 26 to 28 days. The young leave the nest when 24 days old, although they cannot fly for a further ten days. Like other species using open nests, rather than enclosed cavities, the Long-eared Owl has a relatively short fledging period and quickly moves away from the dangerous restriction of the nest site. The young call loud and long to be fed, often betraying their positions in early summer to those who are trying to find or census owls. They make a high-pitched squeaky "*peeyee*" or "*pzeei*" sound, often likened to the noise of a gate swinging on a rusty old hinge.

When disturbed near the nest, young owls will make a great display of aggression and threat, leaning forward and raising their wings clear of the body in a broad semi-circle around the head. This makes the owl appear twice its actual size. Parent owls are very aggressive and fearless in defence of their young.

The Long-eared Owl is certainly formidable. Yet, in competition with other owls and diurnal birds of prey, it often comes off worst. It is smaller and less powerful than the Tawny Owl, which will often kill a Long-eared Owl in a territorial dispute. However, this bird tends to avoid competition with Tawny Owls, Great Horned Owls (*Bubo virginianus*) and Barred Owls (*Strix varia*), being a bird of the forest edge and more open spaces than these deep-woodland dwellers. But quite a large number of Long-eared Owls are killed by Eagle Owls (*Bubo bubo*), Goshawks (*Accipiter gentilis*) and other predators.

The Long-eared Owl has long been persecuted by man and, in many regions, its numbers have been severely reduced or eliminated altogether. Such persecution grows largely out of myth and ignorance. What the Long-eared Owl deserves is praise for its useful way of life, and not the all-too-frequent snap of a trap or blast of hot lead.

STYGIAN OWL
Asio stygius

LENGTH: *380 to 460 mm*   MAP NUMBER: 141
DESCRIPTION: *Large, dark, eared owl; closely mottled; orange eyes*
DISTRIBUTION: *Mexico, Central and South America, Caribbean*
HABITAT: *Forests, mountains, bush*
EGGS: *2. Nest in tree or on ground*
STATUS: *Uncertain, declining and locally threatened*

The eared owls of the genus *Asio* are closely related and the Stygian Owl is particularly close to the Long-eared Owl (*Asio otus*). This bird does actually look like a dark Long-eared Owl, being upright, fairly slim and with noticeable ear tufts. These are closely-set and slightly less obvious than those of the Long-Eared Owl, but its general character shows a close affinity to the commoner bird; indeed, it has a similar fierce expression. However, it has a rather plainer, darker face and also has yellow eyes instead of the fiercely orange orbs of the Long-eared Owl. It is a larger bird than the Long-eared Owls of North America but smaller and less powerfully built than the closely-related birds of Africa. Unlike the Long-eared Owl, it has almost bare toes, although the legs are well feathered.

On the back – terms such as upperparts and underparts seem inappropriate for such an upright bird – the Stygian Owl is almost sooty black, with dull white and buff barring and mottling. The front is rich buff, marked in a very close, herring-bone pattern of black streaks and cross bars.

Whether this blackness warrants the epithet 'as black as Styx' is a matter of choice. The name comes from the legendary Greek river of the Hades, the underworld or hell, across which the mythical ferryman, Charon, ferried the ghosts of the dead. Stygian characteristics are related to infernal and dark attributes, and the evocative name of this owl conjures up a particular air of mystery and dread.

It is an owl of the Americas, found in north-west Mexico, eastern Mexico (including Cozumel Island off the Yucatan Peninsula) and Guatemala, on Cuba and the Isle of Pines, Hispaniola, in southern and central Brazil and in Paraguay and northern Argentina. Each of these six areas has what has been claimed as a separate race. This distribution is, however, incompletely documented for the bird is poorly known in the wild and little-studied. The racial distinctions are, at best, weak.

The Stygian Owl is a bird of the forests, often high in the mountains, but shows a remarkable adaptability in its behaviour. It has been found in both humid and semi-arid forests, in fully-developed tropical rain-forest and in what amounts to little more than low, thorny bush country. In

Venezuela, it apparently has a very wide altitudinal range and it is possible that its nocturnal behaviour may disguise the fact that it is commoner than is generally believed.

Little is really known about the prey of this owl but it is said to feed on bats and has been known to eat doves. In Popayan, in the Andes, ten Stygian Owls were killed on the central plaza as they arrived at dusk to prey on roosting Eared Doves (*Zenaida auriculata*).

The calls and song of this owl remain poorly defined. The best description available is of a hooting "*hu-hu*" or "*hu-hu-hoo*", but a short, cat-like "*miah*" has been heard and recorded from a female in Belize. The calls are probably given at dusk or after dark, when the Stygian Owl becomes active and begins to hunt.

Although reputed to be adaptable, and likely to benefit from its ability to nest both in trees and on the ground if its forest habitat is felled, its breeding biology is virtually unknown. A nest in Cuba was found in a tree and another, built with shredded palm leaves, was found on the ground, but its preference is unclear. The probability is that large, old nests of other birds are used, as they are by the Long-eared Owl. In Cuba, where the forest has been cleared, the Stygian Owl, too, has gone. There must be grounds for fearing that the unchecked clearances of the rain-forest will bring about a serious decline in the populations of the Stygian Owl over much of its range.

ABYSSINIAN LONG-EARED OWL
Asio abyssinicus

LENGTH: *400 mm*   MAP NUMBER: 142
DESCRIPTION: *Large, eared, streaked*
DISTRIBUTION: *East Africa, Zaire*
HABITAT: *Mountain heaths and cedar forests*
EGGS: *? Nest in old nest of bird of prey*
STATUS: *Scarce*

The large long-eared owls of Africa, which are found in Ethiopia and parts of Zaire and Kenya, are separated into this species by many authorities, but grouped by others with the Long-eared Owl (*Asio otus*) of Europe, Asia and North America. The Long-eared Owl is so variable that it becomes a matter of opinion whether some races are really separate species or not. Further study may require them all to be grouped in one superspecies.

Compared with European Long-eared Owls, these African birds are larger, darker in colour and more strongly barred below. They also have larger, more powerful claws and bills, which suggest a rather different, and larger, diet. They live in the depths of highland cedar forests at heights of 10,000 feet (3,000m) or more above sea level, and on the Ruwenzori Mountains and Mount Kenya. The latter birds add a further complication to the overall picture, being darker still but smaller than Ethiopian owls.

On mountain heaths at 12,900 feet (3,940m) above sea level in Ethiopia, Abyssinian Long-eared Owls were found to feed on shrews and seven different kinds of small rodents, including the giant mole, and the average weight of prey was considerably greater than that caught in North America or Europe. On these heathy plateaux, the owls behave much as Long-eared Owls in Europe and are equally likely to form communal roosts close to areas with abundant prey. Up to 30 have been disturbed from the fantastic groves of giant heath.

Like the Long-eared Owl, the Abyssinian Long-eared Owl has a deep, soft hoot and performs a display flight, including a single wing-clap beneath the body, and adopts the old nests of other birds. No significant differences in breeding biology appear to be known to separate this from the widespread species farther north.

MADAGASCAR LONG-EARED OWL
Asio madagascariensis

LENGTH: *320 mm*   MAP NUMBER: 143
DESCRIPTION: *Upright, eared owl; boldly streaked and barred below; dark orange eyes*
DISTRIBUTION: *Eastern Madagascar*
HABITAT: *Humid forest*
STATUS: *Threatened or endangered*

Compared with the Abyssinian Long-eared Owl (*Asio abyssinicus*), there is more widespread agreement that this is a separate species of owl, although it is still classed as part of the Long-eared Owl (*Asio otus*) superspecies group. It is a long-eared owl that has somehow reached an island and become isolated over time, surviving in the restricted and diminishing humid forest of eastern Madagascar. This owl is now so isolated that there is no likelihood that its separateness as a species can be tested by the arrival of long-eared owls flying in from elsewhere.

This is a fairly small bird for a long-eared owl. It is darker above with more orange-buff markings, and pale below with striking cross-bars from the long, narrow black streaks that are relatively sparse over most of the underparts. Despite its size, however, it has particularly long ear tufts and, more significantly, very powerful claws which indicate that it hunts fairly large prey. It is secretive, strictly nocturnal and little known.

SHORT-EARED OWL
Asio flammeus

LENGTH: *330 to 430 mm*   MAP NUMBER: 144
DESCRIPTION: *Large; short ear tufts; dark face surrounding yellow eyes; pale, streaked plumage*
DISTRIBUTION: *North and South America, Caribbean, Europe, Asia*
HABITAT: *Open moors, plantations, grassland, marshes*
EGGS: *3–16. Nest on ground*
STATUS: *Locally frequent*

Over a worldwide range whose sheer scale rivals that of the Barn Owl (*Tyto alba*), the Short-eared Owl is the greatest exponent of low-level hunting over open ground. On dull days and at dusk, it is reminiscent of a harrier in its appearance, behaviour and habitat. It has the same light, effortless flight, full of grace and a joy to watch.

Short-eared Owls breed over much of northern North America, and are winter visitors to the southern half of the United States and northern Mexico. They occur in Hispaniola, Puerto Rico, on the coastal strip of Venezuela, along a narrow band of Colombia and Ecuador, and over the southern half of South America. They are also found on isolated groups of islands, such as the Falkland Islands, Hawaii and the Galapagos Islands. Most of the seven recognized races are island birds.

Short-eared Owls breed in Iceland, the Faeroe Islands and Britain, on the northern and central European mainland, and over a vast stretch of Asia as far as the Bering Sea. They are not found in Ireland, and in large parts of their range, such as most of France and much of Britain, they are very localized and discontinuous in their distribution. The owls move out in winter from the greater part of their northerly range in Europe and Asia, going in almost any direction, to almost any distance, unpredictable and footloose, until they find food.

These are large, handsome owls. In flight, their yellow eyes glow fiercely, with a frosty sparkle that gleams out from deep black sockets. But a clear view of a perched bird shows the colour of the eyes to be the purest lemon. Because they are so often abroad by day, Short-eared Owls often display a feature common to all owls. Unlike man, whose eyes dilate and contract together, the irises of an owl act independently, according to the light. A Short-eared Owl sitting in the sun will often have one eye hugely yellow, the pupil a tiny dot where the sun strikes it. The other eye, in deep shade, may be a large black pupil surrounded by a narrow ring of colour. The eyes are extremely sensitive and fascinating to watch.

In flight, the Short-eared Owl has long, broad, rounded wings that help its featherweight progress and instant manoeuvrability. They have very dark carpal, or wrist, patches, both above and below, with a broad band of pale buff to orange across the flight feathers. The underside of the wing is largely white; the body looks darker but is mostly white and unmarked on the belly, whereas the Long-eared Owl (*Asio otus*) is more streaked over the whole of the underside.

Being so often on the ground, the Short-eared Owl has a more angled, less upright stance than most owls, with the head looking quite long and relatively narrow. The owl is large and rather bulky at rest, with a particularly heavy-bodied look and thickly-feathered flanks. The feet are densely feathered and the toes are equipped with long, curved claws.

The Short-eared Owl does have ear tufts, as its name suggests, but often they cannot be seen. When laid back flat, they are all but indistinguishable, but an owl taken by surprise can raise them into quite substantial 'horns', rather close together over the forehead. At the nest, the adult birds make use of their flexible, expressive facial discs and these horns and put on a frightening exhibition that probably deters many predators. Whatever their function, the feathery tufts are clearly of less importance to this diurnal owl of open country than to the strictly nocturnal, woodland Long-eared Owl.

Short-eared Owls are out and about at any time of day, although they seem most active around dusk. They are particularly active during daylight in winter, in places where diurnal competitors such as harriers are absent, and in summer when they are feeding chicks.

The prey of Short-eared Owls is almost exclusively made up of small mammals, such as mice, voles and shrews. Small birds make up a minor part of the diet. In Finland, 40 pairs survived in less than 8 square miles (20 square kilometres), each pair laying an average of over seven eggs and rearing almost five young in a year when voles were abundant. The owls ate some 50,000 small mammals, of which 42,000 were voles, and under 700 birds.

In North American studies of over 16,000 prey items, almost 95 percent were small mammals. Of these, two-thirds were voles. In the Arctic tundra, Short-eared Owls appear in years when lemmings are plentiful, sharing them with Snowy Owls (*Nyctea scandiaca*) and skuas. In South America, mammals are also the chief food. In the Galapagos Islands, however, local conditions influence the diet and small birds, such as finches, and seabirds, such as petrels and shearwaters, are regularly taken. On the Falkland Islands, the owls eat many Grey-backed Storm-Petrels (*Garrodia nereis*) and diving-petrels, as well as performing the useful service of catching rats.

The prey is caught in a swoop from the air after a low, quartering flight rather like that of a hunting Barn Owl. Sometimes an owl will watch and listen from its perch, often a fence post or even a milestone, and pounce on prey

Short-eared Owl (*Asio flammeus*)

in short aerial forays. Dunes with spiky marram, marshes with reed and sedge, wet pastures, moorland with heather and bilberry, and open, treeless tundra all let the bird drift over large areas in search of prey. It usually avoids trees and bushes but sometimes roosts low in a bush or in long grass sheltered by a willow thicket, where it may be taken for a Long-eared Owl.

In winter, groups of owls roost together, sometimes in large numbers and often in depressions in the ground such as old claypits from which, if disturbed, they come flopping out in all directions. When voles are very numerous, there may be 100 or more owls together, making a strange, eerie sight as they dance silently over the ground at dusk, their wing-patches flashing pale in the fading light. Sometimes they nest, out of their usual range and even out of season, if the food supply remains good.

The territorial call of this owl is a series of deep, booming notes. These are usually given in a high, slow-flapping display flight. This is combined with rapid, multiple wing-claps with the wings held beneath the body. As well as this pulsating "*boo-hoohoohoohoo*" call, there is a quick, sharp alarm of "*chek-chek-chek*" and a wheezy, strained "*keeyow*", which is strongly emphasized. Near the nest, the adults give a variety of sneezing, hissing and tearing sounds, but the range of calls is less than that of the Long-eared Owl. In winter, this is a silent owl, whose call is heard only on rare occasions.

A rough, shallow scrape is the usual rudimentary nest made by a pair of Short-eared Owls. It may be under a tussock of moor grass, or in a broad swathe of old heather, in growing crops, or in old stubble. Some bits of grass and twigs are gathered and placed in the nest by the female, a rare example of an owl actually adding material to the structure of the nest. Only rarely is a nest raised above the ground, in an old nest of some other bird. Nesting begins when the weather is sufficiently mild, if there is enough food. Nests and eggs are not unknown in the winter, provided there are plenty of voles. Normally, however, nesting starts late in the spring.

In North America, five or six eggs are normal, and six are more usual in the north. In Europe, six to eight may be laid and occasionally as many as 12 or even 16. The male hunts, presenting food to the female in special food-passes rather like a Hen Harrier (*Circus cyaneus*). An incubating hen will generally rest with her eyes half-closed, hiding the tell-tale yellow of the iris although keeping the pupil clear so that she can keep an eye on the world. If the nest is approached when the female is incubating, she may sit tight. The male flies nearby, calling noisily until he literally crash-lands and performs a distraction display to take attention away from the nest. Like Hen Harriers, some Short-eared Owls are extremely aggressive and will regularly strike people on the head in terrifying swoops.

When the eggs hatch, the young are of staggered size and age. After about 12 days, they start to move around the vicinity of the nest, hiding in runs or beneath long vegetation. If food is plentiful, only the male hunts. If it is scarce, the female joins in before that stage. When possible, food is brought in to excess and is left around the edge of the nest, which becomes a rather noisome and unwelcoming place.

The young birds may wander as far as 200 yards (200m) from the nest before they can fly, waving their pale wings and calling when they want to be fed. For such large owls, they fly very young, when only 24 to 27 days old. This is a full 10 to 20 days before the tree-bound chicks of the Long-eared Owl. Nevertheless, they rely on their parents for at least seven weeks. The number of young that survive to fledge and become independent depends mainly on the amount of food. In typical owl style, the younger, weaker chicks die first when food is at a premium.

The numbers of Short-eared Owls have declined over a long period in many areas. A temporary abundance in young conifer plantations, which are so common in Scotland, flatters to deceive. It is inevitably followed by a decline when trees become so dense that the owls cannot reach their prey on the ground. Even after clear-felling, the ground is never of much use to them again. Conifer afforestation, despite its short-term benefit, effectively wipes out the owls. Drainage of coastal marshes and pastures has also affected them seriously.

In North America and large parts of Siberia, the owls have adapted to nesting in agricultural areas, but increased mechanization has caused the loss of huge numbers of nests and young. In Canada, Short-eared Owls take advantage of the short grass beside airfields and, between 1965 and 1967 at Vancouver Airport, some 543 birds of prey were trapped, including 426 Short-eared Owls. Others are killed on roads by traffic or in collisions with fences on their low hunting forays.

The modern world could be more hospitable to the Short-eared Owl but it has proved adaptable and mobile enough to survive. Long may it continue to delight the birdwatcher with its elegant flight and flashing eyes.

AFRICAN MARSH OWL
Asio capensis

LENGTH: *305 to 380 mm*   MAP NUMBER: 145
DESCRIPTION: *Large; short ear tufts; dark eyes in pale face*
DISTRIBUTION: *Africa, mostly south of the Sahara*
HABITAT: *Marshy grassland, open savanna*
EGGS: *2–6. Nest in damp grass on ground*
STATUS: *Locally frequent*

The African Marsh Owl gives the impression of being an African equivalent of the Short-eared Owl (*Asio flammeus*). This especially seems so when it flaps away from a grassy hollow in a springy, flexible yet somewhat jerky flight, showing bright buff patches on the outer parts of its wings. It has the same basic pattern but is darker and more grey-looking, with a much more uniform colour. Its face is paler overall, but may be darker around or below the eyes with a grey smudge, as if it had been weeping.

The eyes themselves are brown and much darker, with none of the clear yellow of the Short-eared Owl. Its short, inconspicuous ear tufts are even smaller, with a more pointed shape. But it is built along the same lines and behaves in much the same way.

This is a bird of Africa, including Madagascar. It is found in an isolated area of the north-west, and it is possible that some birds migrate south to Senegal and The Gambia, where small groups roost together outside the breeding season. It is seriously declining in Morocco and has already gone from Algeria. It does occur in isolated patches in a

much larger, separate region in West Africa, although it is in the main probably a non-breeding visitor there. It is more widely distributed in East Africa, from Ethiopia southwards down to the Cape, and westwards into Angola. It may very occasionally drift north into Spain.

The birds on Madagascar are considerably heavier, darker and more barred, with stronger bills. This large-billed tendency is also shown by diurnal, or daytime, birds of prey in Madagascar, and is presumably an adaptation to cope with larger and stronger prey species.

The African Marsh Owl is found in open vleis and swampy moorlands, in the great sudd of the Upper Nile in Sudan, in mountain grassland up to 9,000 feet (2,750m) above sea level in Ethiopia and even in freshly-cultivated

rice fields. Despite its name, it is less of a marsh bird than the Grass Owl (*Tyto capensis*), which tends to be found in the moister regions of any area where these two species occur together.

This is an owl of open spaces, nesting on the ground, often more or less in a tunnel in the vegetation, but occasionally using an old crow's nest. Some scraps of vegetation are added to the nest lining, a trait again recalling the Short-eared Owl. Two to four eggs, and only occasionally five or six, are laid at two-day intervals. Incubation begins with the first one so the chicks hatch out over a week or more. They remain in the nest for two or three weeks before wandering nearby until they can fly.

African Marsh Owls are more nocturnal than Short-eared

Owls, usually hunting at night although they are not infrequently observed before dusk. They seem to hunt more often from a suitable vantage point, but probably most often use a regular, quartering flight, like the Short-eared Owl. Its nocturnal behaviour, and more frequent still-hunting, may mean that it relies more on its ears than its eyes. The complexity of these ears, and therefore their sensitivity, is comparable with that of the Long-eared Owl (*Asio otus*), so the African Marsh Owl is one of the most finely-adapted owls in its hunting skills, perfectly tuned to its specialized role.

This bird was once thought to feed mainly on insects but recent studies have revealed a diet of rodents in Nigeria, and quite a number of small birds in South Africa. It probably eats rodents in the breeding season and later turns to a wider spectrum of prey. That it has a more insectivorous diet than the Short-eared Owl seems clear, and groups may even concentrate around termite nests and catch insects fleeing from grassland fires. One bird was watched hunting insects around street lights in the city of Antananarivo, the capital of Madagascar.

Calls described for this owl include a deep "*kaaa*" with a croaking, frog-like effect, or a more gabbling note like distant geese. Adults grunt in flight and the young have a husky "*queeeep*" and a more musical, rising "*too-eeee*". A squealing note is also given in a distraction display by the male. This display resembles that of the Short-eared Owl and is clearly of great value to a ground-nesting bird. When a nest is approached, the male will fly around and then crash to the ground, thrashing about and squealing as if injured, drawing attention away from the nest, eggs and incubating female.

African Marsh Owls resemble Short-eared Owls in so many ways that some authors have suggested that they are the same species. But sufficient differences exist to preclude that. Indeed, it is not even clear that the Short-eared Owl is a particularly close relative. It may be that the African Marsh Owl is derived from a different branch of the *Asio* group, and has evolved a similar appearance and lifestyle to the Short-eared Owl by a different route.

JAMAICAN OWL

— ONE SPECIES —

JAMAICAN OWL
Pseudoscops grammicus

LENGTH: *310 mm* MAP NUMBER: 146
DESCRIPTION: *Upright; warm brown, eared; whitish edges to face, yellow eyes*
DISTRIBUTION: *Jamaica*
HABITAT: *Woodland and open country*
EGGS: *2. Nest in tree*
STATUS: *Rare, perhaps endangered*

This species remains in a genus of its own but, like the Striped Owl (*Asio (Rhinoptynx) clamator*), its relationship to other species is still unclear. Once considered a close relative of the scops owls – a belief commemorated in its scientific name – the Jamaican Owl is now thought to be closer to the *Asio* group. Yet, according to some authors, elements of the *Athene* and *Aegolius* genera can be traced. It is a little too large for the *Otus* or *Athene* genera and, in outward appearance, superficially resembles the eared owls (*Asio spp*), although its short ear tufts are splayed outwards rather like an eagle owl (*Bubo spp*).

Whatever its origins and close relatives, it is an owl confined to Jamaica, an unusually restricted range for a species of the New World and more reminiscent of island species in Asia. Even in Jamaica it is rare, but it inhabits a variety of countryside, from woodland to more open spaces with scattered trees. It requires at least a few trees of considerable age, for it nests inside hollows in tree trunks

or between the broad bases of two diverging branches, laying two white eggs.

The Jamaican Owl is a nocturnal species, best detected by listening for its quavering hoot or guttural, growling calls after dark. A local name is 'potoo'. Little has been ascertained about the food or the behaviour of this bird, which presents the field scientist with yet another challenge – this time in a pleasant setting.

FEARFUL OWL

ONE SPECIES

FEARFUL OWL
Nesasio solomonensis

LENGTH: *280 to 380 mm* MAP NUMBER: 147
DESCRIPTION: *Warm buff-brown above; pale face with white brows; streaked below; yellow eyes*
DISTRIBUTION: *Solomon Islands*
HABITAT: *Lowland and hillside forest*
STATUS: *Uncertain, probably rare*

Many owls are blessed with evocative English names but none more so than the Fearful Owl, a name conjuring images of a powerful predator, feared by other inhabitants of its woodland domain. It is, indeed, feared. Although not a large owl, it is an effective predator with a large, wickedly-hooked bill and long, sharp claws which would do justice to an owl of much greater size.

The Fearful Owl is a handsome, bright-eyed bird, with piercing yellow eyes surrounded by dusky feathers set beneath white brows. The facial disc is poorly defined but distinctively pale against the tawny-brown of the rest of its head. The underparts are also a rather rich tawny, streaked liberally with dark brown.

This is one of those owls best placed in a genus of its own. Although close to the eared owls (*Asio spp*), despite its lack of ear tufts, it also seems to be related, ecologically speaking, to the eagle owls (*Bubo spp*). It is a forest bird of the lowlands and lower hills of just three of the Solomon Islands to the east of New Guinea: Bougainville, Santa Isabel and Choiseul.

It is known to capture opossums and some birds, and is presumed to specialize in fairly large prey.

FOREST OWLS

FOUR SPECIES

TENGMALM'S OWL/BOREAL OWL
Aegolius funereus

LENGTH: *190 to 230 mm*   MAP NUMBER: 148
DESCRIPTION: *Small, round-headed, high-browed; yellow eyes in pale face*
DISTRIBUTION: *Central and northern Europe, Asia, northern North America and the Rockies*
HABITAT: *Boreal forest*
EGGS: *3–11. Nest in tree hole*
STATUS: *Locally frequent to rare*

Boreal is the American name and an accurate description of the habitat of this northern owl. But it is known as Tengmalm's Owl in Britain and as chouette de Tengmalm in France. It is to be hoped that standardization does not remove the name of Tengmalm from the list of owls. The name Richardson's Owl, its North American title at one time, has already been abandoned. The owl was dedicated to the memory of Sir John Richardson, a Scottish naval surgeon and Arctic explorer, by Prince Charles Lucien Bonaparte in 1838. Sadly, Richardson's Skua is also now known by a different name.

Pehr Gustaf Tengmalm, a Swedish doctor, published local studies of Tawny Owls (*Strix aluco*) in 1781. He died soon afterwards and the ornithologist J.F. Gmelin named this owl in his honour in 1788. Tengmalm was not, in fact, the first to identify this owl; indeed, Linnaeus knew of it some years before Tengmalm was born. Nevertheless, Tengmalm deserves the recognition because of his pioneering work in the classification of owls in his native country. Oddly, in Scandinavia this bird is known not by his name, but as the Pearly Owl.

Tengmalm's Owl has typical features of the *Aegolius* genus, such as a high crown and a high, flat, almost bulging forehead, above big round eyes of deep yellow. These give the owl a distinctive, questioning look. Its facial disc is rather pale, edged neatly in white and dark brown, and the eyes are emphasized by splashes of black. The forehead is speckled with silvery-white. On the bird's back are large, roundish white spots, the pearls of the Scandinavian name. Some birds have a rich, rusty-brown background colour while others are more grey. A perched Tengmalm's Owl shows surprisingly large feet, which are exaggerated by thick, pale feathering.

Young birds have a striking plumage, typical of this genus which has much greater differentiation between juveniles and adults than most. They are extremely dark, rich chocolate brown, with broad spots of white on the wings but solidly dark underparts. The face has a broad, white hour-glass marking between the eyes, but the eyes are of the same vivid yellow as those of their parents.

Although slightly larger than a Little Owl (*Athene noctua*), Tengmalm's Owl looks more like a miniature Tawny Owl, with its upright pose, very large head and strong facial disc. The high, arched eyebrows are quite unlike the frowning brows of the Little Owl. When alarmed, it will raise its crown feathers into two short, blunt horns but it has no proper feathery ear tufts. In flight, Tengmalm's Owl resembles a larger owl more than the Little Owl. Instead of the Little Owl's bounding, woodpecker-like flight, it has a wavering, gentler progress like a Long-eared Owl (*Asio otus*).

On a map of the world, the main range of this species looks like a narrow band drawn right across the northern hemisphere, from the southern half of Alaska skirting south of the bottom edge of Hudson Bay and Newfoundland, then across much of Scandinavia and continuing as a belt across the breadth of Asia. South of this range, the bird is also resident in the Rockies southwards as far as Colorado and even northern New Mexico, and west of the Rockies it occurs southwards to Oregon. These North American populations have been discovered since 1970 but the birds were undoubtedly there all along. There is an isolated population in central Europe, a tiny population in the Pyrenees and a few isolated islands of distribution in the Caucasus Mountains and in central Asia. These pockets were perhaps left behind in high altitude forests when the bulk of the range moved northwards after the most recent Ice Age.

In North America, the Boreal Owl sometimes migrates southwards in large numbers into the northern and north-eastern parts of the United States. These movements are rare, irregular and unpredictable. Occasionally, the birds of northern Europe and Asia also move out in response to the cyclical fluctuations of the small mammals which they eat, but these movements are usually limited to small numbers, even though they move far to the south.

It has been suggested that females and younger birds migrate but adult males are resident, the male's urge to search for food being balanced by the urge to remain in an established territory, ready to claim a nest site early in the spring. Certainly, as American studies have recently confirmed, females are not faithful to territories and are likely to move almost at random.

These owls live mostly in coniferous forests where, in Europe and Asia, they are found alongside Waxwings (*Bombycilla garrulus*), Three-toed Woodpeckers

Tengmalm's Owl/Boreal Owl (*Aegolius funereus*)

(*Picoides tridactylus*) and Pine Grosbeaks (*Pinicola enucleator*) and, in America, alongside Cedar Waxwings (*Bombycilla cedrorum*) and Black-backed Woodpeckers (*Picoides arcticus*). In North America, it has a close relative in the Northern Saw-whet Owl (*Aegolius acadicus*), a bird of very similar appearance and habit, found to the south of the Boreal Owl except for a small range of overlap. It remains unclear why there are two overlapping types in North America, but not in Europe, and whether the European one moved from North America, or vice versa.

In the Alps, Tengmalm's Owls are found in woods at heights up to 6,200 feet (1,900m) above sea level. The owls are found at altitudes of 6,500 feet (2,000m) in central Asia and even at 10,800 feet (3,300m) in the Rocky Mountains. There, they occupy woods of Engelman spruce and balsam, but farther north they tend to be in conifers mixed with birch, aspen, willow and poplar, frequently close to clearings. Across its range, Tengmalm's Owl prefers spruce but the scatter of poplars, willows and other deciduous trees seems to be an essential feature when it searches for a nest site. In Eurasia, it most often uses the old holes chiselled into large trees by Black Woodpeckers (*Dryocopus martius*). In North America, the nest holes of Pileated Woodpeckers (*Dryocopus pileatus*) are chosen where available, though this species is absent from much of the owl's range. Holes made by smaller woodpeckers are also used but may be much more difficult for the owl to enter quickly and inconspicuously, even though they exclude predators more effectively.

One interesting suggestion is that the female owl will sit just inside the nest, with her head filling the entrance to her nest site, to conceal the conspicuous black cavity. Natural holes are scarce and are occupied far less than woodpecker holes. Ornithologists have taken advantage of this lack of nest sites by providing nest boxes, which the owls take to very readily and almost to the exclusion of all other sites, so that their local population can be easily and dramatically increased.

Eggs are laid earlier than those of other owls, to match the spring abundance and activity of voles. Normally there are three to five eggs, but up to 11 have been recorded in good vole years, when the largest number of young are raised. In the leanest years, the owls may not nest at all; in times of plenty, when hunting is easy, the male may be bigamous, or a female may leave her half-grown chicks to be fed by the male while she goes to find another mate and rear a second brood.

In keeping with its cold, northern range, Tengmalm's Owl has thick, soft feathering. This plumage is exceptionally soft and silky in texture and, as with the Great Grey Owl (*Strix nebulosa*), the thick feathering conceals what is, in fact, a small bird beneath. Its ears are complex and highly developed but, rather than being positioned asymmetrically, they differ in shape. The openings are long, equalling the depth of the skull, and are surrounded by a flap of skin and a row of special feathers. Those in front of the ear are soft and allow sound to pass through; those behind are stiff and form the dark outer edge to the face.

The ears are remarkably sensitive to low-frequency sounds, such as the rustling of a mouse on the forest floor, and their elongated shape and wide separation allow the owl to gain a precise appreciation of direction and distance without the extreme bobbing of the head seen in, for example, the Little Owl. No movement is needed because the ears are already sufficiently displaced. This is a perfect example of a bird attuned to the highest level in its ability to hunt a specialized diet in a difficult environment.

Tengmalm's Owls are hard to find in their dark, gloomy forests, which buzz with infuriating insects in the long hours of summer daylight but which are intensely cold, silent and apparently lifeless during the winter frosts. One way is to listen for their calls. The song may be heard sporadically in autumn but reaches a peak in the spring. Even during June and July, the song may still be heard from time to time.

The song is a series of five to eight "*hoop*" notes, each liquid but short and sharp. They are made by the male when seeking a mate or announcing that the territory is occupied. Unmated males call a great deal and one was estimated to give 4,000 songs in one night.

This owl is unlikely to be active in daylight, except in North America, and there only rarely. Even where it extends so far north that it lives through 24-hour, continuous light in summer, it prefers only the dimmest hours. Generally, an owl may be expected to become active and hunt for two hours after sunset and again for two hours before sunrise. This reflects a similar pattern of activity in the woodland vole population.

This species will hunt over forest interiors, woodland glades and even open moors. It is a long-winged owl yet moves with ease through dense forest. Often, it flies low under the thickest branches, sliding silently between the saplings and underbrush and perching every so often on a slender branch to scan for prey. It listens, rather than looks. If a vole is heard, the owl can dive through a thin layer of snow or a dense ground layer of bilberry or other undershrub in order to reach it.

Short-tailed, bank and red-backed voles are commonly eaten in Europe and Asia and red-backed voles and white-footed woodmice in America. Shrews are also taken. Only if voles are in very short supply does this owl turn to small birds as prey. Because it is mainly a resident bird, it is able to profit from caching prey for consumption later in the winter. It may also store food in its nest hole in case of late spring snowstorms which cover the ground and can make hunting temporarily impossible.

Tengmalm's Owls can breed quickly and successfully when voles are abundant but, when their populations crash, as they inevitably do, the owls may have to move elsewhere. However, the cycles of vole populations do not often coincide over large areas, so the owls in one place may move about irregularly, while those elsewhere may be stable. When voles are scarce over very large areas at once, the rare, large-scale eruptions of these owls occur, and many probably die during these enforced migrations. It is then that birdwatchers in the United States or even in Britain may have the rare treat of an unexpected Tengmalm's Owl to add to their life lists.

NORTHERN SAW-WHET OWL
Aegolius acadicus

LENGTH: *170 to 190 mm*   MAP NUMBER: 149
DESCRIPTION: *Small, large-headed; grey-brown above,*
warmer rufous-buff below; orange-yellow eyes
DISTRIBUTION: *North America, northern Mexico*
HABITAT: *Damp woods and forest*
EGGS: *3 — 7. Nest in tree hole*
STATUS: *Locally frequent*

Only four species of small, neat owls make up the genus
Aegolius, but they are among the prettiest and most
individual of owls, with highly expressive faces. All have a
high-browed, high-crowned, almost alien look which
produces an intense, quizzical expression, as if
permanently taken by surprise.

The Northern Saw-whet Owl is a North American
representative, its range lying between that of the Boreal
(Tengmalm's) Owl (*Aegolius funereus*) to the north, with a
slight overlap, and the Unspotted Saw-whet Owl (*Aegolius
ridgwayi*) to the south. It looks very like a Boreal Owl but
is a little smaller, almost a third lighter in weight, paler and
more rusty-coloured above. Its facial disc is less sharply
edged with black and its bill is black, not pale. It is not quite
so densely-feathered and fluffy as the Boreal Owl, which
shows greater adaptation to a colder environment, and it
lacks the heavy feathering on the toes of the more
northerly species. Northern Saw-whet Owls have
gloriously large, orange eyes, the black pupils dilating to
wide, shiny buttons surrounded by narrow circles of
orange in poor light.

These birds have a wide range in North America,
including much of Newfoundland. They occur south of a
band running from the St. Lawrence Seaway, north of the
Great Lakes and Lake Winnipeg to Queen Charlotte Island,
north of Vancouver. To the south, they extend as far as
North Carolina in the east, and southern California and

Arizona in the west, with a southward extension on higher ground into northern Mexico.

They live chiefly in moist, dense woodland, which is often mosquito-ridden, treacherous and swampy. This has made detailed study of this owl extremely difficult. They can be found in trembling aspen thickets along rivers, dense patches of willow isolated in rather more arid prairie, the coniferous forest of northern Canada, with its tamarack bogs and swamps, alderwoods and mountain spruce and fir forests, as well as open pine and oak woods in much more arid regions in the mountains of Mexico.

Unlike the essentially resident Boreal Owl, Northern Saw-whet Owls are apparently regular, if short-distance migrants, with significant numbers passing migration watch-points during clear weather in September. Large numbers may very rarely appear unexpectedly in unlikely places. However, rather than being linked to sudden declines in their major prey, some of these movements are likely to be accidental, in that they involve birds being blown off course during migration and turning up as vagrants, not irruptive visitors searching for food.

In winter these small owls are quiet and inconspicuous and hence rather poorly known. The extent to which they move south in the winter months is not altogether certain. They generally move into swampy, deciduous woods in the eastern United States at least, in areas not used in the summer for breeding.

It is the call of this owl that provides its curious name. The whetting of a saw in a woodcutter's yard is no longer a comparison that would be used to describe the call of a bird but, when the name was coined, it must have been a familiar sound. Audubon himself described the contact call of this owl as resembling 'filing the teeth of a large saw'.

The typical territorial song is a regular, rhythmic repetition of a whistling note with about 130 whistles per minute. It is not unlike the song of the Boreal Owl and even more like that of the Ferruginous Pygmy-Owl (*Glaucidium brasilianum*). The sweet whistles are repeated, unceasing and unvarying, for long periods in late winter and early spring. This is therefore the only period when these owls are at all easy to find. Another call, given when the bird is excited, rings like a bell, or a hammer striking an anvil. The saw-whetting note is described as "*screee-awe, scree-awe*".

Northern Saw-whet Owls are strictly nocturnal. By day, they hide in dense foliage, usually close to the ground rather than high in a tree. They remain quiet and still, usually hunched and rounded with their feathers fluffed out, avoiding the attentions of small birds and predators. When closely approached, the owls become tense in a taut, erect pose. One wing is brought round in front of the body, possibly for protection or perhaps to strengthen its camouflage, and the feathers of the crown are raised.

In this posture, they show a hint of feathered horns or ear tufts, as do the Tawny Owl (*Strix aluco*) and several other species not normally regarded as eared owls. Northern Saw-whet Owls rely on keeping still to escape detection, and will maintain this pose so determinedly that they can sometimes be picked up in the hand.

Mice, voles and shrews are the staple diet of this owl. Pocket mice, deer mice and wandering shrews are eaten according to the habitat, and the vast majority of the prey consists of tiny mammals. Very few birds, frogs and insects are killed. In winter, white-footed mice, meadow voles and house mice have predominated in the prey of Northern Saw-whet Owls studied in Connecticut. The owl hunts in or near scrubby places and inside woods, keeping low and taking animals from the ground.

One bird was caught and fitted with a tiny radio transmitter which allowed its nocturnal activity to be documented. The owl hunted over an area of 280 acres (114ha), from 20 minutes after sunset to 20 minutes before sunrise, spending the night moving from perch to perch or chasing prey in sporadic bursts of activity. It hunted mainly in wooded habitats until the first snow of the winter. It then moved into more open locations, catching the more visible deer mice and meadow voles of grasslands. The regular white-footed mice and red-backed voles were probably less conspicuous in the snow.

To find a nest, this owl searches for suitable old woodpecker holes or, occasionally, natural cavities where branches have broken from trees and, in some places, it uses nest boxes. Between three and seven eggs are laid, with an average of over six in the north and under four in the south and west. Occasionally males may have two or even three mates. A favourite trick of birdwatchers searching for this owl is to rap the trunk of trees with likely holes. If the hole is occupied, the owl is sure to poke its head out to see what is going on. The bird has a frustrating mixture of tameness, dangerous curiosity and extreme inconspicuousness.

Incubation may take up to 28 days and, in common with many owls, the female begins incubating soon after the first egg is laid. Weaker, later chicks may die if food is scarce. Like the Boreal Owl, the juveniles have an unusually obvious plumage, which is basically a deep chocolate brown.

There seems little likelihood that the numbers of the Northern Saw-whet will decline or increase dramatically, provided that its food remains uncontaminated and its favourite woods are not felled. It lives happily out of the public gaze, although it is not averse to entering the edges of towns and villages. If people ignore this owl, it is quite content to get on with its life and ignore them.

UNSPOTTED SAW-WHET OWL
Aegolius ridgwayi

LENGTH: *170 to 190 mm*　　MAP NUMBER: 150
DESCRIPTION: *Warm brown, whiter on face and underparts; long tail*
DISTRIBUTION: *Southern Mexico, Central America*
HABITAT: *Woodland, clearings, mountain forest*
STATUS: *Probably rare and threatened*

This is a rare tropical bird of Central America, found in southern Mexico, Guatemala and Costa Rica. Its restricted range contrasts markedly with that of the Northern Saw-whet Owl (*Aegolius acadius*) and even more so with Tengmalm's/Boreal Owl (*Aegolius funereus*), which it closely resembles.

This species is usually distinguished from the Northern Saw-whet Owl by its lack of spots and other obvious markings. However, there is a report of an owl in Mexico which was intermediate between the two species. It seems

Adult

Juvenile

In Costa Rica, this small, large-headed owl with big feet lives at the edges of forests and in the upper canopy of denser woodland blocks. It likes clearings and pastures where there are still tall trees around the edges, and the oak forests of the high mountains right up to the timber line, as well as the lower, wetter cloud-forests down to 8,200 feet (2,500m) above sea level.

It is a very nocturnal bird, and is therefore hard to see well, if at all. It seems to become active soon after dusk and remains so until shortly before dawn, so the determined birdwatcher should not have long to wait if a suitable vantage point is found. The Unspotted Saw-whet Owl may be best located by its calls, which include a series of four to ten rhythmic, mellow hoots on an even pitch. It also gives a high-pitched trill when alarmed or excited.

Reports of this owl from unexpected, low altitudes are thought to be the result of confusion with the remarkably similar calls of a tree frog. When the Unspotted Saw-whet Owl begins to hunt soon after dusk, it has a quick fluttery and agile flight with rapid wingbeats, which may suggest that it catches more insects, bats and birds than Northern Saw-whet Owls, but the food is thought to be very largely small rodents and shrews.

Little or nothing is known about the nesting behaviour of this species. It is probably as much elusive as it is rare, but it nevertheless presents a challenge to those interested in studying its breeding cycle.

that the Unspotted Saw-whet Owl has a plumage type which is found in the juvenile of the Northern Saw-whet Owl, but it retains this into adulthood.

BUFF-FRONTED OWL
Aegolius harrisii

LENGTH: *200 mm*   MAP NUMBER: 151
DESCRIPTION: *Dark brown, spotted white above; yellow-cream on face and underparts with dark collar*
DISTRIBUTION: *North-west and south-central South America*
HABITAT: *Open areas, forest clearings*
STATUS: *Uncertain, probably rare and threatened*

This owl is an enigma. The Buff-fronted Owl occurs in Venezuela, Colombia, Ecuador and Peru, all in north-west South America, and also in a completely separate area as far away as southern Brazil, Paraguay and northern Argentina. This is a puzzling distribution which raises questions

which are difficult to answer.

It is a very handsome owl, quite unlike the other *Aegolius* species in appearance. It is basically dark brown above, with clear white spots on the scapulars, wing coverts and tail. A broad collar of cream crosses from the sides of the neck over the upper back. From the front, it is a largely unmarked, yellow-buff bird, with a narrow band of dark brown or black across its chest.

A large yellow bill forms the centre of an X-shaped pattern on its face, complemented by shining greenish-yellow eyes and the central mask of dark brown. The forehead is conspicuously creamy-buff, as are the facial discs, which are edged with black. No other owl resembles this strikingly-patterned bird.

Its voice is a quavering trill of "*tutututututututu*", which lasts for three or four seconds. Sometimes there is a brief pause in the middle or a slight change of pitch. A local name in Venezuela is 'surrucucu' which is presumably a representation of this call.

Virtually nothing is known of the nesting habits of the Buff-fronted Owl, except that is has been found nesting in a hollow tree in Argentina. Even its habitat is not entirely clear, but it can be found in rather open areas or forest clearings up to a height of at least 6,500 feet (2,000m) above sea level in Colombia, up to 10,200 feet (3,100m) in Ecuador and up to 12,500 feet (3,800m) in the Paramos, the high windswept plateau of Venezuela. The Andean group is poorly documented, but the south-eastern population is, if anything, even more scantily recorded.

This is one of many owls that illustrate how poorly known some of the world's birds still are. The Buff-fronted Owl is probably not endangered but there is no certainty of this. This bird is so infrequently seen that it might fade into complete obscurity and never be missed. That would be a sad fate for such a beautiful creature.

DISTRIBUTION MAPS

The maps on the following pages show the overall geographical range of each species. However, the exact distribution of a bird within its range will depend on the availability of suitable habitat, and may therefore be much more patchy than these maps can indicate. In addition, it must be remembered that for many species, especially those living in the tropics and on remote islands, information is very scarce and our knowledge is sometimes based solely on a handful of museum specimens. Moreover, the activities of man are at the present time altering habitats on a vast scale, and at an alarming rate, and the distribution of the birds depending on them is also likely to change drastically. Almost all owls are residents, so the maps show a single year-round range. In the case of migratory species, fuller details of the birds' movements are given in the text.

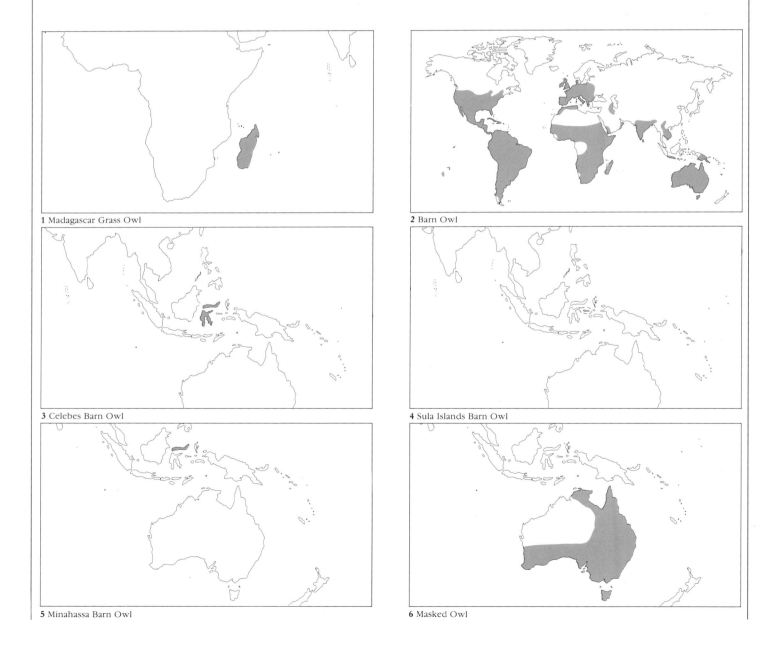

1 Madagascar Grass Owl

2 Barn Owl

3 Celebes Barn Owl

4 Sula Islands Barn Owl

5 Minahassa Barn Owl

6 Masked Owl

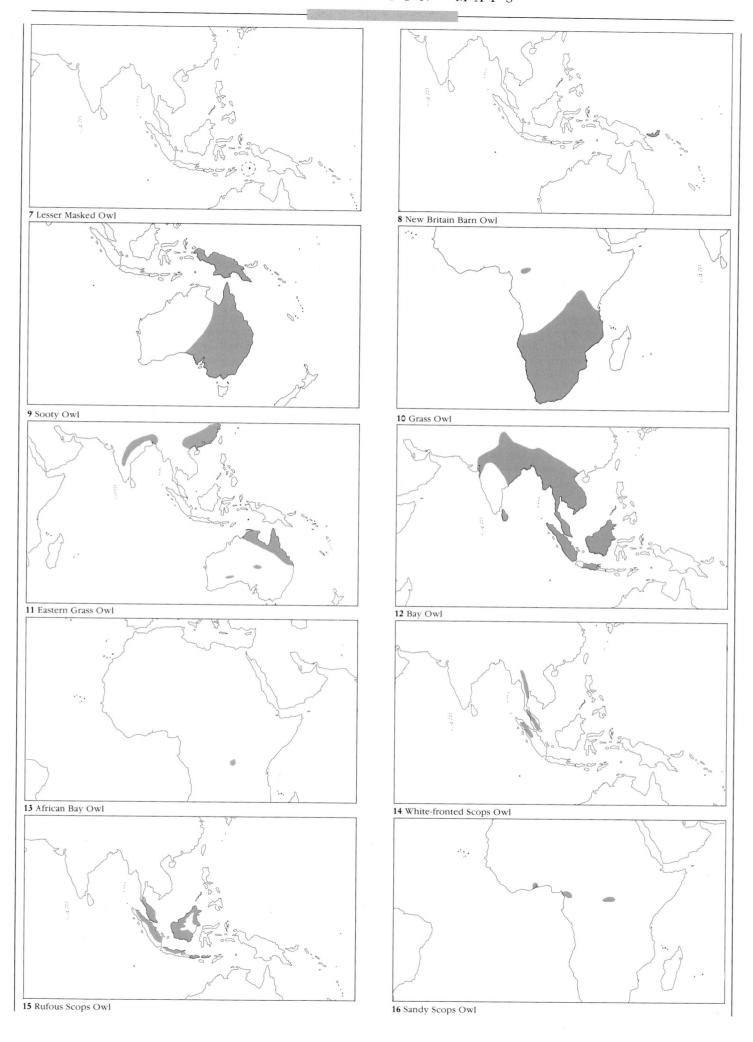

7 Lesser Masked Owl

8 New Britain Barn Owl

9 Sooty Owl

10 Grass Owl

11 Eastern Grass Owl

12 Bay Owl

13 African Bay Owl

14 White-fronted Scops Owl

15 Rufous Scops Owl

16 Sandy Scops Owl

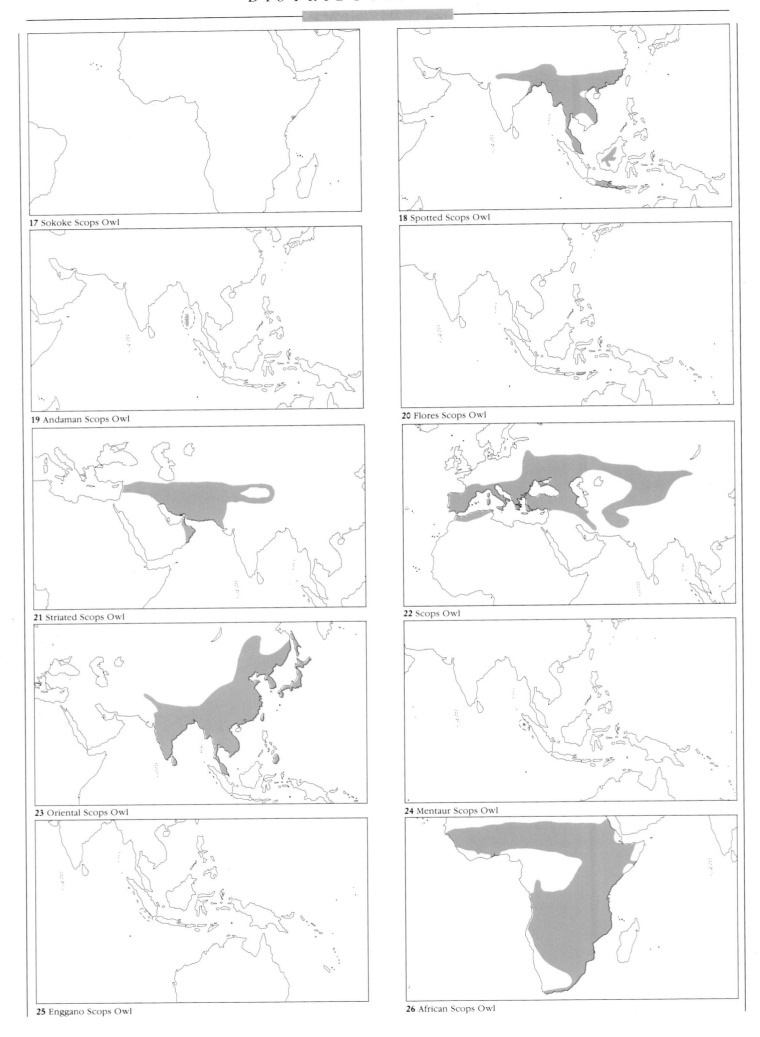

17 Sokoke Scops Owl

18 Spotted Scops Owl

19 Andaman Scops Owl

20 Flores Scops Owl

21 Striated Scops Owl

22 Scops Owl

23 Oriental Scops Owl

24 Mentaur Scops Owl

25 Enggano Scops Owl

26 African Scops Owl

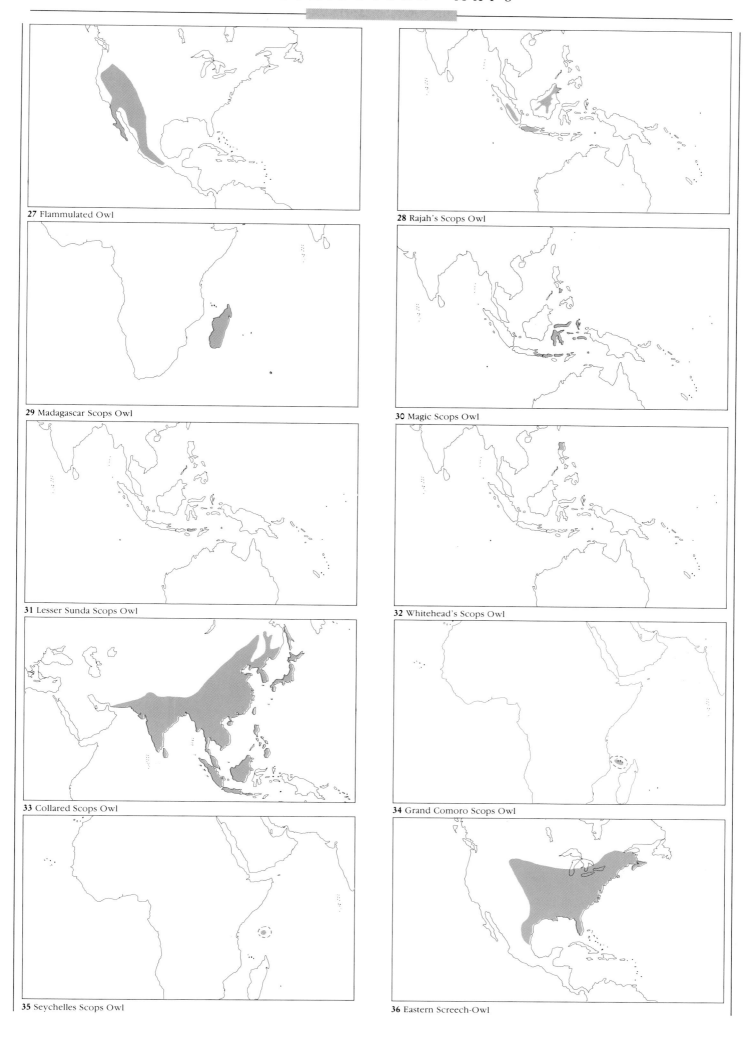

27 Flammulated Owl

28 Rajah's Scops Owl

29 Madagascar Scops Owl

30 Magic Scops Owl

31 Lesser Sunda Scops Owl

32 Whitehead's Scops Owl

33 Collared Scops Owl

34 Grand Comoro Scops Owl

35 Seychelles Scops Owl

36 Eastern Screech-Owl

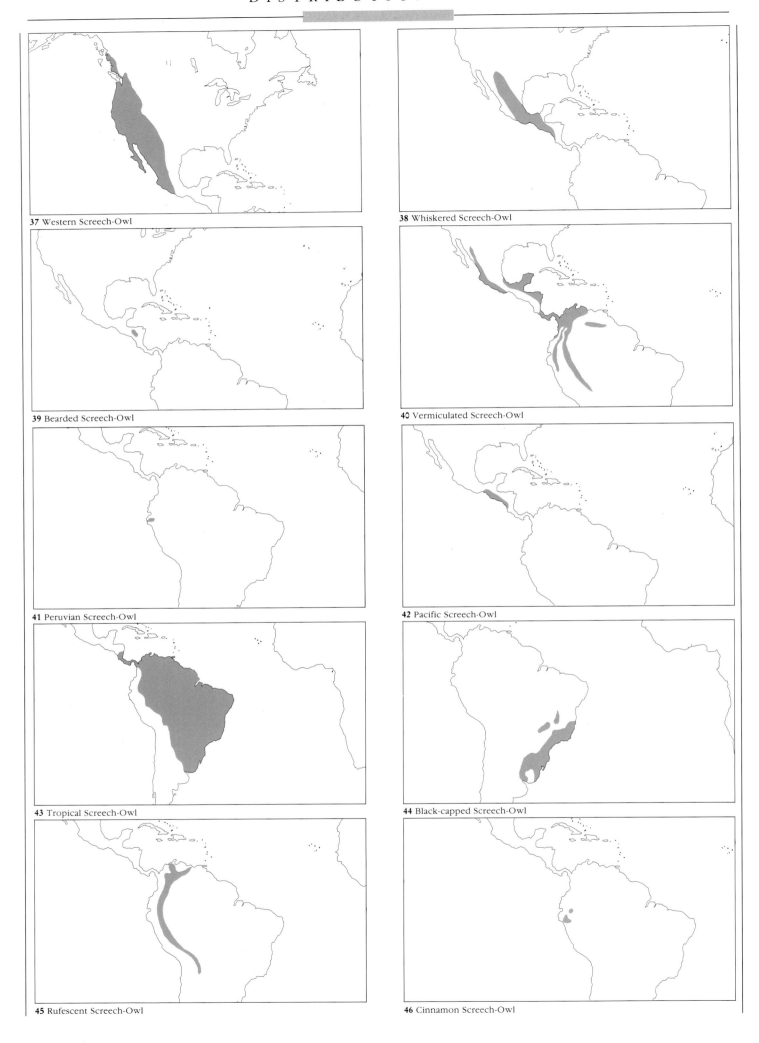

37 Western Screech-Owl

38 Whiskered Screech-Owl

39 Bearded Screech-Owl

40 Vermiculated Screech-Owl

41 Peruvian Screech-Owl

42 Pacific Screech-Owl

43 Tropical Screech-Owl

44 Black-capped Screech-Owl

45 Rufescent Screech-Owl

46 Cinnamon Screech-Owl

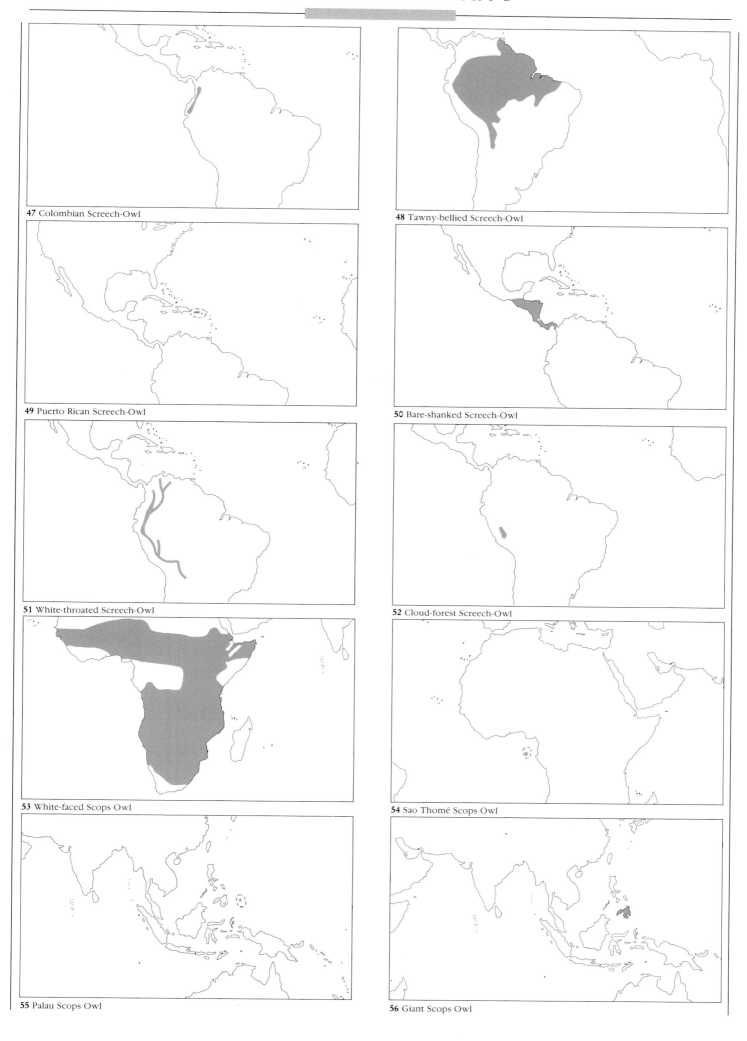

47 Colombian Screech-Owl

48 Tawny-bellied Screech-Owl

49 Puerto Rican Screech-Owl

50 Bare-shanked Screech-Owl

51 White-throated Screech-Owl

52 Cloud-forest Screech-Owl

53 White-faced Scops Owl

54 Sao Thomé Scops Owl

55 Palau Scops Owl

56 Giant Scops Owl

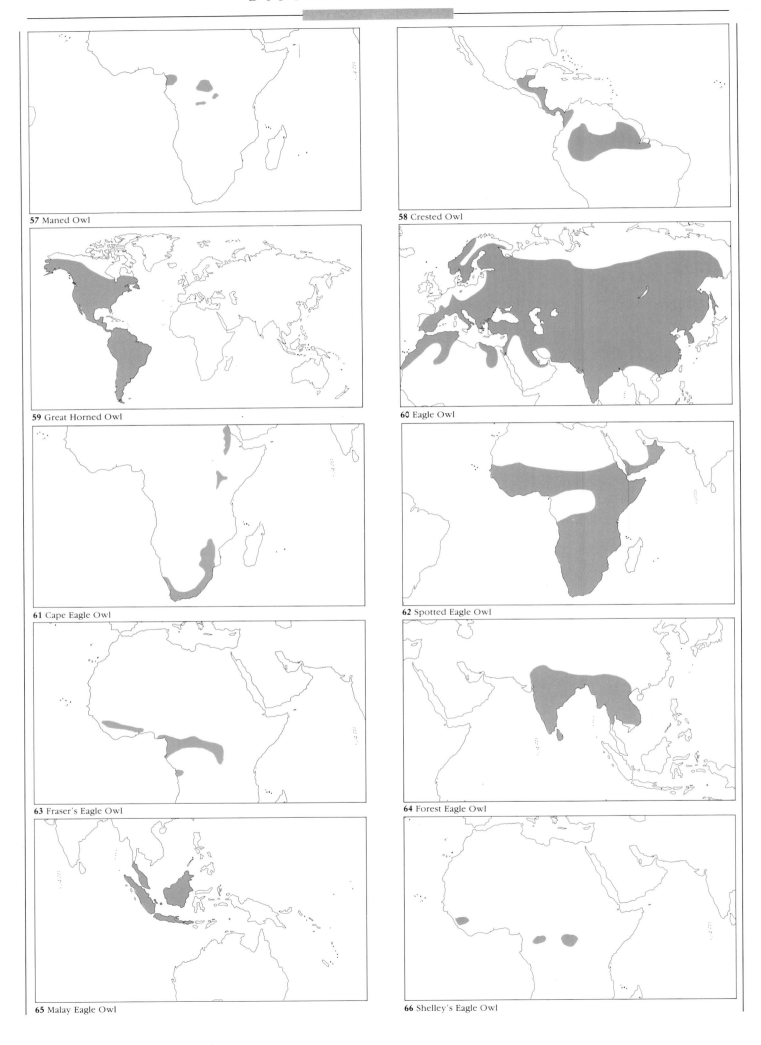

57 Maned Owl

58 Crested Owl

59 Great Horned Owl

60 Eagle Owl

61 Cape Eagle Owl

62 Spotted Eagle Owl

63 Fraser's Eagle Owl

64 Forest Eagle Owl

65 Malay Eagle Owl

66 Shelley's Eagle Owl

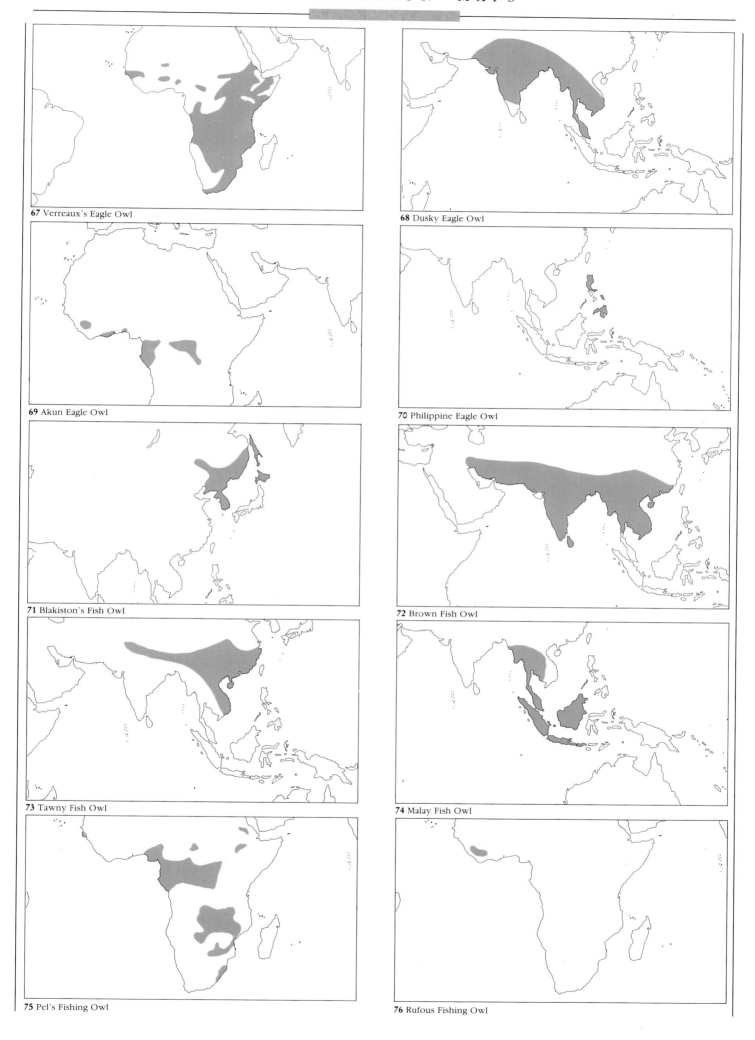

67 Verreaux's Eagle Owl

68 Dusky Eagle Owl

69 Akun Eagle Owl

70 Philippine Eagle Owl

71 Blakiston's Fish Owl

72 Brown Fish Owl

73 Tawny Fish Owl

74 Malay Fish Owl

75 Pel's Fishing Owl

76 Rufous Fishing Owl

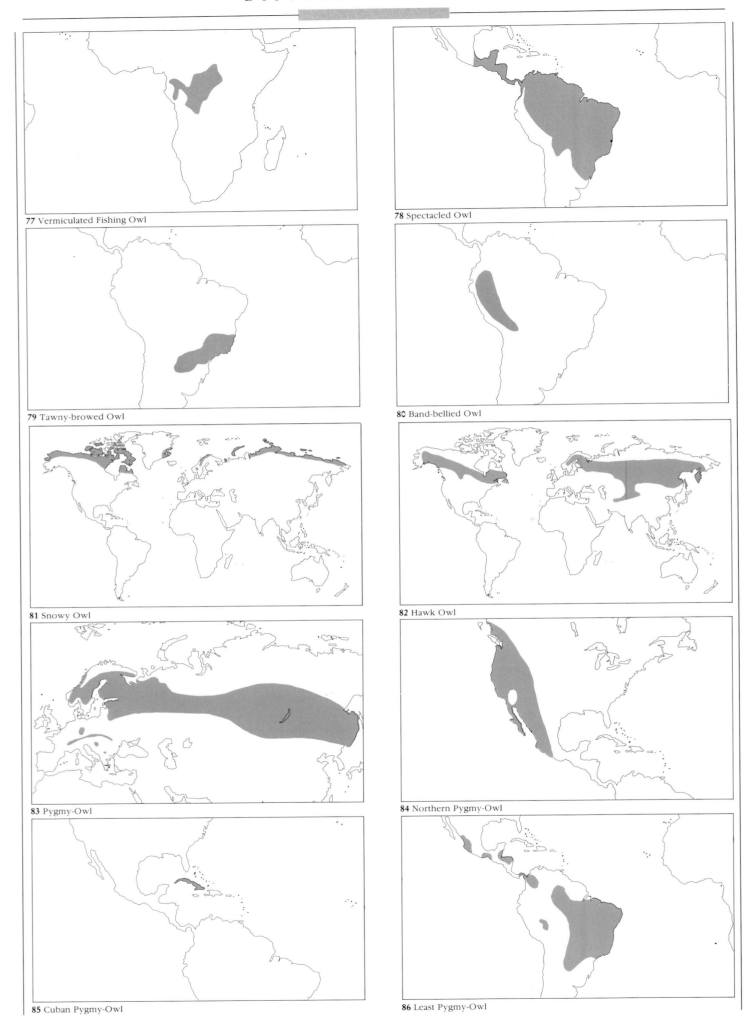

77 Vermiculated Fishing Owl

78 Spectacled Owl

79 Tawny-browed Owl

80 Band-bellied Owl

81 Snowy Owl

82 Hawk Owl

83 Pygmy-Owl

84 Northern Pygmy-Owl

85 Cuban Pygmy-Owl

86 Least Pygmy-Owl

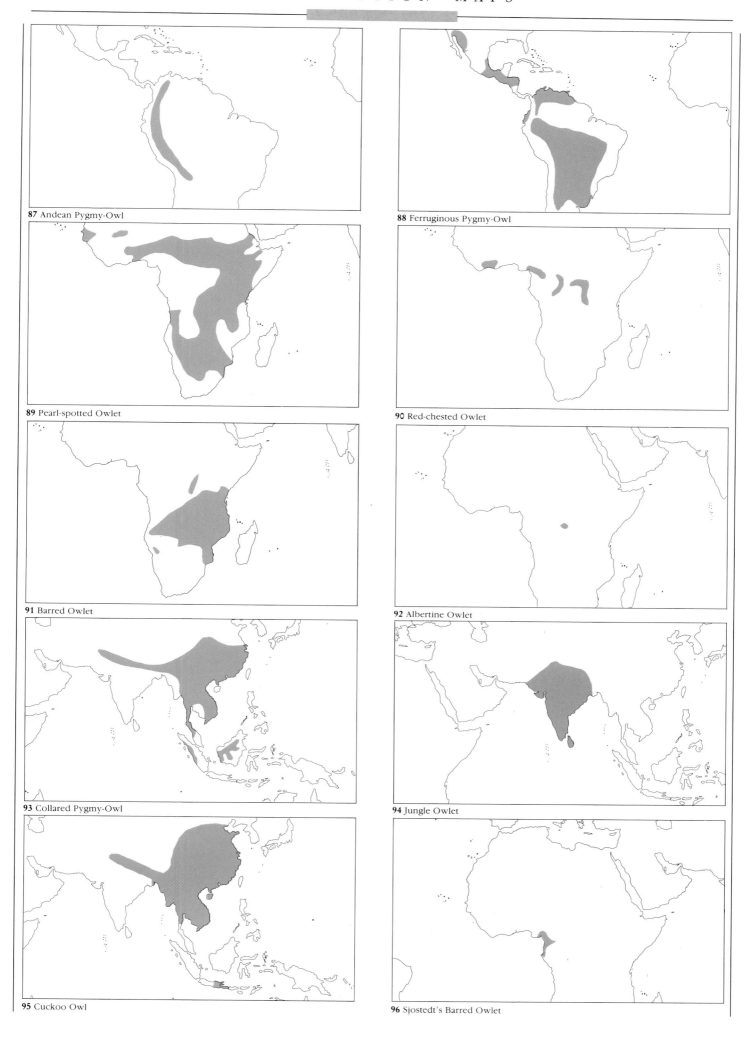

87 Andean Pygmy-Owl

88 Ferruginous Pygmy-Owl

89 Pearl-spotted Owlet

90 Red-chested Owlet

91 Barred Owlet

92 Albertine Owlet

93 Collared Pygmy-Owl

94 Jungle Owlet

95 Cuckoo Owl

96 Sjostedt's Barred Owlet

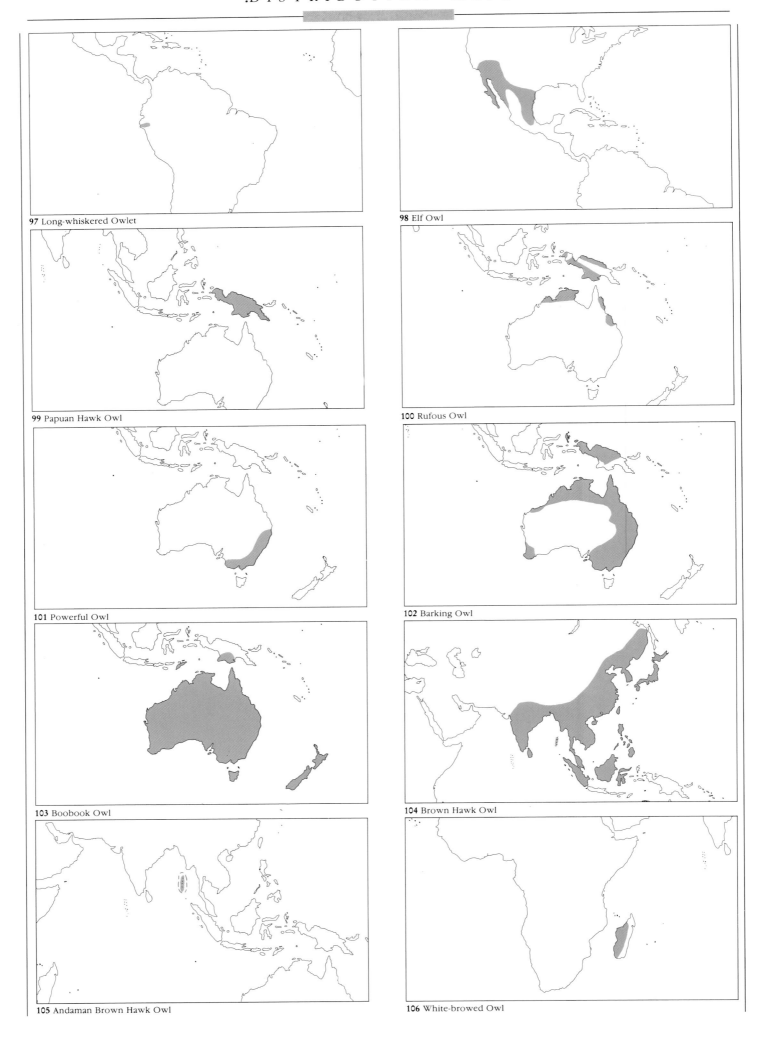

97 Long-whiskered Owlet

98 Elf Owl

99 Papuan Hawk Owl

100 Rufous Owl

101 Powerful Owl

102 Barking Owl

103 Boobook Owl

104 Brown Hawk Owl

105 Andaman Brown Hawk Owl

106 White-browed Owl

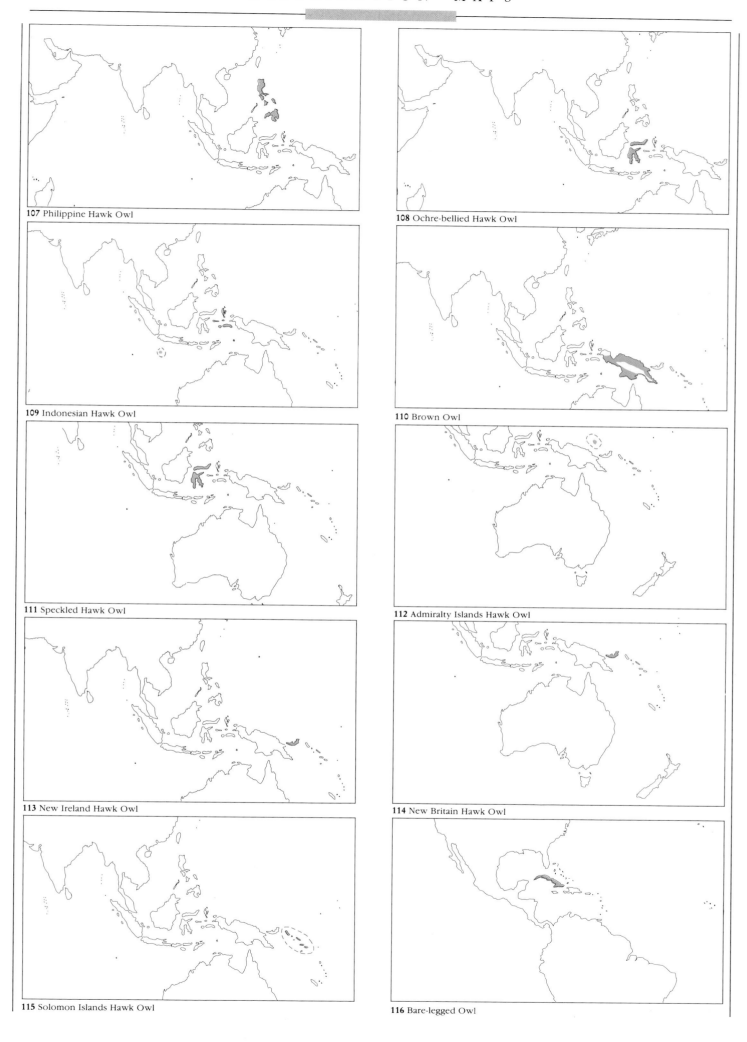

107 Philippine Hawk Owl

108 Ochre-bellied Hawk Owl

109 Indonesian Hawk Owl

110 Brown Owl

111 Speckled Hawk Owl

112 Admiralty Islands Hawk Owl

113 New Ireland Hawk Owl

114 New Britain Hawk Owl

115 Solomon Islands Hawk Owl

116 Bare-legged Owl

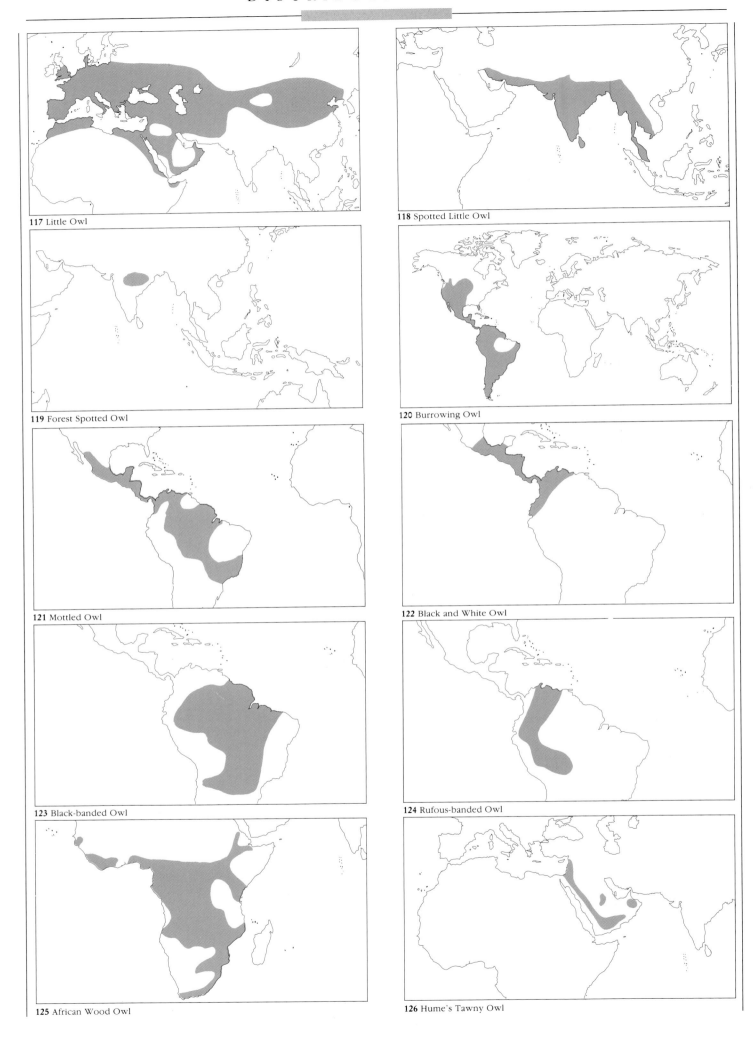

117 Little Owl

118 Spotted Little Owl

119 Forest Spotted Owl

120 Burrowing Owl

121 Mottled Owl

122 Black and White Owl

123 Black-banded Owl

124 Rufous-banded Owl

125 African Wood Owl

126 Hume's Tawny Owl

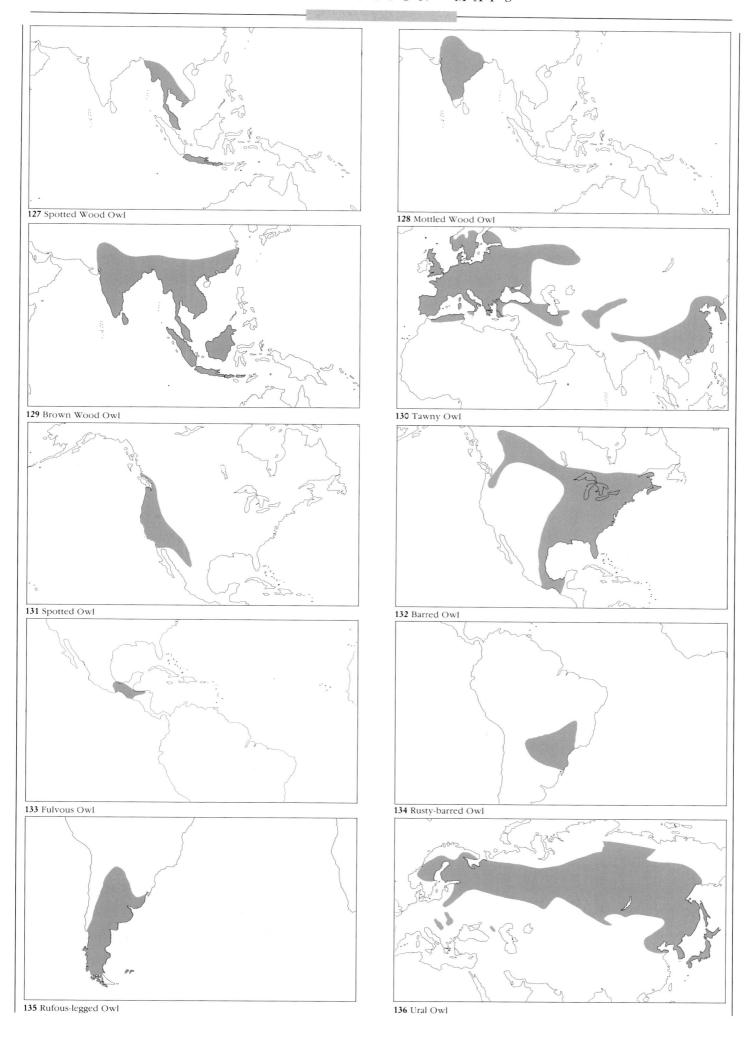

127 Spotted Wood Owl

128 Mottled Wood Owl

129 Brown Wood Owl

130 Tawny Owl

131 Spotted Owl

132 Barred Owl

133 Fulvous Owl

134 Rusty-barred Owl

135 Rufous-legged Owl

136 Ural Owl

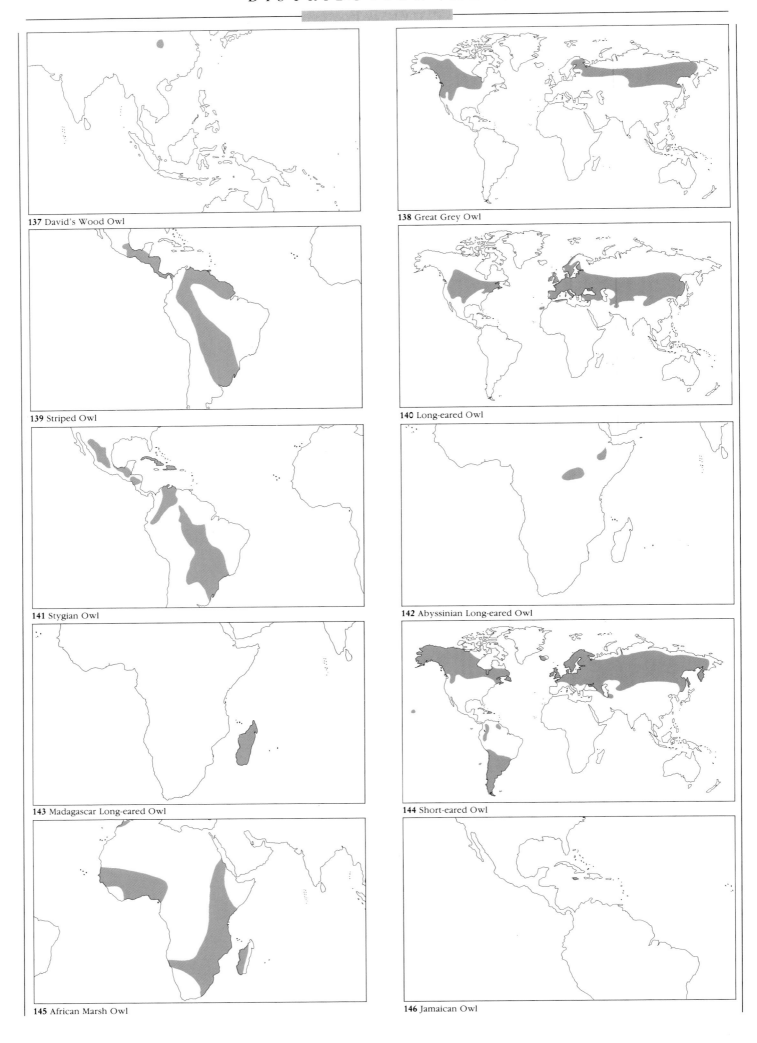

137 David's Wood Owl

138 Great Grey Owl

139 Striped Owl

140 Long-eared Owl

141 Stygian Owl

142 Abyssinian Long-eared Owl

143 Madagascar Long-eared Owl

144 Short-eared Owl

145 African Marsh Owl

146 Jamaican Owl

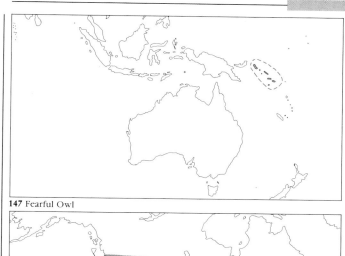

147 Fearful Owl

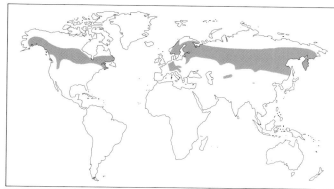

148 Tengmalm's/Boreal Owl

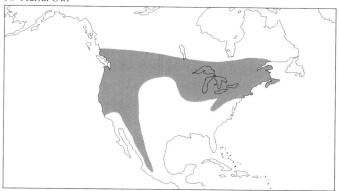

149 Northern Saw-whet Owl

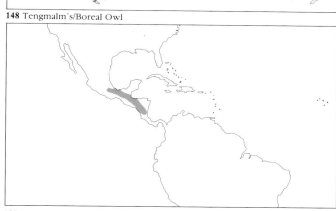

150 Unspotted Saw-whet Owl

151 Buff-fronted Owl

SYSTEMATIC LIST AND MEASUREMENTS

	Length	*Distribution*
FAMILY Tytonidae:		
Madagascar Grass Owl (*Tyto soumagnei*)	10¾″(270mm)	Madagascar
Barn Owl (*Tyto alba*)	13−17″ (330−430mm)	Americas, Europe, South-East Asia, Australasia, Africa
Celebes Barn Owl (*Tyto rosenbergii*)	16¼−20″(410−510mm)	Sulawesi (Celebes)
Sula Islands Barn Owl (*Tyto nigrobrunnea*)	12¼″(310mm)	Sula Islands (in Indonesia)
Minahassa Barn Owl (*Tyto inexspectata*)	10¾−12¼″(270−310mm)	Sulawesi (Celebes)
Masked Owl (*Tyto novaehollandiae*)	19¼−21″(490−530mm)	Australia, Tasmania, New Guinea
Lesser Masked Owl (*Tyto sororcula*)	19¼″(490mm)	Tanimbar Island (in Indonesia)
New Britain Barn Owl (*Tyto aurantia*)	10¾−13″(270−330mm)	New Britain Island (off New Guinea)
Sooty Owl (*Tyto tenebricosa*)	13−15″(330−380mm)	Australia, New Guinea
Grass Owl (*Tyto capensis*)	15−16½″(380−420mm)	Africa
Eastern Grass Owl (*Tyto longimembris*)	15−16½″(380−420mm)	Southern Asia, Australasia
Bay Owl (*Phodilus badius*)	9−13″ (230−330mm)	South-East Asia, Sri Lanka, Borneo, Philippines
African Bay Owl (*Phodilus prigoginei*)	11¾″(300mm)	Zaire
FAMILY Strigidae:		
White-fronted Scops Owl (*Otus sagittatus*)	9¾−11″(250−280mm)	Burma, Thailand, Malaysia
Rufous Scops Owl (*Otus rufescens*)	6−7″(150−180mm)	Malaysia, Sumatra, Java, Borneo, Philippines
Sandy Scops Owl (*Otus icterorhynchus*)	7−7¾″(180−200mm)	West Africa
Sokoke Scops Owl (*Otus ireneae*)	6¼−7″(160−180mm)	Kenya
Spotted Scops Owl (*Otus spilocephalus*)	7″(180mm)	Himalayas, China, South-East Asia, Sumatra, Borneo
Andaman Scops Owl (*Otus balli*)	7″(180mm)	Andaman Islands (in the Indian Ocean)
Flores Scops Owl (*Otus alfredi*)	7½″(190mm)	Flores Island (near Java)
Striated Scops Owl (*Otus brucei*)	6¼″(160mm)	Middle East, central and western Asia
Scops Owl (*Otus scops*)	6¼−7½″(160−190mm)	South-west Europe to eastern Asia
Oriental Scops Owl (*Otus sunia*)	6¼−7″(160−180mm)	Central and South-East Asia, Japan
Mentaur Scops Owl (*Otus umbra*)	6¼″(160mm)	Simeulue Island (near Sumatra)
Enggano Scops Owl (*Otus enganensis*)	6¼″(160mm)	Enggano Island (near Sumatra)
African Scops Owl (*Otus senegalensis*)	7½″(190mm)	Africa south of the Sahara
Flammulated Owl (*Otus flammeolus*)	6¼−6¾″(160−170mm)	Western North America, Central America
Rajah's Scops Owl (*Otus brookii*)	9″(230mm)	Java, Sumatra, Borneo
Madagascar Scops Owl (*Otus rutilus*)	7½−9″(190−230mm)	Madagascar, Pemba Island (off East Africa)
Magic Scops Owl (*Otus manadensis*)	7½−9″(190−230mm)	Indonesia, Philippines
Lesser Sunda Scops Owl (*Otus silvicolus*)	9″(230mm)	Lesser Sunda Islands (in Indonesia)
Whitehead's Scops Owl (*Otus megalotis*)	9″(230mm)	Luzon (in the Philippines)
Collared Scops Owl (*Otus bakkamoena*)	7½−9″(190−230mm)	Central and eastern Asia, Japan, Java
Grand Comoro Scops Owl (*Otus pauliani*)	7¾″(200mm)	Grand Comoro Island (off East Africa)
Seychelles Scops Owl (*Otus insularis*)	7¾″(200mm)	Mahé Island (in the Seychelles)
Eastern Screech-Owl (*Otus asio*)	7½−9″(190−230mm)	Eastern North America
Western Screech-Owl (*Otus kennicotti*)	7¾″(200mm)	Western North America, Mexico
Whiskered Screech-Owl (*Otus trichopsis*)	7½″(190mm)	Arizona, Central America
Bearded Screech-Owl (*Otus barbarus*)	7¾−9″(200−230mm)	Guatemala, southern Mexico
Vermiculated Screech-Owl (*Otus guatemalae*)	7¾″(200mm)	Mexico to north-west Argentina
Peruvian Screech-Owl (*Otus roboratus*)	7¾−9″(200−230mm)	South-west Ecuador, north-west Peru
Pacific Screech-Owl (*Otus cooperi*)	9″(230mm)	Central America
Tropical Screech-Owl (*Otus choliba*)	7½−9″(190−230mm)	Central and South America
Black-capped Screech-Owl (*Otus atricapillus*)	9″(230mm)	Brazil
Rufescent Screech-Owl (*Otus ingens*)	7¾−9″(200−230mm)	Andes from Venezuela to Bolivia
Cinnamon Screech-Owl (*Otus petersoni*)	8¼″(210mm)	Ecuador, Peru
Colombian Screech-Owl (*Otus colombianus*)	9″(230mm)	Colombia, Ecuador

	Length	Distribution
Tawny-bellied Screech-Owl (*Otus watsonii*)	7½–9"(190–230mm)	Northern and central South America
Puerto Rican Screech-Owl (*Otus nudipes*)	8¾"(220mm)	Virgin Islands and Puerto Rico
Bare-shanked Screech-Owl (*Otus clarkii*)	9"(230mm)	Central America, Colombia
White-throated Screech-Owl (*Otus albogularis*)	7½–9"(190–230mm)	Andes from Venezuela to Bolivia
Cloud-forest Screech-Owl (*Otus marshalli*)	7¾"(200mm)	Peru
White-faced Scops Owl (*Otus leucotis*)	7½–9½"(190–240mm)	Africa south of the Sahara
Sao Thomé Scops Owl (*Otus hartlaubi*)	7"(180mm)	Sao Thomé Island (off West Africa)
Palau Scops Owl (*Pyrroglaux podargina*)	8¾"(220mm)	Palau Islands (in the South Pacific)
Giant Scops Owl (*Mimizuku gurneyi*)	11¾"(300mm)	Philippines
Maned Owl (*Jubula lettii*)	17¼"(440mm)	West Africa
Crested Owl (*Lophostrix cristata*)	15¾"(400mm)	Central America, Amazon basin
Great Horned Owl (*Bubo virginianus*)	17–21"(430–530mm)	North and South America
Eagle Owl (*Bubo bubo*)	22¾–28"(580–710mm)	Europe, North Africa, Middle East, Asia
Cape Eagle Owl (*Bubo capensis*)	19¾–22¾"(500–580mm)	East and southern Africa
Spotted Eagle Owl (*Bubo africanus*)	17¾"(450mm)	Arabia, Africa south of the Sahara
Fraser's Eagle Owl (*Bubo poensis*)	15¼–17¾"(390–450mm)	West Africa
Forest Eagle Owl (*Bubo nipalensis*)	20–24"(510–610mm)	Himalayas, India, South-East Asia
Malay Eagle Owl (*Bubo sumatrana*)	15¾–18"(400–460mm)	Burma, Malaysia, Sumatra, Java, Borneo
Shelley's Eagle Owl (*Bubo shelleyi*)	24"(610mm)	West Africa
Verreaux's Eagle Owl (*Bubo lacteus*)	23½–25½"(600–650mm)	Africa south of the Sahara
Dusky Eagle Owl (*Bubo coromandus*)	17–19"(430–480mm)	India, South-East Asia
Akun Eagle Owl (*Bubo leucostictus*)	15¾–18"(400–460mm)	West Africa
Philippine Eagle Owl (*Bubo philippensis*)	15¾"(400mm)	Luzon and Mindanao (in the Philippines)
Blakiston's Fish Owl (*Ketupa blakistoni*)	24"(600mm)	Eastern Asia, Japan
Brown Fish Owl (*Ketupa zeylonensis*)	19–20"(480–510mm)	Middle East, southern Asia
Tawny Fish Owl (*Ketupa flavipes*)	19–20"(480–510mm)	Southern Asia
Malay Fish Owl (*Ketupa ketupu*)	15–17¼"(380–440mm)	Malaysia, Sumatra, Java, Borneo
Pel's Fishing Owl (*Scotopelia peli*)	20–24"(510–610mm)	Africa south of the Sahara
Rufous Fishing Owl (*Scotopelia ussheri*)	18–20"(460–510mm)	West Africa
Vermiculated Fishing Owl (*Scotopelia bouvieri*)	18–20"(460–510mm)	West Africa
Spectacled Owl (*Pulsatrix perspicillata*)	17–18"(430–460mm)	Mexico, Central and South America
Tawny-browed Owl (*Pulsatrix koeniswaldiana*)	17¼"(440mm)	Brazil, Paraguay, Argentina
Band-bellied Owl (*Pulsatrix melanota*)	19"(480mm)	Colombia, Ecuador, Peru, Bolivia
Snowy Owl (*Nyctea scandiaca*)	21–26"(530–660mm)	Circumpolar Arctic
Hawk Owl (*Surnia ulula*)	14¼–16¼"(360–410mm)	North America, northern Europe and Asia
Pygmy-Owl (*Glaucidium passerinum*)	6¼–6¾"(160–170mm)	Northern and central Europe, northern Asia
Northern Pygmy-Owl (*Glaucidium gnoma*)	6¾"(170mm)	Western North and Central America, Mexico
Cuban Pygmy-Owl (*Glaucidium siju*)	6¾"(170mm)	Cuba and Isle of Pines
Least Pygmy-Owl (*Glaucidium minutissimum*)	4¾–5½"(120–140mm)	Mexico south to Brazil and Paraguay
Andean Pygmy-Owl (*Glaucidium jardinii*)	6"(150mm)	Costa Rica, Panama, Andes
Ferruginous Pygmy-Owl (*Glaucidium brasilianum*)	6½"(165mm)	Extreme southwestern USA to Argentina
Pearl-spotted Owlet (*Glaucidium perlatum*)	6¾–7¾"(170–200mm)	Africa south of the Sahara
Red-chested Owlet (*Glaucidium tephronotum*)	6¾–7"(170–180mm)	West, central and East Africa
Barred Owlet (*Glaucidium capense*)	8¼–8¾"(210–220mm)	Liberia, Kenya south to Angola and Mozambique
Albertine Owlet (*Glaucidium albertinum*)	7¾"(200mm)	Zaire, Rwanda
Collared Pygmy-Owl (*Glaucidium brodiei*)	6"(150mm)	Himalayas, China, South-East Asia, Sumatra, Borneo
Jungle Owlet (*Glaucidium radiatum*)	6¾"(170mm)	India, Pakistan, Bangladesh, Sri Lanka, western Burma
Cuckoo Owl (*Glaucidium cuculoides*)	9–9¾"(230–250mm)	Himalayas, China, South-East Asia, Java, Bali
Sjostedt's Barred Owlet (*Glaucidium sjostedti*)	9¾"(250mm)	West central Africa
Long-whiskered Owlet (*Xenoglaux loweryi*)	5–5½"(130–140mm)	Peruvian Andes
Elf Owl (*Micrathene whitneyi*)	5–5½"(130–140mm)	Extreme southern USA, Mexico
Papuan Hawk Owl (*Uroglaux dimorpha*)	11¾–13"(300–330mm)	New Guinea, Yapen Island
Rufous Owl (*Ninox rufa*)	15¾–19¾"(400–500mm)	New Guinea, northern Australia
Powerful Owl (*Ninox strenua*)	24¾–25½"(630–650mm)	South-east Australia
Barking Owl (*Ninox connivens*)	15–17¼"(380–440mm)	Australia, New Guinea, Moluccas
Boobook Owl (*Ninox novaeseelandiae*)	13¾"(350mm)	Indonesia, Australian islands, New Zealand
Brown Hawk Owl (*Ninox scutulata*)	11–12½"(280–320mm)	India, east and South-East Asia, Philippines, Japan
Andaman Brown Hawk Owl (*Ninox affinis*)	9¾–11"(250–280mm)	Andaman and Nicobar Islands (in the Indian Ocean)
White-browed Owl (*Ninox superciliaris*)	9–11"(230–280mm)	Madagascar
Philippine Hawk Owl (*Ninox philippensis*)	7¾"(200mm)	Philippines
Ochre-bellied Hawk Owl (*Ninox perversa*)	9¾–10¼"(250–260mm)	Sulawesi (Celebes)
Indonesian Hawk Owl (*Ninox squamipila*)	11¾–13¾"(300–350mm)	Moluccas, Christmas Island, Lesser Sundas
Brown Owl (*Ninox theomacha*)	7¾–9¾"(200–250mm)	New Guinea archipelago
Speckled Hawk Owl (*Ninox punctulata*)	7¾–10¼"(200–260mm)	Sulawesi (Celebes)

	Length	Distribution
Admiralty Islands Hawk Owl (*Ninox meeki*)	7¾−9¾″(200−250mm)	Admiralty Islands (off Papua New Guinea)
New Ireland Hawk Owl (*Ninox solomonis*)	9¾−11¾″(250−300mm)	New Ireland, New Britain and New Hanover Islands (off Papua New Guinea)
New Britain Hawk Owl (*Ninox odiosa*)	7¾−9″(200−230mm)	New Britain Island (off Papua New Guinea)
Solomon Islands Hawk Owl (*Ninox jacquinoti*)	9¾−12¼″(250−310mm)	Solomon Islands (east of New Guinea)
Bare-legged Owl (*Gymnoglaux lawrencii*)	7¾−9″(200−230mm)	Cuba and Isle of Pines
Little Owl (*Athene noctua*)	7½−9″(190−230mm)	Europe, North Africa, Middle-East, Asia
Spotted Little Owl (*Athene brama*)	7½−8¼″(190−210mm)	Iran, India, South-East Asia
Forest Spotted Owl (*Athene blewitti*)	9″(230mm)	India
Burrowing Owl (*Athene cunicularia*)	7¾−10¼″(200−260mm)	Canada, USA, Central and South America
Mottled Owl (*Ciccaba virgata*)	13¾″(350mm)	Mexico, Central and South America
Black and White Owl (*Ciccaba nigrolineata*)	13¾−15″(350−380mm)	Mexico to Ecuador
Black-banded Owl (*Ciccaba huhula*)	13¾″(350mm)	Northern and central South America
Rufous-banded Owl (*Ciccaba albitarsus*)	11¾″(300mm)	Venezuela, Colombia, Ecuador, Peru, Bolivia
African Wood Owl (*Ciccaba woodfordii*)	13¾″(350mm)	Africa south of the Sahara
Hume's Tawny Owl (*Strix butleri*)	13″(330mm)	Middle East
Spotted Wood Owl (*Strix seloputo*)	15¾−17¾″(400−450mm)	South-East Asia, some Asian islands
Mottled Wood Owl (*Strix ocellata*)	15−18″(380−460mm)	India, western Burma
Brown Wood Owl (*Strix leptogrammica*)	18−21″(460−530mm)	India, south China, South-East Asia, Indonesia
Tawny Owl (*Strix aluco*)	14¼−18″(360−460mm)	Europe, Asia, North Africa, Middle East
Spotted Owl (*Strix occidentalis*)	16−19″(405−480mm)	Western North America, Mexico
Barred Owl (*Strix varia*)	16−23½″(405−600mm)	North America, Mexico
Fulvous Owl (*Strix fulvescens*)	16−17¾″(405−450mm)	Southern Mexico, northern Central America
Rusty-barred Owl (*Strix hylophila*)	14″(355mm)	Brazil, Uruguay, Argentina
Rufous-legged Owl (*Strix rufipes*)	13−15″(330−380mm)	Paraguay, Argentina, Chile
Ural Owl (*Strix uralensis*)	22¾″(580mm)	North and central Europe, central Asia, Japan
David's Wood Owl (*Strix davidi*)	22¾″(580mm)	China
Great Grey Owl (*Strix nebulosa*)	24−33″(610−840mm)	North America, northern Europe, northern Asia
Striped Owl (*Asio clamator*)	12−15″(305−380mm)	Mexico, Central and South America
Long-eared Owl (*Asio otus*)	13¾−15¾″(350−400mm)	North America, Europe, Middle East, Asia, North Africa
Stygian Owl (*Asio stygius*)	15−18″(380−460mm)	Mexico to Argentina, West Indies
Abyssinian Long-eared Owl (*Asio abyssinicus*)	15¾″(400mm)	Ethiopia, Zaire, Kenya
Madagascar Long-eared Owl (*Asio madagascariensis*)	12½″(320mm)	Madagascar
Short-eared Owl (*Asio flammeus*)	13−17″(330−430mm)	North and South America, Caribbean, Europe, Asia
African Marsh Owl (*Asio capensis*)	12−15″(305−380mm)	Morocco, Africa south of the Sahara
Jamaican Owl (*Pseudoscops grammicus*)	12¼″(310mm)	Jamaica
Fearful Owl (*Nesasio solomonensis*)	11−15″(280−380mm)	Solomon Islands (east of New Guinea)
Tengmalm's/Boreal Owl (*Aegolius funereus*)	7½−9″(190−230mm)	North America, north and central Europe, Asia
Northern Saw-whet Owl (*Aegolius acadicus*)	6¾−7½″(170−190mm)	North America, northern Mexico
Unspotted Saw-whet Owl (*Aegolius ridgwayi*)	6¾−7½″ (170−190mm)	Southern Mexico, Central America
Buff-fronted Owl (*Aegolius harrisii*)	7¾″(200mm)	Venezuela and Colombia to northern Argentina and southern Brazil

READING LIST

General Works

Burton, J.A. 1984: *Owls of the World*. William Collins, London.
    A popular illustrated review, dealing especially with taxonomy and ecology. Due to be revised.

Clark *et al.* 1978: *Working Bibliography of Owls of the World*. National Wildlife Federation.
    Though a little dated, a useful guide to the literature and taxonomy.

Everett, M.J. 1977: *A Natural History of Owls*. Hamlyn, London.
    A popular general study, illustrated by photographs.

Grossman, M.L. and J. Hamlet 1965: *Birds of Prey of the World*. Cassell, London.
    A comprehensive work, dealing with diurnal raptors and owls.

Hosking, E. and J. Flegg 1982: *Eric Hosking's Owls*. Pelham, London.
    Photographs of many of the world's owls by a master.

Howard, R. and A. Moore 1980; 3rd edition 1991: *A Complete Checklist of the Birds of the World*. Oxford.

King, B. and B. Warren 1981: *Endangered Birds of the World — the ICBP Bird Red Data Book*. Washington D.C.
    A review of threatened species.

Regional Works and Monographs

Bent, A.C. 1937: *Life Histories of North American Birds — Birds of Prey*. Dover.
    Dated but a discursive look at habitats and behaviour.

Bunn, D.S. *et al.* 1982: *The Barn Owl*. T. & A.D. Poyser, Calton.
    A complete study of a well-known species.

Collar, N.J. and S.N. Stuart 1985: *Threatened Birds of Africa and Related Islands*. ICBP, Cambridge.

Johnsgard, P.A. 1988: *North American Owls — Biology and Natural History*. Smithsonian.
    Detailed accounts of the lives of 19 species.

Kemp, A. and S. Calburn 1987: *The Owls of Southern Africa*. Struik Winchester, Capetown.
    Essays on each species with paintings and sketches showing behaviour.

Mikkola, H. 1983: *Owls of Europe*. T. & A.D. Poyser, Calton.
    A series of mini-monographs with chapters on aspects of owls.

Steyn, P. 1982: *Birds of Prey of Southern Africa*. Croom Helm, Beckenham.

Voous, K.H. and A. Cameron 1988: *Owls of the Northern Hemisphere*. William Collins, London.
    A thought-provoking look at relationships and ecology, with excellent paintings.

Field Guides, Handbooks and Atlases

Ali, S. 1977: *Birds of the Eastern Himalayas*. Oxford.

Ali, S. and S. Dillon Ripley 1983: *The Handbook of the Birds of India and Pakistan*. Oxford.

Beehler, B.M. *et al.* 1986: *Birds of New Guinea*. Princeton.

Blakers, M. *et al.* 1984: *The Atlas of Australian Birds*. Melbourne.

Cadman, M.D. *et al.* 1987: *Atlas of the Breeding Birds of Ontario*. University of Waterloo Press.

Cramp, S. *et al.* 1985: *The Birds of the Western Palearctic*, vol IV. Oxford.

Dee, T.J. 1986: *The Endemic Birds of Madagascar*. ICBP, Cambridge.

Fry, C.H. *et. al.* 1988: *The Birds of Africa*, vol III. Academic Press, London.

Haverschmidt, F. 1968: *Birds of Surinam*. Constable.

Hilty, S.L. and W.L. Brown 1986: *A Guide to the Birds of Colombia*. Princeton.

King, B. *et al.* 1975: *A Field Guide to the Birds of South-East Asia*. William Collins, London.

Lewis, A. and D. Pomeroy 1989: *A Bird Atlas of Kenya*. Balkema, Netherlands.

Macdonald, J.D. 1973: *Birds of Australia*. Witherby, London.

Mayr, E. 1945: *Birds of the Southwest Pacific*. Tuttle.

McLachlan, G.R. and R. Liversidge 1978: *Roberts' Birds of South Africa*. South African Bird Book Fund, Capetown.

Paz, U. 1987: *Birds of Israel*. Christopher Helm, London.

Pizzey, G. and R. Doyle 1980: *A Field Guide to the Birds of Australia*. William Collins, London.

Rand, A.L. and E.T. Gilliard 1967: *Handbook of New Guinea Birds*. Weidenfeld & Nicholson, London.

Ridgely, R.S. 1976: *A Guide to the Birds of Panama*. Princeton.

Ryser, F.A., Jr. 1985: *Birds of the Great Basin*. University of Nevada Press, Nevada.

de Schauensee, R.H. and W.H. Phelps, Jr. 1978: *A Guide to the Birds of Venezuela*. Princeton.

Van Marle, J.G. and K.H. Voous 1988: *The Birds of Sumatra*. British Ornithologists' Union, London.

White, C.M.N. and M.D. Bruce 1986: *The Birds of Wallacea*. British Ornithologists' Union, London.

INDEX

Page numbers in **bold** refer to the main entry.
Map numbers are printed in *italic*.